ADOBE® ILLUSTRATOR® CS3

CLASSROOM IN A BOOK®

The official training workbook from Adobe Systems

Adobe

Adobe Press books are published by Peachpit, Berkeley, CA. To report errors, please send a note to errata@peachpit.com.

Printed in the USA

ISBN-13: 978-0-321-49200-5
ISBN-10: 0-321-49200-5

9 8 7 6 5 4 3 2 1

Phil Guindi
Illustrator Product Manager

Welcome to Adobe Illustrator CS3 Classroom in a Book, the official training workbook for the vector drawing tool that lets you create content that goes everywhere—to print, web and interactive, mobile, and motion designs.

For Illustrator CS3, the thirteenth full release, we focused on four major areas: creative power, ease of use, runtime performance, and integration. Live Color is an amazing new color environment for inspiration and exploration, as well as precise color control and production. For those of you who always thought that Illustrator's basic drawing tools needed a tune up, we've done just that, making point selection and path editing faster and more natural. On the integration front, Flash aficionados will be blown away by the tight integration between Illustrator and Flash. And users who take their content to video applications will love the new Crop Area tool and the video-specific document profiles and templates.

Whether you're an Illustrator newbie or consider yourself a seasoned pro, we've something in Illustrator CS3 to please each member of our creative family. So jump in and enjoy!

Best regards,

Phil Guindi
Illustrator Product Manager

Lesson files . . . and so much more

The *Adobe Illustrator CS3 Classroom in a Book* CD includes the lesson files that you'll need to complete the exercises in this book, as well as other content to help you learn more about Adobe Illustrator and use it with greater efficiency and ease. The diagram below represents the contents of the CD, which should help you locate the files you need.

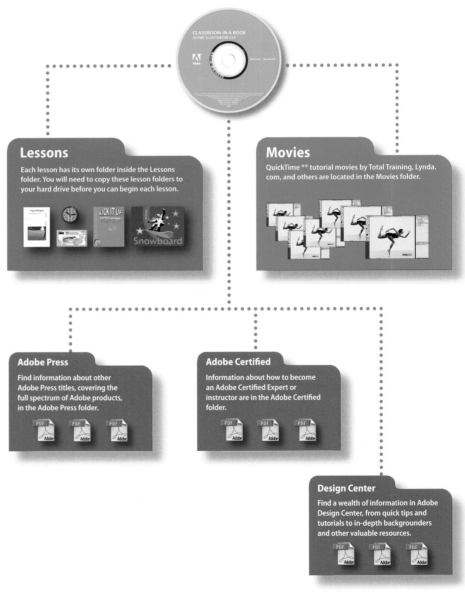

Lessons

Each lesson has its own folder inside the Lessons folder. You will need to copy these lesson folders to your hard drive before you can begin each lesson.

Movies

QuickTime ** tutorial movies by Total Training, Lynda.com, and others are located in the Movies folder.

Adobe Press

Find information about other Adobe Press titles, covering the full spectrum of Adobe products, in the Adobe Press folder.

Adobe Certified

Information about how to become an Adobe Certified Expert or instructor are in the Adobe Certified folder.

Design Center

Find a wealth of information in Adobe Design Center, from quick tips and tutorials to in-depth backgrounders and other valuable resources.

**The latest version of Apple QuickTime can be downloaded from http://www.apple.com/quicktime/download/.

Contents

Getting Started

What's New in Adobe Illustrator CS3

A Quick Tour of Adobe Illustrator CS3

1 Getting to Know the Work Area

2 Selecting and Aligning

3 Creating Shapes

4 Transforming Objects

5 Drawing with the Pen tool

6 Color and Painting

7   Working with type

8   Working with Layers

9   Blending Shapes and Colors

10 Working with Brushes

11 Applying Effects

12   **Applying Appearance Attributes and Graphic Styles**

13   **Working with Symbols**

14 Combining Illustrator CS3 Graphics with the Creative Suite

15 Printing Artwork and Producing Color Separations

Getting Started

Adobe® Illustrator® CS3 is the industry-standard illustration program for print, multimedia, and online graphics. Whether you are a designer or a technical illustrator producing artwork for print publishing, an artist producing multimedia graphics, or a creator of web pages or online content, the Adobe Illustrator program offers you the tools you need to get professional-quality results.

About Classroom in a Book

Adobe Illustrator CS3 Classroom in a Book® is part of the official training series for Adobe graphics and publishing software from Adobe Systems, Inc.

The lessons are designed so that you can learn at your own pace. If you're new to Adobe Illustrator, you'll learn the fundamentals you need to master in order to put the program to work. If you are an experienced user, you'll find that *Classroom in a Book* teaches many advanced features, including tips and techniques for using the latest version of Adobe Illustrator.

Although each lesson provides step-by-step instructions for creating a specific project, there's room for exploration and experimentation. You can follow the book from start to finish, or do only the lessons that correspond to your interests and needs. Each lesson concludes with a review section summarizing what you've covered.

Prerequisites

Before beginning to use *Adobe Illustrator CS3 Classroom in a Book*, you should have a working knowledge of your computer and its operating system. Make sure you know how to use the mouse and standard menus and commands, and also how to open, save, and close files. If you need to review these techniques, see the printed or online documentation included with your Windows or Mac OS.

Note: When instructions differ by platform, Windows commands appear first, and then the Mac OS commands, with the platform noted in parentheses. For example, "press Alt (Windows) or Option (Mac OS) and click away from the artwork." Common commands may be further abbreviated with the Windows commands first, followed by a slash and the Mac OS commands, without any parenthetical reference. For example, "press Alt/Option" or "Ctrl/Command+click."

Installing the program

Before you begin using *Adobe Illustrator CS3 Classroom in a Book*, make sure that your system is set up correctly and that you've installed the required software and hardware.

The Adobe Illustrator CS3 software is not included on the Classroom in a Book CD; you must purchase the software separately. For complete instructions on installing the software, see the Adobe Illustrator Read Me file on the application DVD or on the web at www.adobe.com/support/.

Installing the Classroom in a Book fonts

The Classroom in a Book lesson files use the fonts that come with Adobe Illustrator CS3. You'll find some of the fonts on the product DVD; others install with the product for your convenience. These fonts are installed in the following locations:

- Mac OS X: [startup drive]/Library/Fonts/
- Windows: [startup drive]\Windows\Fonts\

For more information about fonts and installation see the Adobe Illustrator CS3 Read Me file on the application DVD or on the web at www.adobe.com/support/

Copying the Classroom in a Book files

The Classroom in a Book CD includes folders containing all the electronic files for the lessons. Each lesson has its own folder. You must install these folders on your hard disk to use the files for the lessons. To save room on your hard disk, you can install the folders for each lesson as you need them.

To install the Classroom in a Book files

1   Insert the *Adobe Illustrator CS3 Classroom in a Book* CD into your CD-ROM drive.

2   Create a folder on your hard disk and name it AICIB.

3   Do one of the following:

• Copy the Lessons folder into the AICIB folder.

• Copy only the single lesson folder you need.

Restoring default preferences

The preference files control how panels and command settings appear on your screen when you open the Adobe Illustrator program. Each time you quit Adobe Illustrator, the position of the panels and certain command settings are recorded in the preference files. If you want to restore the tools and panels to their original default settings, you can delete the current Adobe Illustrator CS3 preferences files. Adobe Illustrator creates preference files, if they don't already exist, the next time you start the program and save a file.

You must restore the default preferences for Illustrator before you begin each lesson. This ensures that the tools and panels function as described in this book. When you have finished the book, you can restore your saved settings.

To save your current Illustrator preferences

1   Exit Adobe Illustrator CS3.

2   Locate the AIPrefs (Windows) or Adobe Illustrator Prefs (Mac OS) and the AIWSPrefs file, as follows.

• In Windows, the AIPrefs file is located in the Documents and Settings\username\ Application Data\Adobe\Adobe Illustrator CS3 Settings folder. The AIWSPrefs file is located in the Documents and Settings\username\Application Data\Adobe\Adobe Illustrator CS3 Settings\Workspaces folder.

Note: You may have to click on the View tab in the Folder Options dialog box from the Control panel to show hidden files to locate these preferences. Check the radio button to the left of Show hidden files and folders.

• In Mac OS, the Adobe Illustrator Prefs file is located in the Users/username/Library/ Preferences/Adobe Illustrator CS3 Settings folder. The AIWSPrefs file is located in the Users/username/Library/Preferences/Adobe Illustrator CS3 Settings/Workspaces folder.

Note: If you cannot locate the preferences file, use your operating system's Find command, and search for AIPrefs (Windows) or Adobe Illustrator Prefs (Mac OS) and AIWSPrefs.

If you can't find the files, either you haven't started Adobe Illustrator CS3 yet or you have moved the preferences file. The preferences file is created after you quit the program the first time, and is updated thereafter.

3 Make a duplicate copy of these files and save to another folder on your hard drive.

Note: To locate and delete the Adobe Illustrator preferences file quickly each time you begin a new lesson, you can create a shortcut (Windows) or an alias (Mac OS) for the Illustrator CS3 Settings folder.

To delete the current Illustrator preferences

1 Exit Adobe Illustrator CS3.

2 Locate the AIPrefs (Windows) or Adobe Illustrator Prefs (Mac OS) and the AIWSPrefs file, as follows.

• In Windows, the AIPrefs file is located in the Documents and Settings\username\ Application Data\Adobe\Adobe Illustrator CS3 Settings folder. The AIWSPrefs file is located in the Documents and Settings\username\Application Data\Adobe\Adobe Illustrator CS3 Settings\Workspaces folder.

Note: You may have to click on the View tab in the Folder Options dialog box from the Control panel to show hidden files to locate this preference. Check the radio button to the left of Show hidden files and folders.

• In Mac OS, the Adobe Illustrator Prefs file is located in the Users/username/Library/ Preferences/Adobe Illustrator CS3 Settings folder. The AIWSPrefs file is located in the Users/username/Library/Preferences/Adobe Illustrator CS3 Settings/Workspaces folder.

3 Delete the AIPrefs (Windows) or Adobe Illustrator Prefs (Mac OS) file and the AIWSPrefs file.

4 Launch Illustrator. The application will create a new set of preferences files with the original default settings.

To restore your saved preferences after completing the lessons

1 Exit Adobe Illustrator CS3.

2   Delete the current AIPrefs (Windows) file or Adobe Illustrator Prefs file (Mac OS) and the AIWSPrefs file and return the original files you saved (AIPrefs file (Windows) or Adobe Illustrator Prefs file (Mac OS) and the AIWSPrefs) to the Adobe Illustrator CS3 Settings folder.

Note: You can relocate the original preferences file rather than renaming it.

Additional resources

Adobe Illustrator CS3 Classroom in a Book is not meant to replace documentation that comes with the program. Only the commands and options used in the lessons are explained in this book. For comprehensive information about program features, refer to these resources:

· Adobe Illustrator CS3 Help, which you can view by choosing Help > Illustrator Help.
· Printed copies of Adobe Illustrator CS3 documentation (a subset of Help) are available for purchase from www.adobe.com/go/buy_books
· Adobe Design Center provides you with hundreds of tutorials from experts and authors in the community, as well as thoughtful articles about design and technology. Go to www.adobe.com/designcenter/
· Adobe CS3 Video Workshop DVD, included in the product box, provides you with 250 instructional movies on Illustrator CS3 and other products across the Adobe Creative Suite 3 lineup.

Useful links
· Illustrator product home page www.adobe.com/products/illustrator/
· Illustrator User Forums www.adobe.com/support/forums/
· Illustrator Exchange www.adobe.com/cfusion/exchange/
· Illustrator plug-ins www.adobe.com/products/plugins/illustrator/
· Illustrator training resources www.adobe.com/products/illustrator/training.html

Adobe certification

The Adobe Certification program is designed to help Adobe customers improve and promote their product-proficiency skills. The Adobe Certified Expert (ACE) program recognizes the high-level skills of expert users. Authorized Training Centers (AATC) use only Adobe Certified Experts to teach Adobe software classes. For Adobe Certified information, visit www.adobe.com/support/certification.

What's New in Adobe Illustrator CS3

Illustrator CS3 is packed with new and innovative features to help you produce artwork more efficiently, whether for print, web, or digital video publication. In this chapter, you'll learn about many of these new features - how they function, and how you can use them in your work.

Workspace improvements

Panels, which were called palettes in previous versions, can now be docked along the edge of the workspace, giving you flexible, efficient control over the workspace. When you drag a pane narrow enough the panels switch to icon mode, which can be used to pop up the associated panel. In addition, you can also now display the Tools panel as a single or double column using new arrows that appear above the Tools panel.

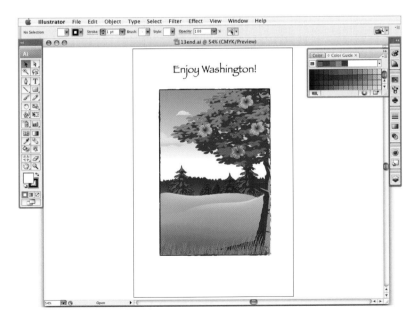

Control panel enhancements

The Control panel now provides you with access to anchor controls if you select one, or multiple anchor points in a path. Note that this exposes another handy new feature, the ability to delete multiple anchor points without breaking a path. The Control panel now also gives you direct access to Envelope Distortion options. It also lets you apply a rectangular Clipping Mask to an image, and gives you access to Select Similar options. If there isn't enough room to display all of the icons, specific groups of icons are collapsed, based on what is selected in the document. Clicking on a collapsed icon link gives you quick access to that panel.

Document startup profiles

In Illustrator CS3 you can select between Print, Web, Video, Mobile, and Basic RGB/ Basic CMYK workflows. When creating a new document, you can select from several workflow types, which populates the interface with the appropriate Document Raster setting, Color Profile, and other settings. All of these settings can be customized as well.

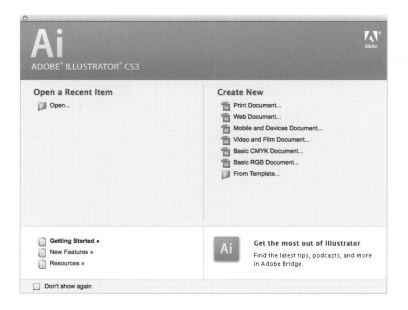

Drawing enhancements

Drawing in Illustrator CS3 is more efficient, thanks to improved rendering performance. You also have more control when working with anchors and anchor point handles. In addition to being able to change the size and shape of anchor points and anchor point handles, the selection logic for anchor points has been improved. When you click to select an anchor point, Illustrator now selects the closest point, instead of the anchor point that is highest in the stacking order. Also, alignment controls now work on anchor points, and there is now a selection threshold, which you can set in the Preferences. Learn more about drawing in Lesson 5, "Drawing with the Pen tool."

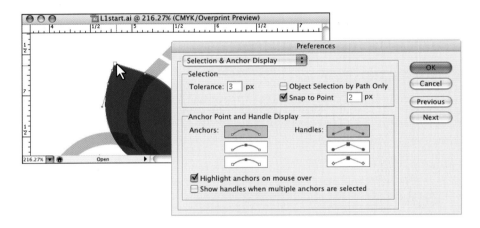

The Eraser tool

The new interactive Eraser tool is an exciting addition to the program, as it erases any vector content. It is also selection aware, meaning that it won't erase anything outside of a selection. It is also tablet aware, and by default, it should be associated to the back end (eraser end) of a tablet stylus. Read more about the Eraser tool in "A Quick Tour of Adobe Illustrator CS3."

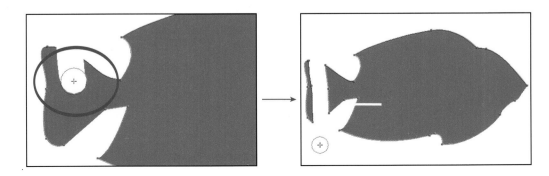

Live Color

Live Color is new in Illustrator CS3 and a large step towards helping you find "good" colors, experiment with colors right on your artwork, and manage your colors as a group. Live color is composed of 3 major parts:
1. The Color Guide panel, which is a lightweight interface to find compelling color groups. 2. Changes to the Swatches panel, which include the ability to save a set of colors as a group, view grouping structure from within the Swatches panel, and extract all used colors from specific selected artwork. 3. The Live Color dialog box, which allows you to find compelling color groups right on an interactive color wheel and to define custom color groups. It also gives you the ability to constrain color group selection to specific Color Panels/Color Spaces (for instance WebSafe or Pantone®). Read more about the Live Color in Lesson 6, "Color and Painting."

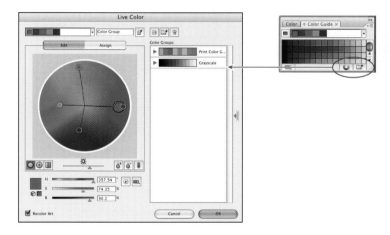

Layers panel enhancements

Layers have long been a part of Illustrator, but this enhancement is a big productivity boost. You now have a small color proxy beside each layer so that you can easily tell which layer you've got selected by color. Read more about layers in Lesson 8, "Working with Layers."

The Crop tool

The new interactive Crop tool, which is fully integrated into the Control panel, allows you to easily change crop size, and/or move a crop, as well as define multiple crop areas within a single document. For video content creators, there are many overlays to help create content that shows video safe areas, pixel rulers that show aspect scaling, and more. Read more about the Crop tool in Lesson 14, "Combining Illustrator CS3 Graphics with the Creative Suite."

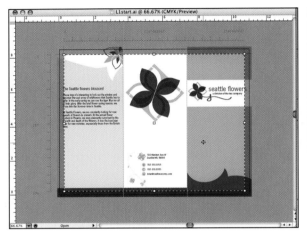

Symbol workflow improvements

Symbols in Illustrator now work more like they do in Flash. This means that you can double-click on a symbol instance to edit the symbol definition. When you create a symbol, you can decide whether it should be a Graphic or Movie Clip symbol. All of the key symbol attributes, including the ability to name a symbol instance, can now be accessed right from the Control panel.

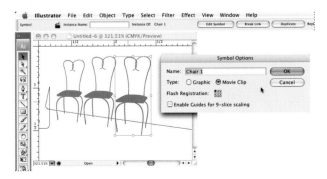

Enhanced support for digital video workflows

Video content creators will appreciate new overlays that help create content that shows video safe areas, pixel rulers that show aspect scaling, and more. The new document startup profiles also include Video and Mobile workflows as a starting point for documents.

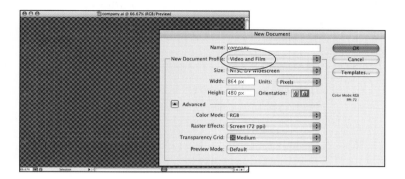

Dynamic and input text

To enhance integration between the programs, Illustrator CS3 now lets you define text objects as Flash Dynamic or Input text via the new Flash Text panel. If you specify an Illustrator text object as either Dynamic Text or Input Text, it will be exported as the correct Flash type when using SWF Export, and it should also File > Import or Copy > Paste as the appropriate Flash object. Illustrator also now allows you to name these objects, so that they can be accessed programmatically.

While this list is by no means an exhaustive description of the new features of Illustrator CS3, it exemplifies Adobe's commitment to providing the best tools possible for your publishing needs. We hope you enjoy working with Illustrator CS3 as much as we do.

—**The Adobe Illustrator CS3 Classroom in a Book Team**

take the ride

Snowboard

This interactive demonstration of Adobe Illustrator CS3 is designed to give an overview of new and exciting features in the program. You will discover new features like color groups and Live Color, and learn key fundamentals of the program.

A Quick Tour of Adobe Illustrator CS3

This interactive demonstration of Adobe Illustrator CS3 is designed to give an overview of the program and some of the exciting new features in about an hour.

Getting started

You will work with one file during this tour. All art files are located on the *Adobe Classroom in a Book* CD that is located on the inside back cover of this book. Make sure that you copy the AICIB folder from the CD to your hard drive before starting this exercise. Before you begin, you need to restore the default preferences for Adobe Illustrator CS3. Then you'll open the finished art file for this lesson to see what you will create on your own.

Note: If you are new to Adobe Illustrator or to vector-drawing applications, you might want to begin with Lesson 1, "Getting to Know the Work Area."

1   To ensure that the tools and panels function exactly as described in this tour, delete or deactivate (by renaming) the Adobe Illustrator CS3 preferences file. See "Restoring default preferences" on page 3.

2   Start Adobe Illustrator CS3. When the Welcome Screen appears, choose Open, or choose File > Open.

3   Open the tour_done.ai file in the Lesson00 folder located inside the Lessons folder within the AICIB folder on your hard drive. If a Missing Profile warning appears, click OK.

Choose View > Zoom Out to make the finished artwork smaller, and leave it on your screen as you work. Use the Hand tool (✋) to reposition the artwork to the upper left of the window, then drag the lower right corner of the document window to make the window smaller. If you don't want to leave the image open as you work, choose File > Close.

The completed tour illustration.

1   Choose File > New or by using the keyboard shortcut Ctrl+N (Windows) or Command+N (Mac OS). For the tour file, you will start with a blank document.

2   When the New Document dialog box appears, with the New Document Profile set at Print, type in snowboard for the Name. Next, choose the landscape button for the Orientation, select Inches from the Units menu and click OK. A new blank document window appears.

💡 *Adobe Illustrator CS3 offers pre-built New Document Profiles when you open a new document. These profiles are tailored for different kinds of projects—mobile, print, web, and video, for example.*

3   Choose File > Save As. In the Save As dialog box, the name should be **snowboard. ai**. Leave Illustrator (*.AI), as the file format and click Save. In the Illustrator Options dialog box, leave the options at their defaults and click OK.

4   Choose View > Show Rulers, or use the keyboard shortcut Ctrl+R (Windows) or Command+R (Mac OS) to show rulers on the top and left part of your artboard.

5   Select the Rectangle tool (▭) and click once on the artboard; do not click and drag. The Rectangle dialog box appears.

6   Enter **11** for the Width, and **8.5** for the Height, then click OK. A rectangle appears on the page. You will reposition it in the next step.

With any shape tool, you can click once on the artboard to enter exact values for the shape.

Note: *If your document is not measuring in increments of inches, you can still enter "in" after the value to create the rectangle in inches.*

7   Select the Selection tool (↖) from the Tools panel. With the rectangle still selected, click the Align to Artboard option in the Control panel to show more align options. This will align the rectangle to the artboard instead of other objects. Choose Horizontal Align Center and Vertical Align Center to align the rectangle in the center of the artboard.

Align the rectangle to the artboard.

8   With the rectangle still selected, notice at the bottom of the Tools panel that there are controls for the fill and the stroke. The stroke is essentially a border, the fill is the interior of a shape. When the Fill box is forward, any selected color will become assigned to the interior of the selected object. Activate the fill by clicking the solid Fill box. Read more about strokes and fills in Lesson 6, "Color and Painting."

Fill box is   Stroke box is
forward.   forward.

For this example, you will assign colors using the Selection tool and the Swatches panel. Before you get started, notice that when you move the cursor over the swatches on the Swatches panel, a tooltip appears, providing you with the name of the color. Keep this in mind, as you will need to reference certain colors in the next few steps.

9   Choose Window > Swatches to show the Swatches panel.

10   Make sure the rectangle is still selected and choose the C=85 M=50 Y=0 K=0 swatch from the Swatches panel; the rectangle now has a blue fill.

Move the cursor over the swatches
in the Swatches panel to see color names.

11   Double-click the blue color swatch and in the Swatch Options dialog box, enter **71** in the C field and **42** in the M field to edit the color. Click OK. Keep the rectangle selected.

Pathfinder effects

Next you'll create the curved shape on the left side of the page.

1   Choose Edit > Copy, Edit > Paste in Front to make a copy of the rectangle on top of the other.

2   Click the Rectangle tool, hold down the mouse button and select the Ellipse tool (   ). Click somewhere on the page to reveal the Ellipse dialog box. Enter **14.1** in the Width field and **13.1** in the Height field. Click OK.

Next you will position, then punch the circle out of the rectangle.

3   Select the Selection tool ( ). In the Control panel, make sure that the center in the reference point locator (   ) is selected, and in the X field enter **9.8** and in the Y field enter **6.4.** Press Enter or Return. The Reference panel is discussed in further detail in Lesson 4, "Transforming Objects."

Note: If you don't see the X or Y in the Control panel, click on the word Transform to reveal the Transform panel or choose Window > Transform.

Edit the X and Y position of the ellipse.

4　With the Selection tool (⬆), Shift-click the circle and the rectangle behind it to select both. Open the Pathfinder panel by choosing Window > Pathfinder.

5　Option-click (Mac) or Alt-click (Windows) on the Subtract from shape area button (⬚) to cut the circle out of the rectangle. Close the Pathfinder panel. Choose File > Save. Next you will choose a tint/shade of the blue color applied to the subtracted shape.

Working with color groups and Live Color

A color group is an organization tool that lets you group related color swatches together in the Swatches panel. In addition, a color group can be a container for color harmonies, which you create using the Live Color dialog box or the Color Guide panel. Next you will create a variation of the blue color.

1　Choose Window > Color Guide. With the new shape still selected, and the fill box selected in the Tools panel, click the Set base color to the current color icon in the Color Guide panel. Choose the Shades category from the Harmony rules pop-up menu.

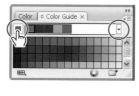
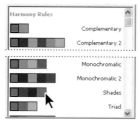

Click to set the base color.　　*Choose the Shades harmony rule.*

2　In the Color Guide panel, click a dark blue color from the top row of color shades. This should fill the new subtracted shape with the new color. Click the Set base color to the current color icon.

Choose a color.　　*Set the base color.*

3 Click the Edit Colors button (⬤) at the bottom of the Color Guide panel. The Live Color dialog box will appear.

4 In the Live Color dialog box, click the Edit tab at the top. Click the Color Mode button and select Global Adjust from the menu. Move the Saturation slider to the left until the value in the field is -29%. The Color Guide panel and Live Color adjustments will be discussed in greater detail in Lesson 6, "Color and Painting." Click OK.

5 Choose Select > Deselect.

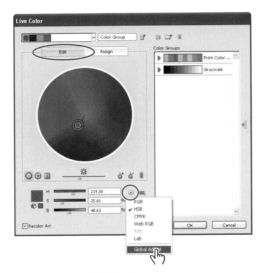

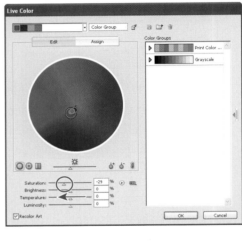

Select Edit and Global Adjust.   *Desaturate the color.*

Placing Photoshop images in Illustrator CS3

Illustrator can place Photoshop files as well as assign Layer Comps before you place the image on the artboard. Layer Comps are a Photoshop feature that allow you to save combinations of layers, using the Layer Comp palette in Photoshop. Layer Comps can be based upon visibility, position, and Layer appearance. Get more details about Layer Comps in Lesson 14, "Combining Illustrator CS3 Graphics with the Creative Suite."

1 Choose File > Place.

2 When the Place window appears, navigate to your AICIB folder to Lesson00, and select the file snowboard.psd. Make sure that the Link checkbox in the lower left corner is checked and click Place.

Illustrator recognizes when a file has been saved with Layer Comps, and opens a Photoshop Import Options window. The file in this example has been saved with two different Layer Comps.

3 In the Photoshop Import Options window, check the Show Preview checkbox and use the Layer Comp pop-up menu to select the comp named No background, and click OK. If you receive a color warning, disregard it for this example and click OK. The image of snowboarder is placed on the page.

Illustrator recognizes Layer Comps saved in Photoshop files.

4 Choose File > Save.

Using Live Trace

Live Trace provides incredible tracing options. Use it to trace logos, artwork, or even create vector color images from photographs. In this example, you will trace a Photoshop file to create a piece of black and white line art.

1 With the image still selected, click the Live Trace button in the Control panel.

As you see, the image is converted to a black and white image.

2   In the Control panel, enter 190 in the Threshold text field.

The Threshold is what Illustrator automatically chooses to be white or black. This can be helpful when working with images with fine lines that might get lost in the translation. The Live Trace feature is discussed in more detail in Lesson 3, "Creating Shapes."

Change the Threshold value.   *The result.*

Note: *Live Trace lives up to its name. If you were to edit the live trace image in Photoshop, the file would update the Live Trace image in Illustrator.*

3   With the traced object still selected, click Expand in the Control panel. This converts the traced image to paths.

4   Choose Select > Deselect and then, using the Direct Selection tool (⬚), click on the white background outside of the snowboarder. This activates only that white area. This is a bounding box that we want to remove.

5   Press the Delete or Backspace key to remove the white object, such as the background, but keep the traced image intact. Repeat these steps for the white space between the snowboarder's boots.

Traced image with background selected.   *Traced image with most of background removed.*   *All the white gone from the background.*

6   Choose File > Save. Keep the file open.

Using the Live Paint feature

The Live Paint tool will automatically fill paint regions. You explore this feature in the tour, but get more details in Lesson 6, "Color and Painting."

1   With the Selection tool (➤), select the snowboarder. Choose Select > Save Selection just in case you need to reference it again in the future. In the Save Selection dialog window, name the selection **snowboarder**. Click OK. Leave the snowboarder selected.

2   Choose Object > Live Paint > Make to turn this into a Live Paint group.

3   Select the Live Paint Bucket tool (🪣) from the Tools panel and hover over the snowboarder (don't click!). Even though this shape is created from many circles, Live Paint recognizes the visual shapes and highlights them as move over them.

4   Choose Window > Swatches and select the light orange color (C=0 M=35 Y=85 K=0). Move the cursor over the bottom of the snowboard, until the bottom is highlighted and notice the cursor (🪣). Click and the orange is applied.

The color squares above the paint bucket represent the color before and after the selected color in the Swatches panel (which is the color square in the middle).

Note: The color you choose may look different. That's OK.

The Live Paint feature automatically detects paint regions.

5   Now click your left arrow on the keyboard to choose the red/orange color (■)from the three swatches above the Paint Bucket tool. Using the Live Paint Bucket tool, apply the fill to the tip of the snowboard.

Note: You can also choose a swatch from the Swatches panel first before you click.

6   Choose File > Save.

Using the Control panel for typesetting

Before getting started, make sure that you choose Window > Workspace > [Basic]. This ensures that the Control panel is at the top of the Document window.

1   Select the Type tool (T), and click once on the artboard. Don't worry about location, the text will be repositioned later in the lesson.

Note: Make sure that you click and release on the artboard where there are no other objects. Also, do not click and drag, this creates a small, limited text area. More on type is discussed in Lesson 7, "Working with Type."

2   Type the word **Snowboard**. Still with the Type tool, choose Select > All, or use Ctrl+A (Windows) or Command+A (Mac OS).

3   In the Control panel, set the font size to **148 pts**. Press Enter after typing the new size.

4   Make sure the text is still selected and then do the following:

•   Click and drag over the font name in the Font text field in the Control panel.

Select the font in the Control panel.

•   Begin typing "**My**" while the font name is selected. This will filter the font list to Myriad. You may need to click the arrow to reveal the pop-up menu and choose Myriad Pro.

5   From the Font Style pop-up menu, choose Semibold.

💡 *Would you rather see the entire Character panel? Simply click on the underlined word Character in the Control panel. You can also use the Control panel to access the Stroke, Paragraph, and Transparency panels.*

6   Switch to the Selection tool (➤). The text area becomes active. Click the word Transform in the Control panel and making sure that the reference point locator (▦) is set to center, type **5.5** in the X Value and **1.2** in the Y Value. Press Enter.

Note: *If you don't see the Transform link, but see the X and Y value fields in the Control panel, enter the value in them.*

Position the text using the Transform panel.   *The result.*

Creating outlines of text

In the next part of this exercise, you will convert the text from font to outlines. An outline of a font is a vector shape of the font. It no longer is editable text but can be used in a variety of ways.

1   With the type still selected, choose Type > Create Outlines. The text is converted into vector shapes.

2   The outlined text is grouped together as a default. Before accessing individual letters and attributes, choose Object > Ungroup, or use Shift+Ctrl+G (Windows) or Shift+Command+G (Mac OS).

3   While the letters are still selected, choose Select > Save Selection. When the Save Selection window appears, name the selection **snowboardtext** and click OK. This makes it easier to reselect the text later in the exercise.

4   Choose Select > Deselect and File > Save.

Using the Appearance panel

1   Choose Window > Appearance.

The Appearance panel is an incredibly powerful panel that allows you to specifically control an object's attributes such as stroke, fills and other effects. Discover more about Effects in Lesson 11, "Applying Effects."

2   Choose Select > snowboardtext to reactivate the outlined text. If you do not have a saved selection, you can also select the first outlined letter S then hold down the Shift key and click on each outlined letter. This adds them to the selection.

Note in the Appearance panel that the selection is listed as a Compound Path and that both a stroke and fill are listed as attributes.

3   Select the word Stroke in the Appearance panel and then choose Window > Swatches to show the Swatches panel. Click on the None swatch (⊘) in the Swatches panel.

4   Open the Appearance panel again and choose Fill in the Appearance panel and click on an orange swatch in the Swatches panel. Your text now has no stroke and an orange fill.

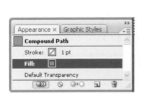 

The Appearance panel can be used for simple fills and strokes, as well as complex object attributes that include multiple strokes and fills.

Applying Effects

Now comes the fun part, using the Appearance panel to create some simple effects that might be difficult to create otherwise.

1   If the Snowboard text outline is no longer selected, choose Select > snowboardtext to reactivate the selection.

2   Choose Window > Appearance, then choose Compound Path in the Appearance panel.

3   Choose Effect > Stylize > Round Corners. When the Round Corners window appears, enter the amount of radius as **1 in**. Click OK. The text has now been rounded by 1 in. Keep the text outlines selected.

Choose Compound Path.   *The Round Corners effect.*   *The result.*

Saving the appearance as a graphic style

Perhaps you like the combination of attributes you have applied to an object and want to store them for later use. This can easily be done by saving a Graphic Style.

1   Choose Window > Graphic Styles.

The Graphic Styles panel can be used to store combinations of attributes applied to objects. This is discussed more in Lesson 12, "Applying Appearance Attributes and Graphics Styles."

2   Click the New Graphic Style button at the bottom of the Graphic Styles panel. Double-click the new graphic style that appears in the panel. When the Graphic Styles Options window appears, type **orange-rounded** in the Style Name text box; click OK. The Graphic Style you just created appears as the last thumbnail on the panel.

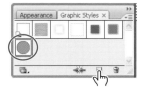

Save combinations of object attributes as a style in the Graphic Styles panel.

3   Choose Select > Deselect, then select the Type tool (T). Click and type "take the ride" anywhere on the artboard, but off your existing artwork. Choose Select > All to select the text. Make sure that the text attributes are set as Myriad Pro, Condensed, 40 pt. Enter those values using the Control panel.

4   Select the Selection tool (⬆) and click on the word Transform in the Control panel, making sure that the reference point locator (⊞) is set to center. Enter **3.2** in the X Value and **6.7** in the Y Value. Also, change the rotation value (∠:) in the Transform panel to **-93** and press Enter to accept.

Note: If you don't see the Transform link, but see the X and Y value fields in the Control panel, enter the value in them.

5   In the Graphic Styles panel, click on the thumbnail of the orange-rounded graphic style you saved. Your saved attributes are applied to the text.

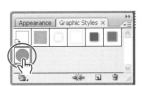

Apply the orange-rounded   *The "take the ride" text has the*
graphic style.   *Graphic Style applied.*

6   In the Tools panel make sure that the Fill box is forward and choose white for the text fill from the Swatches panel. Graphic Styles allow you to override properties.

Note: If you click on the Fill box in the Tools panel and it was already forward, the Color panel may appear. If so, open the Swatches panel again before continuing.

7   Choose File > Save. Leave this file open for the rest of the tour exercise.

Applying Warp to the text

The take the ride text is not quite following the curve it's next to. In this next section, you will learn how to apply a warp to text using the Control panel. Working with envelopes will be discussed further in Lesson 7, "Working with Type."

1   With the text frame still selected, click the Make Envelope button (⬛▪) in the Control panel. This will let you warp the text using preset templates such as envelope, flag, etc.

2   In the Warp Options dialog box, choose Vertical for the direction and move the slider for the Bend to the right until 9% is reached. The text will be warped, following the curve more closely. Click OK.

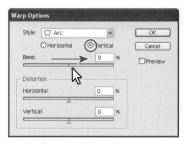

Apply the text warp.   *The result.*

3   Choose File > Save.

Applying a blending method

Next you will apply a blending mode to the shape. A blending mode determines how the object and its colors interact with the underlying objects.

1   Choose File > Place and locate the file named curve.ai in the Lesson00 folder. Make sure that the Link option is deselected and click Place.

The file is placed as an Adobe PDF document. The Place PDF dialog box will appear so click OK.

2   Click the Edit Clipping Path button (![icon]) on the left end of the Control panel. Press Backspace (Windows) or Delete to delete the clipping path that comes in with the curved shape. Use the Selection tool (![icon]) to click on the curved shape to select it again.

3   Click the Align to Artboard button (![icon]) in the Control panel. Click on the Vertical Align Top button (![icon]).

4   In the Control panel, make sure that the center in the reference point locator (![icon]) is selected, and enter **5.5** in the X text box. Press Enter or Return.

Note: If you don't see the X text box or Y text box in the Control panel, click on the word Transform to reveal the Transform panel or choose Window > Transform.

5   Choose Window > Layers.

6 With the curve still selected, and the Layers panel showing, click the Create New Layer button (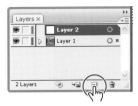) at the bottom of the Layers panel. This will make a new layer.

7 Choose Select > Deselect. Using the Selection tool Shift-click on the 3 background shapes (the blue rectangle, the new curve you placed and the darker blue shape). In the Layers panel, click and drag the color box in the selection column to the new layer, named Layer 2. The shapes will now have a red outline indicating that they are on Layer 2. Click and drag Layer 2 beneath Layer 1. You will see a line appear in the Layers panel when dragging underneath Layer 1. You can learn more about layers in Lesson 8, "Working with Layers."

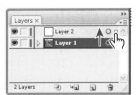
Drag selected objects to Layer 2.

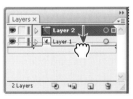
Drag Layer 2 beneath Layer 1.

The result.

8 Choose Select > Deselect.

9 With the Selection tool, click on the curve shape that was placed.

10 If the Transparency panel is not visible, choose Window > Transparency.

11 Choose Soft Light from the Blending Mode pop-up menu. This will blend the shape's color into the other two shapes beneath it. You can learn more about transparency and blending modes in Lesson 12, "Applying Appearance Attributes and Graphic Styles."

12 Double-click the Eraser tool (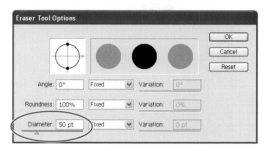) in the Tools panel to open the Eraser Tool Options dialog box. Change the Diameter to **50pt** and click OK.

13 Drag the cursor along the right edge of the curved shape to create a ripple effect.

Note: The Eraser only erases selected objects, but you need to make sure to touch the object to erase parts of it.

Click and drag to erase only the selected shape.

The result.

14 Choose File > Save.

Working with Symbols

A symbol is an art object that you store in the Symbols panel, and can be reused over and over again You will now take the snowflake that was pasted in from pieces.ai in the previous steps. Get more details about Symbols in Lesson 13, "Working with Symbols."

1 If the Symbols panel is not visible, choose Window > Symbols.

2 Open the snowflake.ai file in the Lesson00 folder located inside the Lessons folder within the AICIB folder on your hard drive.

3   Click on the snowflake with the Selection tool (➤), then choose Edit > Copy. Choose File > Close to close the snowflake.ai file. In the snowboard.ai file that is still open, choose Edit > Paste in Front.

4   Click the New Symbol button (⊡) at the bottom of the Symbols panel. The Symbol Options dialog box will appear. Type snowflake into the Name field and choose Graphic as the Type. Click OK.

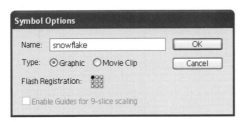

💡 *Adobe Illustrator CS3 has tighter integration with Adobe Flash. For instance, symbols are able maintain their structure and editability when you copy/paste them into Flash.*

A snowflake should appear in the Symbols panel. This symbol has been saved in the Symbol library for this document only. To learn more about symbols, view Lesson 13, "Working with Symbols."

5   From the Symbols panel, drag out the snowflake symbol onto the artboard. This creates an instance of the symbol. Drag out several more to create a loose snowflake pattern.

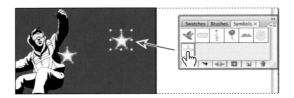

6   After dragging several snowflakes onto the artboard, use the Selection tool and the Shift key (to keep proportions) to select a few and resize them.

7   Choose File > Save and keep the file open.

Creating a clipping mask

To finish up with this project, you will create a clipping mask. A clipping mask essentially blocks or covers the object area not included in the object defined as the mask. This can be adjusted, of course. Details relating to this are found in Lesson 8, "Working with Layers."

1   If the Layers panel is not visible, choose Window > Layers. Click Layer 2 to select it. This will place the new object you are going to create on Layer 2.

2   In the Tools panel, click and hold down on the Rectangle tool (▢) and select the Rounded Rectangle tool (▢).

3   Click once on the artboard. This opens the Rounded Rectangle dialog box.

4   Enter a Width of **10.75 in**, a Height of **8.25 in**, and change the Corner Radius to **.5 in.** Click OK. The rounded rectangle appears on the page. It does not matter what color the fill or stroke is for this object.

5   In the Control panel, choose None (⊘) from the Fill color and None (⊘) from the Stroke color.

6   With the rectangle still selected, click on the Align to Artboard button (▦) in the Control panel. Choose Horizontal Align Center (▤) and Vertical Align Center (▥) to align the shape to the center.

The rounded rectangle in position.

7   Choose Select > Deselect.

8   In the Layers panel, click the Make/Release Clipping Mask button (◑) at the bottom of the panel.

Congratulations, your artwork is completed, and you have completed the tour of Adobe Illustrator CS3.

9   Choose File > Save and File > Close.

The Seattle flowers blossom!

These days it's interesting to look out the window and discover the vast array of wildflowers that Seattle has to offer. In the early spring we can see the tiger lillys ion all of hteir glory. After the brief flower spring season, we move into the Summer time in Seattle.

At Seattle Flowers, we are constantly looking for new breeds of flowers to present. At the annual flower festival in Phoenix, we were pleasantly surprised by the breadth and depth of the fflowers. It was the best year ever for new varieties, espeecially those from the British Isles.

seattle flowers
a division of the tea company

159 Western Ave W
Seattle WA, 98000

p 555 555.5555
r 555 555.5555
e brian@seaflowercomp.com

To the make best use of the extensive drawing, painting, and editing capabilities in Adobe Illustrator CS3, it's important to learn how to navigate the workspace. The workspace consists of the menu bar, Tools panel, Control panel, document window, and the default set of panels.

1 | Getting to Know the Work Area

In this introduction to the work area, you'll learn how to do the following:

- Use the Welcome Screen.
- Open an Adobe Illustrator CS3 file.
- Select tools in the Tools panel.
- Use viewing options to enlarge and reduce the document window.
- Work with panels, including the Control panel.
- Use Illustrator Help.

Getting started

You'll be working in one art file during this lesson, but before you begin, restore the default preferences for Adobe Illustrator CS3. Then, open the finished art file for this lesson to see an illustration.

1   To ensure that the tools and panels function exactly as described in this lesson, delete or deactivate (by renaming) the Adobe Illustrator CS3 preferences file. See "Restoring default preferences" on page 3.

Note: Due to the differences in Color Settings from one system to another, Missing Profile alert messages may appear as you open various exercise files. Click OK when you see this message. Color Settings are discussed in Lesson 15, "Printing Artwork and Producing Color Separations."

Note: If you have not already copied the resource files for this lesson onto your hard disk from the Lesson01 folder from the Adobe Illustrator CS3 Classroom in a Book CD, do so now. See "Copying the Classroom in a Book files" on page 2.

2   Double-click the Adobe Illustrator CS3 icon to start the Adobe Illustrator program.
When started, Adobe Illustrator CS3 displays a Welcome Screen with hyperlinked
options.

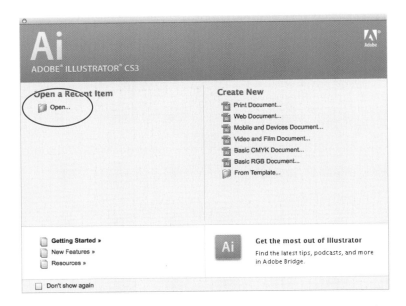

Use the Welcome Screen to find out what's new in Adobe Illustrator CS3, gain access to
resources and a list of new features. The resources include videos, fonts, templates, and
much more. The Welcome Screen also offers the option to create a new document from
scratch, from a template, or to open an existing document. The Open a Recent Item
includes the Open link and a list of recently viewed files. This area will be blank when
first starting Adobe Illustrator CS3. For this lesson you'll open an existing document.

*Note: If you prefer not to have the Welcome Screen appear at startup, check the Don't show
again checkbox. You can open the Welcome Screen at any time by selecting Welcome Screen
from the Help menu.*

3 Click Open on the left side of the Welcome Screen, or choose File > Open, and open the L1start.ai file in the Lesson01 folder, located within the AICIB folder on your hard drive.

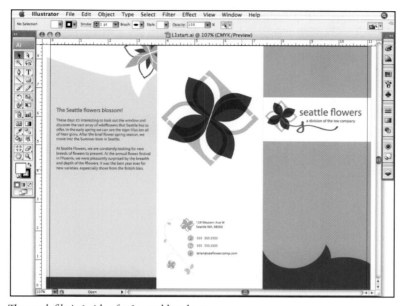

The work file is 1 side of a 3 panel brochure.

When the file is opened, and Adobe Illustrator CS3 is fully launched, the menu bar, the Tools panel, Control panel and panel groups appear on the screen. Notice how the panels are docked on the right side of the screen. This is where some of the program's panels are stored by default. Adobe Illustrator CS3 also consolidates many of your most frequently accessed panel items into the Control panel just below the menu bar. This lets you operate with fewer visible panels, giving you a large workspace.

You will use the L1start.ai file to practice navigating, zooming, and investigating an Adobe Illustrator CS3 document and work area.

4 Choose File > Save As, name the file **Flowers.ai**, and select the Lesson01 folder in the Save As menu. Leave the type of file format set to Illustrator(.AI), and click Save. If a warning message appears referencing spot colors and transparency, click Continue. The Illustrator Options window appears; leave the options at the default settings and click OK.

About the artboard

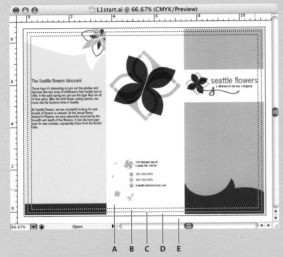

A. *Printable area.* B. *Nonprintable area.* C. *Edge of the page.*
D. *Artboard.* E. *Scratch area.*

The artboard represents the entire region that can contain printable artwork. However, the artboard's dimensions do not necessarily match the current page size. For example, your artboard may be 10 x 20 inches while your print settings specify 8.5 x 11 inch paper. You can view the page boundaries in relation to the artboard by showing page tiling (View > Show Page Tiling). When page tiling is on, the printable and nonprintable areas are represented by a series of solid and dotted lines between the outermost edge of the window and the printable area of the page.

Printable area is bounded by the innermost dotted lines and represents the portion of the page on which the selected printer can print. Many printers cannot print to the edge of the paper. Don't get confused by what is considered nonprintable.

Nonprintable area is between the two sets of dotted lines representing any nonprintable margin of the page. This example shows the nonprintable area of an 8.5" x 11" page for a standard laser printer.

The printable and nonprintable area is determined by the printer selected in the Print Options dialog box. (See Lesson 15, "Printing Artwork and Producing Color Separations" for more information about assigning a printer.) If you are saving an Illustrator document to be placed in a layout program, such as InDesign, the printable and nonprintable areas are irrelevant; the artwork outside the bounds will still appear.

Edge of the page is indicated by the outermost set of dotted lines.

Artboard is bounded by solid lines and represents the entire region that can contain printable artwork. By default, the artboard is the same size as the page, but it can be enlarged or reduced. The U.S. default artboard is 8.5" x 11", but it can be set as large as 227" x 227".

Scratch area is the area outside the artboard that extends to the edge of the 227" square window. The scratch area represents a space on which you can create, edit, and store elements of artwork before moving them onto the artboard. Objects placed onto the scratch area are visible on-screen, but they do not print.

—From Illustrator Help

Viewing artwork

When you open a file, it is automatically displayed in Preview mode, which shows how the artwork will print. When you're working with large or complex illustrations, you may want to view only the outlines, or wireframes, of objects in your artwork, so that the screen doesn't have to redraw the artwork each time you make a change. Outline mode can also be helpful when selecting objects as you will see in Lesson 2, "Selecting and Aligning."

1   Choose View > Outline. Only the outlines of the objects are displayed. Use this view to find objects that might not be visible in Preview mode.

2   Choose View > Preview to see all the attributes of the artwork. If you prefer keyboard shortcuts, Ctrl+Y (Windows) or Command+Y (Mac OS) toggles between these two modes.

3   Choose View > Logo Zoom (at the bottom of the View menu) to zoom in to a preset area of the image. This custom view was saved with the document.

Note: To save time when working with large or complex documents, you can create your own custom views within a document to quickly jump to specific areas and zoom levels. You set up the view that you want to save, and then choose View > New View. Name the view; it is saved with the document.

4   Choose View > Overprint Preview to view any lines or shapes that are set to overprint. This view is helpful for those in the print industry who need to see how inks interact when set to overprint. See Lesson 15, "Printing Artwork and Producing Color Separations" for more information on overprinting.

5   Choose View > Pixel Preview to view how the artwork will look when it is rasterized and viewed on-screen in a Web browser.

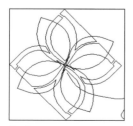   

Outline view.   *Preview view.*   *Overprint preview.*   *Pixel preview.*

6   Choose View > Fit in Window to view the entire page.

About page tiling

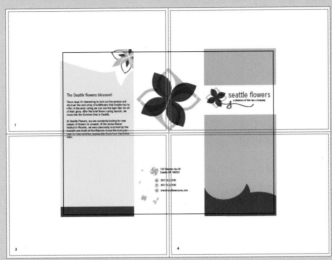

Artboard divided into multiple page tiles.

Adobe Illustrator CS3 is generally not meant to create multi-page documents. That would be more a function of a page layout program such as InDesign. Adobe Illustrator CS3 can, however, tile multiple pages for the purposes of accommodating artwork that is too large for an output device.

What is Tiling?

By default, Illustrator prints your artwork on a single sheet of paper. However, if the artwork is larger than the page sizes available on your printer, you can print onto multiple sheets of paper.

Dividing the artboard to fit a printer's available page sizes is called tiling. You can choose a tiling option in the Setup section of the Print dialog box. To view the page tiling boundaries on the artboard, choose View > Show Page Tiling.

When you divide the artboard into multiple page tiles, the pages are numbered from left to right and from top to bottom, starting with page 1. These page numbers appear on-screen for your reference only; they do not print. The numbers enable you to print all the pages in the file or specify particular pages to print.

—From Illustrator Help

Using the Illustrator tools

The Adobe Illustrator CS3 Tools panel contains selection tools, drawing and painting tools, editing tools, viewing tools, and the Fill and Stroke boxes. As you work through the lessons, you'll learn about each tool's specific function.

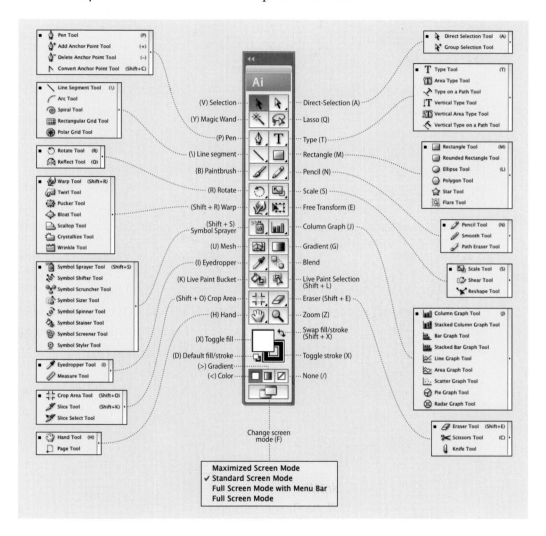

Note: The Tools panel shown here is a double column. You may see a Tools panel composed of only one column.

1   Position the cursor over the Selection tool (▸) in the Tools panel. Notice that the name and shortcut are displayed.

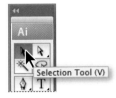

Note: The Tools panel shown here is a double column. You may see a Tools panel composed of only one column.

💡 *You can select a tool by either clicking the tool in the Tools panel or by using the keyboard shortcut for a particular tool. Because the default keyboard shortcuts work only when you do not have a text insertion point, you can also add other key commands to select tools, even when you are editing text. To do this, use the Edit > Keyboard Shortcuts command. For more information, select Keyboard Shortcuts in Illustrator Help.*

2   Position the cursor over the Direct Selection tool (▹) and hold down the mouse button—additional Selection tools appear. Drag down and to the right, and release the mouse button over one of the additional tools to select it. Any tool in the Tools panel that displays a small black triangle at the bottom right corner contains additional tools that can be selected by clicking and holding down the tool.

Next you will focus on resizing and floating the Tools panel.

3   Select hidden tools using the following methods:

• Click and hold the mouse button on a tool that has additional hidden tools. Then drag to the desired tool, and release the mouse button.

• Hold down Alt (Windows) or Option (Mac OS), and click the tool in the Tools panel. Each click selects the next hidden tool in the hidden tool sequence.

• Click and drag to the right of the hidden tools and release on the arrow. This tears off the tools from the Tools panel so that you can access them at all times.

4   The Tools panel can be changed to either a one column or two column panel. Click the double arrow in the upper left corner of the Tools panel to contract to one column. Click the same double arrow to expand to two columns again. This can conserve screen space.

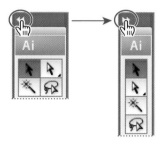

5   The Tools panel can also be removed from its position on the left side of the workspace. To move the Tools panel and float it in the workspace, click and drag it from the title bar above the Illustrator icon or the Illustrator icon into the workspace.

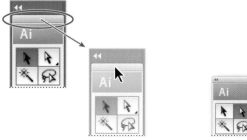

Click and drag to move the Tools panel.   *The result.*

6   When the Tools panel is free-floating, it can become one column. With the Tools panel floating, click the double arrow in the upper left corner at the top of the Tools panel. This will give you a one column Tools panel. Click again to turn the Tools panel back into two columns.

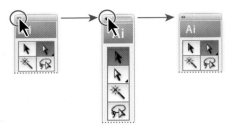

7   To dock the Tools panel again, click and drag from the light gray area or the AI logo area at the top of the Tools panel to the left side of the application window (Windows) or screen (Mac OS). A translucent area with a blue border to the left will appear. Let go of the Tools panel and it will fit neatly into the side of the workspace.

Note: If you click the double-arrows in the upper left corner of the Tools panel, it may not let you drag it.

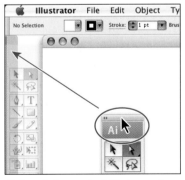 

Click and drag to dock Tools panel.   *The result.*

The Control panel

The Control panel (Window > Control) offers quick access to options, commands, and other panels related to the current page item or objects you select (this is called context-sensitive). By default, the Control panel is docked at the top of the application window (Windows) or screen (Mac OS); however, you can dock it to the bottom of the application window (Windows) or screen (Mac OS), float it, or hide it altogether. When text in the Control panel is blue and underlined, you can click the text to display a related panel. For example, click the word Stroke to display the Stroke panel.

1   Take a look at the Control panel located below the menus. With the Selection tool, click the middle of orange/blue flower at the top, left of the page. Notice the Control panel information. "Group" appears on the left side of the Control panel as well as the Stroke, Style, Opacity, etc. of that group of objects. Choose Select > Deselect so the group is no longer selected.

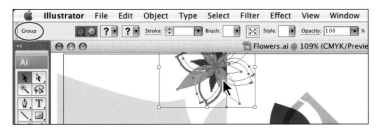

2   With any tool, click the light gray bar on the left side of the Control panel, hold down and drag into the workspace. A vertical bar should be visible on the left side of the Control panel for you to move it. The Control panel can be docked on the top of the workspace again or at the bottom of the workspace or float freely.

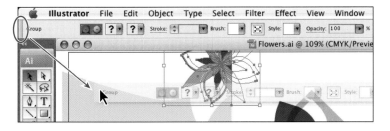

3   Click the left side of the Control panel (the gripper bar) and drag it back to the top of the workspace below the menus. A blue line will appear telling you that it will be docked when you let go.

💡 *To put the Control panel back at the top of the page you could choose Window > Workspace > Basic. This will reset the workspace.*

Working with panels

Panels give you quick access to many of Illustrator's tools, which make modifying artwork easier. By default, some of the panels are docked and appear as icons on the right side of the workspace.

Here you'll experiment with hiding, closing, and opening panels.

1   Choose Window > Workspace > [Basic] to reset the panels to their original location.

2   Click the Swatches panel icon (▦) to expand the panel, or choose Window > Swatches. Notice how the Swatches panel appears with two other panels (Brushes and Symbols). They are all part of a panel group. Click the Symbols panel tab to expand the Symbols panel. Try clicking other panel icons like the Color panel (🎨). Notice how a new group appears, closing the group that contained the Swatches panel.

Panel Dock ──────►

Click the Swatches icon to show the Swatches panel.

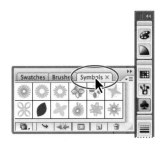
Click the Symbols tab to show the Symbols panel.

Note: *Be careful not to click the x to the right of a panel name like Symbols. This will close the panel. The panel can be opened by choosing Window > Swatches, for example.*

3   Click the Symbols panel tab (or whichever panel is showing) to collapse the panel back to its icon.

💡 *To find a hidden panel, choose the panel name from the Window menu. A check mark to the left of the panel name indicates that the panel is already open and in front of other panels in its panel group. If you choose a checked panel name on the Window menu, the panel and its group will close.*

💡 *To collapse a panel back to an icon, you can click its tab, its icon, or the double arrow in the panel's title bar.*

4　Click the double arrow at the top of the dock to expand the panels. Click the double arrow to collapse the panels again.

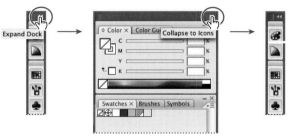

Click to expand.　Click to collapse.　　　　The result.

5　To change the width of all the panels in a dock, drag the gripper (▥) at the top of the dock to the left until text appears. To undo what you just did, click the gripper (▥) again and drag to the right until you can drag no further.

Click and drag
to change the width.

Click and drag back
to put it back.

The result.

6　Choose Window > Workspace > [Panel] to expand the panels. You are now going to resize a panel group. This can make it easier to see more important panels. Click the Symbols panel tab and drag the dividing line between the Symbols panel group and the Stroke panel group down to resize the group.

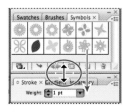

Next you'll reorganize a panel group.

7 Drag the Symbols panel tab outside the group to remove the panel from the dock.

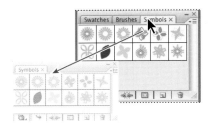 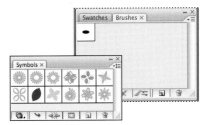

Drag the panel tab   *The result.*
to separate from the group.

You can also move panels from one panel group to another to create custom panel groups of the panels you use most often.

> 💡 *Press Tab to hide all open panels and the Tools panel. Press Tab again to display them all again. You can hide or display just the panels (not the Tools panel) by pressing Shift+Tab.*

Next you'll organize the panels to create more space in your work area.

8 You can double-click the tab containing the name of the panel to reduce the size of the panel. Double-click the tab again to minimize the panel. This can also be done when a panel is docked.

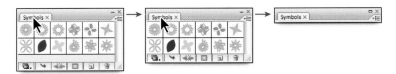

Note: You can double-click a third time on some panels to return to the full-size view of the panel. Also, be careful not to click the X that appears in the tab because this will close the panel.

Customizing your workspace

You can reset your panels and Tools panel to their default position. You can also save the position of panels and easily access them at any time by creating a workspace. Next you will create a workspace to access a group of commonly used panels.

1   To reset the workspace back to the default settings, choose Window > Workspace > [Basic].

Next you'll open some panels, align them on the side, and save the workspace.

2   Choose Window > Align and position the group of panels so that they are all visible on the left side of the screen, below the Tools panel.

3   Choose Window > Workspace > Save Workspace. The Save Workspace window opens. Enter the name **Navigation,** then click OK.

4   Return to the default panel layout by choosing Window > Workspace > [Basic]. Note that the panels return to their default positions. Toggle between the two workspaces using the Window > Workspace command and selecting the workspace you wish to use; return to the [Basic] workspace before going on to the next exercise.

Using panel menus

Most panels have a panel menu in the upper-right corner of the panel. Clicking this button (⊡≡) opens a menu with additional commands and options for the selected panel. You can use this to change options for the panel display or to access additional commands relating to the panel.

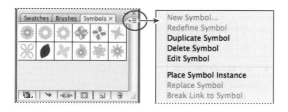

Next you will change the display of the Symbols panel.

1   Click the Symbols panel icon on the right side of the workspace. You can also choose Window > Symbols to display this panel.

2   Position the cursor on the panel menu (⊡≡) in the upper-right corner of the Symbols panel, and click to display the panel menu.

3   Choose Small List View from the panel menu. This shows the symbols as a list with a thumbnail, allowing for you to see the name of the symbol as well as the thumbnail. This command affects only the Symbols panel rows, not the other panels visible on the screen. The commands in the panel menu apply only to the active panel.

4   Click the Symbols panel menu, and choose Thumbnail View to return the symbols to their original view. Click the Symbols panel tab to hide it again.

In addition to the panel menus, context-sensitive menus display commands relevant to the active tool, selection, or panel.

To display context-sensitive menus, position the pointer over the artwork, panel list, scrollbar, or Document magnification level. Then click with the right mouse button (Windows) or press Ctrl and hold down the mouse button (Mac OS).

*Options for a
context-sensitive menu.*

Changing the view of artwork

You can reduce or enlarge the view of artwork at any magnification level from 3.13% to 6400%. Adobe Illustrator displays the percentage of the artwork's actual size in the title bar, next to the filename, and at the lower-left corner of the document window. Using any of the viewing tools and commands affects only the display of the artwork, not the actual size of the artwork.

Using the view commands

To enlarge or reduce the view of artwork using the View menu, do one of the following:

• Choose View > Zoom In to enlarge the display of the Flowers.ai artwork.

• Choose View > Zoom Out to reduce the view of the Flowers.ai artwork.

Each time you choose a Zoom command, the view of the artwork is resized to the closest zoom preset level. The preset zoom levels appear at the lower left corner of the window in a menu, indicated by a down arrow next to the percentage.

You can also use the View menu to fit the artwork to your screen, or to view it at actual size.

1   Choose View > Fit in Window. A reduced view of the entire document is displayed in the window. A helpful keyboard command for this view is Ctrl+0 (zero) (Windows) or Command+0 (Mac OS).

Note: With a Scratch area that extends to 227", you can easily lose sight of your illustration. By using View > Fit in Window, or the keyboard shortcuts, or Ctrl+0 (Windows) or Command+0 (Mac OS), artwork is centered in the viewing area.

2   To display artwork at actual size, choose View > Actual Size. The artwork is displayed at 100%. The actual size of your artwork determines how much of it can be viewed on-screen at 100%.

3   Choose View > Fit in Window before continuing to the next section.

Using the Zoom tool

In addition to the View commands, you can use the Zoom tool to magnify and reduce the view of artwork. Use the View menu to select predefined magnification levels or to fit your artwork inside the document window.

1   Click the Zoom tool (🔍) in the Tools panel to select the tool, and move the cursor into the document window. Notice that a plus sign (+) appears at the center of the Zoom tool.

2   Position the Zoom tool in the upper-left corner of the blue and orange flower and click once. The artwork is displayed at a higher magnification.

3   Click two more times on the blue and orange flower . The view is increased again, and you'll notice that the area you clicked is magnified. Next you'll reduce the view of the artwork.

4   With the Zoom tool still selected, position the pointer over the blue and orange flower and hold down Alt (Windows) or Option (Mac OS). A minus sign (-) appears at the center of the Zoom tool.

5   With the Alt/Option key still pressed, click the artwork twice. The view of the artwork is reduced.

For a more controlled zoom, you can drag a marquee around a specific area of your artwork. This magnifies just the selected area.

6 With the Zoom tool still selected, hold down the mouse button and drag over the area of the illustration you want to magnify; watch as a marquee appears around the area you are dragging, then release the mouse button. The area that was included in the marqueed area is now enlarged to fit the size of the document window.

7 Choose View > Fit in Window before proceeding. Drag a marquee around the large blue flower in the center of the document window.

The percentage at which the area is magnified is determined by the size of the marquee you draw with the Zoom tool—the smaller the marquee, the higher the level of magnification.

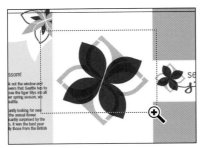
Area selected with marquee.

Resulting view.

Note: *Although you can draw a marquee with the Zoom tool to enlarge the view of artwork, it is not efficient to draw a marquee when reducing the view of artwork.*

You can also use the Zoom tool to return to a 100% view of your artwork, regardless of the current magnification level.

8 Double-click the Zoom tool in the Tools panel to return to a 100% view.

Because the Zoom tool is used frequently during the editing process to enlarge and reduce the view of artwork, you can select it from the keyboard at any time without deselecting any other tool you may be using.

9 Before selecting the Zoom tool from the keyboard, select any other tool in the Tools panel and move the cursor into the document window.

10   Now hold down Ctrl+spacebar (Windows) or Command+spacebar (Mac OS) to use the Zoom tool without actually choosing that tool. Click or drag to zoom in on any area of the artwork, and then release the keys.

11   To zoom out using the keyboard, hold down Ctrl+Alt+spacebar (Windows) or Command+Option+spacebar (Mac OS). Click the desired area to reduce the view of the artwork, and then release the keys.

12   Double-click the Zoom tool in the Tools panel to return to a 100% view of your artwork.

Scrolling through a document

You use the Hand tool (🖐) to scroll to different areas of a document. Using the Hand tool allows you to push the document around much like you would a piece of paper on your desk.

1   Click the Hand tool (🖐) in the Tools panel.

2   Drag downward in the document window. As you drag, the artwork moves with the hand.

As with the Zoom tool (🔍), you can select the Hand tool with a keyboard shortcut without deselecting the active tool.

3   Click any other tool except the Type tool (T) in the Tools panel and move the pointer into the document window.

4   Hold down the spacebar to select the Hand tool from the keyboard, and then drag to bring the artwork back into view.

You can also use the Hand tool as a shortcut to fit all the artwork in the window.

5   Double-click the Hand tool to fit the document in the window.

Note: The spacebar shortcut will not work when the Type tool is active and your cursor is within a text area.

Using the Navigator panel

The Navigator panel lets you scroll through a document. This is useful when you need to see the entire illustration in one window and edit it in a zoomed-in view.

1   Choose Window > Navigator to open the Navigator panel. It will be floating in the workspace.

2   In the Navigator panel, drag the slider to the right to approximately 200% to magnify the view of the document. As you drag the slider to increase the level of magnification, the red outline in the Navigator window becomes smaller, showing the area of the document that is being magnified.

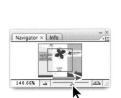 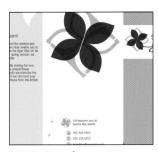

Drag the slider to 150%.   150% view of image.

3   Position the pointer inside the Navigator window. The pointer becomes a hand.

4   Drag the hand in the Proxy Preview Area (the red box) of the Navigator panel to scroll to different parts of the artwork.

Drag the zoom window.   View of image after dragging.

5   With the pointer (hand) still positioned in the Navigator panel, hold down on the Ctrl (Windows) or Command (Mac OS) key. When the hand changes to a magnifier, drag a marquee over an area of the artwork. The smaller the marquee you draw, the greater the magnification level in the document window.

6   Close the Navigator panel.

Using Illustrator Help

For complete information about using panels and tools, you can use Illustrator Help. Illustrator Help includes keyboard shortcuts and additional information.

Illustrator Help is easy to use because you can look for topics in these different ways:

- Scanning a table of contents.
- Searching for keywords or phrases.
- Using an index.
- Jumping from topic to topic using related topic links.

Displaying the Help contents

First you'll look for a topic using the Contents screen.

1 To display the Help Contents menu, choose Help > Illustrator Help, or press F1.

2 Drag the scroll bar, or click the arrows, to navigate through the contents. The contents are organized in a hierarchy of topics, much like the chapters of a book.

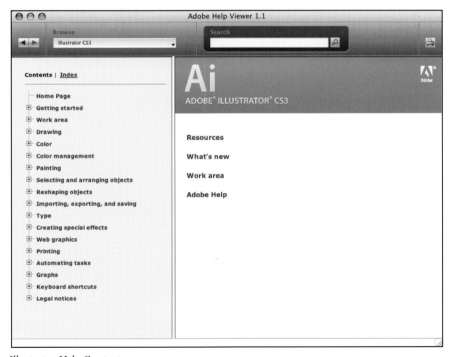

Illustrator Help Contents screen.

3 If the Contents link on the left is not selected, click it, and click the plus sign to the left of Work area. The plus + turns into a minus -, revealing topics to the Adobe Illustrator CS3 work area.

4 Click the plus sign to the left of Tools. A sub-menu appears.

5 Locate the topic "Tools panel overview" and click to display it. An illustration of the Tools panel appears along with its tool tip.

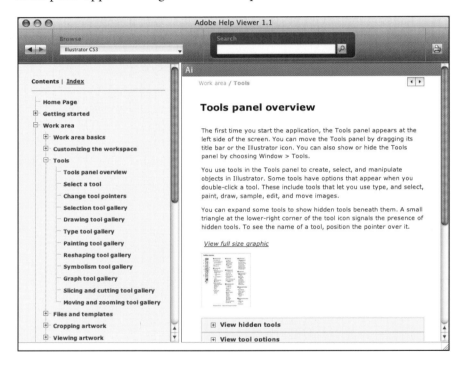

Using keywords, links, and the index

If you can't find the topic you want to review by viewing the Contents page, you can try using Search. You can search using keywords or phrases.

1 In the Search field at the top of the Help Viewer, type **Brushes**. Click the Search button to go to that topic. A list appears of the items containing information about brushes.

2 Click "Create or modify brushes" to learn about creating brushes. Notice, under Related Information, that there are several subtopics available for further research.

3   Click Create a brush to read about creating different kinds of brushes.

Locating a topic using the index

1   Click the Index tab in the left column to go to an alphabetical listing of topics. You will see an alphabet.

2   Click the letter H to get a listing of all the topics starting with H.

3   Click "hanging punctuation" to reveal a hanging punctuation sub category. Click the subtopic "hanging punctuation" to see how to create this text formatting attribute.

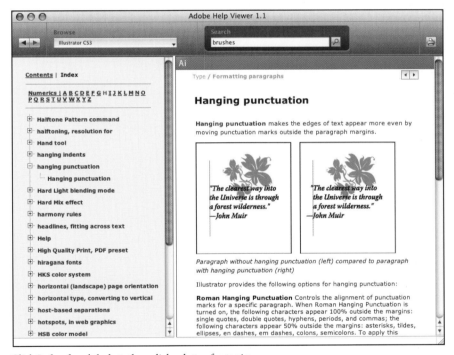

Click Index for alphabet, then click a letter for topics.

4   When you are finished investigating Illustrator Help, close the window and return to the document window.

Exploring on your own

Open a sample file from Adobe Illustrator CS3 to investigate and use some of the navigational and organization features learned in this lesson.

1   Open the file named Yellowstone Map.ai in the Lesson01 folder.

Note: A missing profile dialog box may appear. Click OK to continue.

2   Perform the following on this artwork:

•   Practice zooming in and out. Notice that at the smaller zoom levels the text is "greeked," appearing as though it is a solid gray bar. As you zoom in closer the text can be viewed more accurately.

•   Save zoomed in views using View > New View for different areas such as; Mammoth Springs, Tower-Roosevelt and Canyon Village.

•   Create a zoomed in view of Madison in the Outline View. Create a Preview view of the entire map.

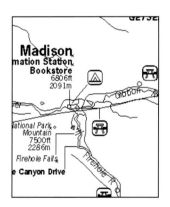 

•   Enlarge the Navigator panel and use it to scroll around the document and to zoom in and out.

•   Create a Saved workspace that shows only the Tools panel, Control panel and Layers panel. Save it as map tools.

Review

▶ **Review questions**

1   Describe two ways to change your view of a document.

2   How do you select tools in Illustrator?

3   Describe three ways to change the panel display.

4   Describe how to get more information about the Illustrator program.

5   How do you save panel locations and visibility preferences?

▶ **Review answers**

1   You can choose commands from the View menu to zoom in or out of a document, or fit it to your screen; you can also use the Zoom tool in the Tools panel, and click or drag over a document to enlarge or reduce the view. In addition, you can use keyboard shortcuts to magnify or reduce the display of artwork. You can also use the Navigator panel to scroll artwork or change its magnification without using the document window.

2   To select a tool, you can either click the tool in the Tools panel or press the tool's keyboard shortcut. For example, you can press **V** to select the Selection tool from the keyboard. Selected tools remain active until you click a different tool.

3   You can click a panel's tab or choose Window > Panel Name to make the panel appear. You can drag a panel's tab to separate the panel from its group or to remove it from a dock and create a new group, or drag the panel into another group. You can drag a panel group's title bar to move the entire group. Double-click a panel's tab to cycle through a panel's various sizes. You can also press Shift+Tab to hide or display all panels.

4   Adobe Illustrator contains Help, plus keyboard shortcuts and some additional information and full-color illustrations. Illustrator also has context-sensitive help about tools and commands, and online services for additional information on services, products, and Illustrator tips.

5   Choose Window > Workspace > Save Workspace to create custom work areas and make it easier to find the controls you need.

In this lesson, you will learn how to correctly locate and select objects using the Selection tools, as well as how to protect others by hiding and locking them.

You will also learn how to align objects and points to each other and the artboard.

2 Selecting and Aligning

In this lesson, you'll learn how to do the following:

- Differentiate between the various selection tools.
- Group and ungroup items.
- Clone items with the Selection tool.
- Lock and hide items for organizational purposes.
- Save selections for future use.
- Use tools and commands to align basic shapes to each other.

Getting started

When changing colors, size, adding effects or any number of attributes, you must first select the object to which you are applying the changes. Consider this lesson a primer in the fundamentals of the Selection tools. More advanced selection techniques using layers are available, and are discussed in Lesson 8, "Working with Layers."

Before you begin, you'll need to restore the default preferences for Adobe Illustrator CS3. Then you will open the art file that you will be working with for this exercise.

1 To ensure that the tools and panels function exactly as described in this lesson, delete or deactivate (by renaming) the Adobe Illustrator CS3 preferences file. See "Restoring default preferences" on page 3.

2 Start Adobe Illustrator CS3.

Note: If you have not already copied the resource files for this lesson onto your hard disk from the Lesson02 folder from the Adobe Illustrator CS3 Classroom in a Book CD, do so now. See "Copying the Classroom in a Book files" on page 2.

3   Choose File > Open, and open the L2start_01.ai file in the Lesson02 folder, located inside the Lessons folder within the AICIB folder on your hard drive.

Using the Selection tool

1   Select the Selection tool (↖) in the Tools panel. Position the cursor over the different shapes without clicking. Note the icon that appears as you pass over objects (↖▪), indicating that there is an object that can be selected under the pointer. Click the black airplane in the upper left corner. A bounding box with eight handles appears.

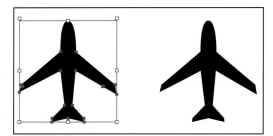

The bounding box.

The bounding box is used for transformations such as resizing and rotating; it also indicates that this item is selected and ready to be edited. This could mean changing its size, color, position, or any number of other things. The color of the bounding box also indicates which layer the object is on, but that will be discussed more in Lesson 8, "Working with layers."

2   Using the Selection tool, click the airplane to the right and notice that the first airplane is now deselected and only the second airplane is selected.

3   Add another airplane to the selection by holding down the Shift key and clicking the first airplane. Both airplanes are now selected.

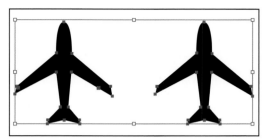

Add other items to a selection by
holding down the Shift key.

4   Reposition the airplanes anywhere on the document by clicking in the center of either selected airplane and dragging. Since both are selected, they travel together.

Note: *If selecting an item without a fill, you must click the stroke (border).*

5   Deselect the airplanes by clicking the artboard where there are no objects. If you prefer, choose Select > Deselect.

6   Revert to the last saved version of the document by pressing the F12 key or choose File > Revert. In the Revert dialog box, click Revert.

Using the Direct Selection tool

1   With the same file open, L2start_01.ai switch to the Direct Selection tool ( ). Again, don't click, but move the mouse over the different points on the airplanes with the Direct Selection tool. When the Direct Selection tool is over an anchor point of an unselected or selected path or object, it has a hollow square next to it. Click the top point of the first airplane and drag the anchor point. Note that only the point you dragged is solid, indicating that it is selected, while the other points in the airplane are hollow and not selected.

Only the point that is
selected is solid.

2   With the Direct Selection tool still active, click and drag the individual point down. This allows you to edit the shape of an object. Try clicking on other points, and notice that the initial point is then deselected and you can edit other points individually.

Note: Using the Shift key, you can select multiple points to move them together.

3   Revert to Saved by choosing File > Revert. In the Revert dialog box, click Revert.

About Selecting Points

Illustrator CS3 has Selection & Anchor Display preferences that allow you to set options for selecting points with the Direct Selection tool (↕).

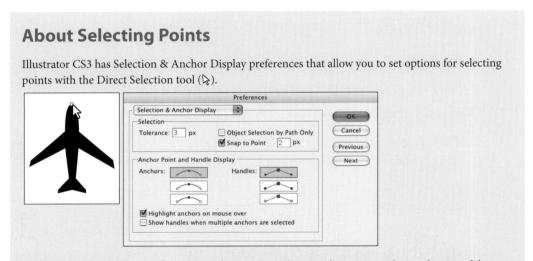

By choosing Illustrator > Preferences > Selection & Anchor Display, you can change the size of the anchor points (called Anchors in the dialog box that appears). You can also turn off the highlighting of anchor points on mouse-over by deselecting it in the Selection & Anchor Display preferences. You will learn more about anchor points and anchor point handles in Lesson 5, "Drawing with the Pen tool."

As you move the cursor over anchor points, they are highlighted. Revealing points in this way makes it easier to determine which point you are about to select.

Creating selections with a marquee

Some selections may be easier to make by creating a marquee around the objects that you want to select.

1   With the same file open, L2start_01.ai, switch to the Selection tool (▸). Instead of Shift-clicking to select the first two airplanes, position the mouse above the upper left airplane and then click and drag downward and to the right to create a marquee that overlaps just two points of the airplanes.

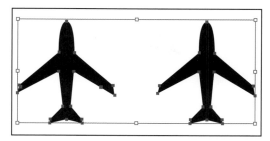

When dragging with the Selection tool, you only need to encompass a small part of an object to include it in the selection.

2   Try dragging a marquee starting outside the airplanes and crossing over both points in the top row. The airplanes become active.

3   Select > Deselect or click where there are no objects.

4   Using the same method, but with the Direct Selection tool (⬆), click outside the first airplane and drag to select the nose of each of the airplanes in the top row.

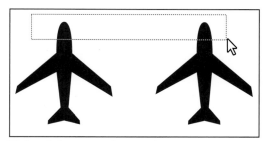

Click and drag across the top points.   *The result.*

Only the top points become selected. You can tell the top anchor points are selected because they are solid filled. Click one of the anchor points and drag to see how they reposition together. Use this method when selecting a single point. That way, you don't have to click exactly on the anchor point that is to be edited.

5   Choose Select > Deselect.

Creating selections with the Magic Wand

1   With the same file open, L2start_01.ai, switch to the Magic Wand tool (⚒). The Magic Wand will select objects of the same relative color fill. Click the apple and notice the fish being selected as well. No bounding box (box surrounding the two shapes) will appear because the Magic Wand tool is still selected.

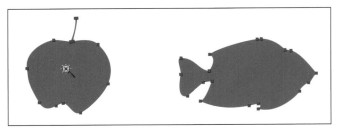

When clicking with the Magic Wand, objects with a similar color fill to the object being selected will be chosen as well.

2 Try clicking one of the baseball hats with the Magic Wand tool. Hold down the Shift key+(✎) and click back on the apple. This will add the apple and fish to the selection because they are both red. Hold down Alt (Windows) or Option (Mac)+(✎) and click the apple again to remove the red objects from the selection.

3 Select > Deselect or click where there are no objects.

Grouping items

You can combine several objects into a group so that the objects are treated as a single unit. This way, you can move or transform a number of objects without affecting their attributes or relative positions.

1 With the same file open, L2start_01.ai, switch to the Selection tool (▶). Click outside the top right airplane and drag a marquee that touches both airplanes, the fish and apple to select all four.

2 Choose Object > Group, then choose Select > Deselect.

3 With the Selection tool (▶), click the apple. Notice that since it is grouped with the other three objects, all four are now selected. Also notice that, with it still selected, on the left end of the Control panel you see "Group."

Adding to a group

Groups can also be nested; that is, they can be grouped within other objects or groups to form larger groups.

1 With the grouped objects still selected, Shift-click the left hat in the third row. With this added to the selection, choose Object > Group. The bounding box is expanded to include this new selection.

2   Shift-click the right hat in the third row and also choose Object > Group

3   Choose Select > Deselect when finished.

You have created a nested group. You may think of them as groups within groups. This is a common technique used when designing artwork.

4   Choose the Selection tool (↖) and click any one of the grouped objects. They all become selected.

5   Click off the objects in a blank area on the artboard to deselect them.

6   Hold down on the Direct Selection tool (↖) in the Tools panel, and drag to the right to access the Group Selection tool (↖).

7   Click the left airplane once. Only the airplane you clicked becomes active. Click again and the initial group of airplanes, apple and fish becomes active. As you continue to click, each individual group you create is selected.

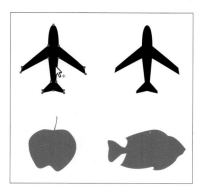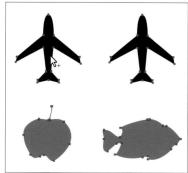

The Group Selection tool allows you to add selections within groups.

8   Ungroup the items by choosing Object > Ungroup. Note that you will have to repeat this action for each of the groups created. In this case, to get these back to individual objects, you would have to choose Object > Ungroup four times.

9   Choose File > Close, do not save the file.

Isolate selected group

As you work with grouped objects, you may find yourself repeatedly grouping and ungrouping when you need to access a single object within a group. This gets tedious, which is why you may want to isolate a group of objects to focus on.

To do this, choose the Selection tool and double-click a grouped object. As an example, if the airplanes from the previous exercise were grouped, and you double-clicked them, you would put the group into isolation mode. When that happens, the other objects on the page appear dimmed and a gray bar shows up at the top of the page to indicate that you've isolated a group. In isolation mode, using the Selection tool, you can select each object separately without having to ungroup. To exit the isolated group, double click outside of the group or click the arrow that appears in the gray bar at the top of the page.

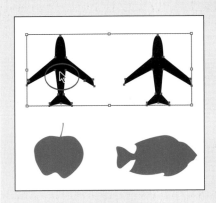 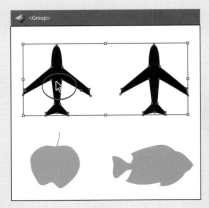

Applying the selection techniques

In this next lesson, you will use some of the techniques discussed previously in this lesson, as well as other selection options.

1   Choose File > Open, and open the L2start_02.ai file in the Lesson02 folder, located inside the Lessons folder within the AICIB folder on your hard drive. You will work on the original document and save it at the end of the lesson.

2   Make sure that the entire artboard is visible by choosing View > Fit in Window. On the right you see the completed project; on the left are the objects needed to create the finished flower.

3   Start this lesson by hiding the panels; you won't need them for this lesson. Hold down Shift+Tab to hide the panels, or hide panels individually, or by groups, using the Window menu.

4   With the Selection tool (➤), select the white flower (the daisy) on the left. To avoid grabbing a bounding box handle and accidently resizing the circle, click and drag the center of the flower to slide it to its new location as the head of the green flower stem on the left.

5   Using the Selection tool, drag the yellow/orange sunflower base, the brown sunflower center, and the leaf veins into position.

Note: *Be careful with the leaf veins. It contains three objects, so, using the Selection tool, Shift-click (or drag across) to select all of the objects and click one of the lines to move them together.*

*Use the selection tools
to move parts into place.*

6   Select the orange and brown sunflower shapes and choose Object > Lock > Selection to keep it in position. You will not be able to select it until you choose Object > Unlock All. Leave it locked for now.

7 Using the Direct Selection tool, click the anchor point in the tip of the left leaf. When the individual point is selected it appears as a solid point (active), whereas the other anchor points are hollow (inactive). Click and drag the individual anchor point to change its position.

If you are having difficulty accessing only one anchor point, remain on the Direct Selection tool and choose Select > Deselect. Then click and drag a marquee around the point, encompassing it with the selection marquee.

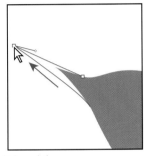

Using the Direct Selection tool, click and drag individual anchor points.

8 Individually select other anchor points in the leaf shape and position them in different directions. You are reshaping the leaf.

9 Select the Selection tool. The sunflower center (in the upper-left corner) is made of 4 small, light brown circles. Use either the marquee selection technique or the Shift key to select all four parts of the flower center. Choose Object > Group. Drag the group into position in the center of the orange and brown sunflower.

10 While still using the Selection tool, hold down the Alt (Windows) or Option key (Mac OS) and drag the selected flower center group into the center of the white flower (the daisy). This should make a copy. Position the cloned object as the white flower's center. Make sure to let go of the mouse before releasing the Alt/Option key.

Note: If you also hold down the Shift key when cloning, the newly cloned object is constrained and snaps to a straight 45°, 90°, or 180° angle.

11 Choose File > Save and close the file.

Hiding selected objects

As you create more complex artwork, existing objects may get in the way and make it difficult to select objects. A common technique is to hide selected artwork. Do this by choosing Object > Hide > Selection. The shortcut is Ctrl+3 (Windows) or Command+3 (Mac OS). A hidden object cannot be moved or selected; it is essentially an object that no longer exists on the active artboard. Bring all hidden objects back at the same time by choosing Object > Show All, or use Ctrl+Alt+3 (Windows) or Command+Option+3 (Mac OS).

Advanced selection techniques

When working on complex artwork, selections may become more difficult to control. In this section, you'll combine some of the techniques you've already learned with some additional features that make selecting objects easier.

1   Choose File > Open. Open the file named L2start_03.ai in the Lesson02 folder of AICIB lessons. If the Swatches panel is not visible, choose Window > Swatches.

2   Note that the large words make it difficult to select items underneath. Using the Selection tool (▶), select the word, Fries, and choose Object > Hide > Selection or hold down Ctrl+3 (Windows) or Command+3 (Mac OS). The word will come back in the exact same location when you choose Object > Show All at the end of the lesson.

3   Select any red star and choose Select > Same > Fill and Stroke. All the other red stars are now selected. Make sure that the fill box is selected (forward) in the Tools panel and select white from the Swatches panel. The red stars all change to white.

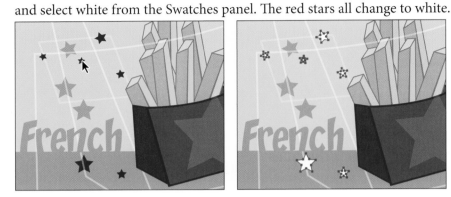 

4   Select one of the shapes within the french fries and then choose Select > Same > Stroke Weight. The french fry shape has a 1.5 pt stroke, so all strokes that are 1.5 pt are now activated. In the Control panel, type **3** into Stroke weight and press Enter to increase the stroke weight to 3 pt. Keep these items selected.

5   With the previous selection still active, choose Select > Save Selection. Name the selection **3 pt stroke**. Click OK. This allows you to reactivate this selection at a later time.

6   Choose Select > Deselect to deselect the objects. Choose Select > 3 pt stroke from the bottom of the Select menu to make the selection active.

 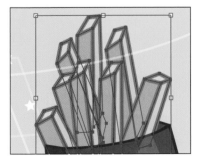

7   Choose Object > Show All to bring back the words French Fries. Choose Select > Deselect. Keep the file open for the next exercise.

Aligning objects

Multiple objects may need to be aligned or distributed to each other, the artboard or the crop area. In this section, you will explore the options for aligning objects and aligning points.

1   With the same file open, L2start_03.ai, Shift + click the text french and fries with the Selection tool (↖)(they should each be grouped objects). Choose Window > Align, or simply click the word Align in the Control panel to reveal the Align panel.

Note: The Align options are visible in the Control panel when an object is selected. If they do not appear, choose Align from the Control panel menu. So, throughout this lesson, you can use the Control panel or the Align panel.

2   In the Align panel, click the Horizontal Align Left button (🖿). Notice how the fries text moves to align with the word french.

3   Choose Edit > Undo Align to undo the last step.

4   With the two objects still selected, click the word fries with the Selection tool. In the Align panel, choose the horizontal align left option from the Align Objects options again. This time notice how the word french moves to align with the word fries. You just set an object to align to, otherwise known as a key object.

Next you'll align two points to each other, again using the Align panel.

5   Choose Edit > Undo Align to undo the last step. Choose Select > Deselect.

6   With the Direct Selection tool (➤), Shift + click to choose two points on the left side of the dark red shape in the french fries box.

Notice when the cursor moves over an anchor point a hollow square appears beneath the pointer.

7   In the Align panel, or in the Control panel, click Horizontal Align Left (▣).

Next you'll align all of the art to the center of the artboard.

8   With the Selection tool, choose Select > All to select all of the artwork on the artboard.

9   Choose Object > Group to group the objects together.

This is an important step when aligning more than one object to the artboard. If this isn't done, then centering everything horizontally on the artboard, for instance, would move all of the objects to the center independent of each other. Grouping moves the objects together, as one object, relative to the artboard.

10 From the Align panel, click the Align to Artboard button (⬛▾). This will lock the option so that all future alignments will be aligned to the artboard. Click the Horizontal Align Center button (⬛) to align the objects to the horizontal center of the artboard.

11 Choose File > Save and then choose File > Close.

About align options

The Align panel has a lot of features that are very useful in Illustrator. Not only can you align objects, but you can also distribute objects as well. The following is a summary of the options available to you in the Align panel.

Select the objects to align or distribute. To align an anchor point on the object, use the Direct Selection tool and select the anchor point.

In the Align panel, do any of the following:

• To align or distribute relative to the bounding box of all selected objects, click the button for the type of alignment or distribution you want.

• To align or distribute relative to one of the selected objects, click that object again (you don't need to hold down Shift as you click this time). Then click the button for the type of alignment or distribution you want.

• To stop aligning and distributing relative to an object, choose Cancel Key Object from the Align panel menu.

• To align relative to a crop area, specify the crop area you want to align to by selecting it with the Crop tool. Click the Align To Crop Area button (⌗) or click the Align menu and choose Align To Crop Area. Then click the button for the type of alignment you want.

• To align relative to the artboard, click the Align To Artboard button (⊞) or click the Align menu (▯) and choose Align To Artboard. Then click the button for the type of alignment you want.

By default, Illustrator calculates alignment and distribution based on the objects' paths. However, when working with objects that have different stroke weights, you can use the edge of the stroke to calculate alignment and distribution instead. To do this, select Use Preview Bounds from the Align panel menu

—From Illustrator Help

Exploring on your own

Experiment by cloning a star from L2start_03.ai. Clone it several times using the Alt/Option key. Apply different colors and strokes to the shapes and reselect them using the Select Same menu item. Select three stars from L2start_03.ai and try some of the Distribute Objects options in the Align panel.

Review

▶ ## Review questions

1   Why might an object that has no fill not become selected when you click on it?

2   How can you select one item in a group?

3   How do you edit the shape of an object?

4   What should be done after spending a lot of time creating a selection that is going to be used repeatedly?

5   If something is blocking your view of a selection, what can you do?

6   To align objects to the artboard, what must be selected in the Align panel before you choose an alignment option?

Review answers

1   Items that have no fill must be selected by clicking the stroke.

2   Using the Group Selection tool, you can click once for an individual item within a group. Continue to click to add the next grouped items to the selection. Read Lesson 9, "Working with Layers," to see how you can use layers to make complex selections.

3   Using the Direct Selection tool, you can select one or more individual anchor points and make changes to the shape of an object.

4   For any selection that you will need to use again, choose Select > Save Selection. Name the selection and reselect it at any time from the Select menu.

5   If something is blocking your access to a selection, you can choose Object > Hide > Selection. The object is not deleted, just hidden in the same position until you choose Object > Show All.

6   The align to artboard option must be selected first.

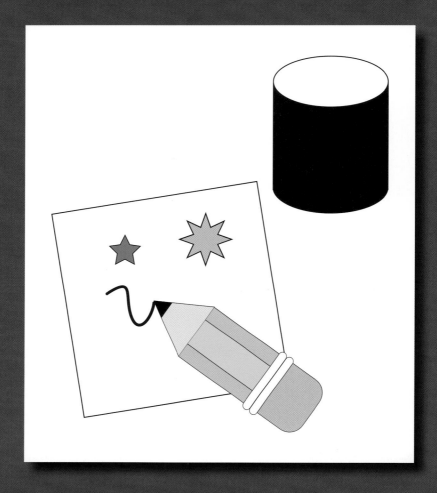

Many objects in illustrator can be created by starting with basic shapes and then editing them to create new shapes. In this lesson, you will use some basic shapes to create a logo.

3 | Creating Shapes

In this lesson, you'll learn how to do the following:

- Create basic shapes.
- Move, scale, and rotate objects using a variety of methods.
- Draw with the Pencil tool.
- Work with Smart Guides.
- Position objects precisely.
- Work with line segments.
- Use Live Trace.

Getting started

In this lesson, you'll create a logo composed of a pencil, paper and a pencil can. Before you begin, you'll restore the default preferences for Adobe Illustrator CS3, then open a file containing a composite of the finished artwork to preview what you'll create.

1   To ensure that the tools and panels function exactly as described in this lesson, delete or deactivate (by renaming) the Adobe Illustrator CS3 preferences file. See "Restoring default preferences" on page 3.

2   Start Adobe Illustrator CS3.

Note: If you have not already copied the resource files for this lesson onto your hard disk from the Lesson03 folder from the Adobe Illustrator CS3 Classroom in a Book CD, do so now. See "Copying the Classroom in a Book files" on page 2.

Creating basic shapes

You'll begin this exercise by creating a new document and setting the ruler units to inches, displaying a grid to use as a guideline for drawing, and closing the panels that you won't use.

1   Choose File > New to open a new, untitled document. Choose Print from the New Document Profile menu and change the units to inches. Leave the rest of the settings as they are, and click OK.

2   Choose File > Save As, name the file **Pencil.ai**, and save in the Lesson03 folder. Leave the type of file format set to Adobe Illustrator Document, and click Save. In the Illustrator Options, leave the default settings unchanged and click OK.

3   Reset the workspace by choosing Window > Workspace > [Basic].

4   Choose View > Show Grid to display a grid that's useful for measuring, drawing, and aligning shapes. This grid won't print with the artwork.

5   Choose View > Show Rulers, or hold down Ctrl+R (Windows) or Command+R (Mac OS) to display rulers along the top and left side of the window if they are not already showing. The ruler units are inches because of the change you made in the New Document dialog box.

You can change the ruler units of measure used for all documents or for only the current document. The ruler unit of measure applies to measuring objects, moving and transforming objects, setting grid and guide spacing, and creating ellipses and rectangles. It does not affect the units in the Character, Paragraph, and Stroke panels. These are controlled by the options in the Units & Display Performance dialog box in the program preferences.

6   To change options such as artboard size and units after a document is created, choose File > Document Setup.

You can change the units of measure for rulers by right-clicking (Windows) or Ctrl-clicking (Mac OS) a ruler in your active document. Choose the unit of measure from the context-sensitive menu that appears.

Document Startup Profiles

A document is the space in which you create artwork. In Illustrator, you can create documents destined for many different types of output.

You start a new document by choosing a new document profile based on your intended output. Each profile includes preset values for size, color mode, units, orientation, transparency, and resolution. For example, the Video And Film Document profile uses pixels instead of points, and you can choose a device-specific crop area, such as NTSC DV Widescreen, to create a document in the exact dimensions required, with video-safe guides in place to help you lay out your design for optimal viewing.

—From Illustrator Help

At left you can see the New Document dialog box with the Video and Film New Document profile chosen. The Advanced options (click the arrow to the left of Advanced to toggle open) are context-sensitive, which means that the options change based on which document profile is chosen.

Using basic shape tools

In this lesson, you'll create a simple logo using the basic shape tools. The shape tools are organized under the Rectangle tool. You can tear this group off the Tools panel to display it as a separate free-floating panel.

1   Hold down the mouse button on the Rectangle tool (▣) until a group of tools appears, and then drag to the tear-off triangle at the end and release the mouse button.

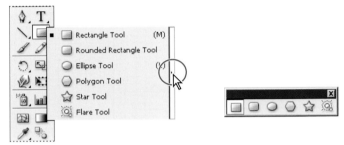

Tearing off the Rectangle tool group.

2   Move the Rectangle tool group away from the Tools panel.

Drawing the pencil shape

In Adobe Illustrator CS3, you control the thickness and color of lines that you draw by setting stroke attributes. A stroke is the paint characteristic of a line, or the outline of an object. A fill is the paint characteristic of the inside of an object. The default settings let you see the objects you draw with a white fill and a black outline.

First you'll draw a series of rectangles and triangles that make up the pencil. You'll display Smart Guides to align your drawing.

1   Select the Zoom tool (🔍) in the Tools panel, and click the middle of the window once or twice until you are zoomed in to 150%. Notice that 150% is displayed in the bottom-left corner of the window.

2   Choose View > Smart Guides to turn them on. Smart Guides automatically snap the edges of objects to nearby objects or their intersecting points as you move them. Smart Guides also show Text Label Hints that display information about the position the pointer is currently snapped to (such as "center") as you manipulate the pointer.

About Smart Guides

When Smart Guides are turned on and you move the cursor over your artwork, the cursor looks for objects, page boundaries, and intersections of construction guides to snap to that area within the tolerance range set in Smart Guides Preferences.

Smart Guides are temporary snap-to guides that help you create, align, edit, and transform objects relative to other objects. To activate Smart Guides, choose View > Smart Guides.

You can use Smart Guides in the following ways:

• When you create an object with the pen or shape tools, use the Smart Guides to position a new object's anchor points relative to an existing object.

• When you move an object, use the Smart Guides to align your cursor to construction guides and existing paths. The alignment is based on the position of the pointer, not the edges of the object, so be sure to click to the exact point you want to align to.

• When you transform an object, Smart Guides automatically appear to assist the transformation. You can change when and how Smart Guides appear by setting Smart Guide preferences.

Note: When Snap to Grid is turned on, you cannot use Smart Guides (even if the menu command is selected).

—From Illustrator Help

3   Choose Window > Transform to display the Transform panel. Then choose Window > Info.

4   Select the Rectangle tool (▣), and drag it to draw a rectangle that's approximately 0.75 inch wide and 1 inch tall. Use the rulers and the grid as guides. This will be the body of the pencil. You can also use the Info panel to determine the size.

When you release the mouse button, the rectangle is automatically selected and its center point appears. All objects created with the shape tools have a center point that you can drag to align the object with other elements in your artwork. You can make the center point visible or invisible using the Attributes panel, but you cannot delete it.

5   In the Transform panel, note the rectangle's width and height. If necessary, enter **.75 inch** in the width text field and **1 inch** in the height text field.

The Transform panel displays rectangle's width and height.

You'll draw another rectangle centered inside the first one to represent the two vertical lines on the pencil.

6   With the Rectangle tool still selected, position the pointer over the center point of the rectangle, hold down Alt (Windows) or Option (Mac OS), and drag out diagonally from the center point to draw a rectangle that's centered inside the other. Release the mouse button and then the Alt/Option key when the rectangle is the same height as the first rectangle (1 inch).

Holding down Alt/Option as you drag the Rectangle tool draws the rectangle from its center point rather than from its top left corner. Smart Guides indicate when you've snapped to the first rectangle's edge, by displaying the text label hint "path."

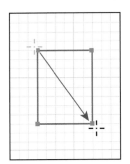 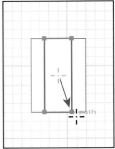

Drag to draw first rectangle.   *Alt/Option+drag to draw second rectangle.*

Besides dragging a tool to draw a shape, you can click with the tool to open a dialog box of options. Now you'll create a rounded rectangle, which will be the eraser, by setting options in a dialog box.

7 Select the Rounded Rectangle tool (⬛), and click once in the artwork to open the Rounded Rectangle dialog box. Type **0.75** in the Width text field, press Tab, and type **0.75** in the Height text field. Then press Tab again, and type **0.20** in the Corner Radius text box (the radius is the amount of the curve on the corners). Click OK.

💡 *To automatically enter identical Width and Height values in the Ellipse or Rectangle dialog box, enter a Width or Height value, and then click the name of the other value to enter the same amount.*

You'll use Smart Guides to help you align the eraser to the top of the pencil body.

8 Choose View > Hide Bounding Box to hide the bounding boxes of selected objects. This will prevent you from accidentally distorting the eraser shape when you move and align it.

The bounding box appears as a temporary boundary around selected objects. With the bounding box, you can move, rotate, duplicate, and scale objects easily by dragging the selection or a handle (one of the hollow squares surrounding the selected objects).

9 With the Rounded Rectangle tool still selected, hold down Ctrl (Windows) or Command (Mac OS) to access the Selection tool (▶) temporarily. Select the right edge of the eraser without releasing the mouse button, and then drag the right side of the eraser to align with the right side of the pencil body. (Smart Guides indicate the path of the right side.) Release the mouse button to drop the eraser on top of the pencil body.

10 Hold down Ctrl (Windows) or Command (Mac OS), select the bottom edge of the eraser, and drag it up to the intersect point at the top of the pencil body. Release the mouse button.

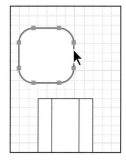 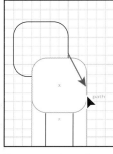 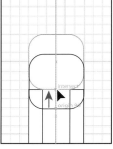 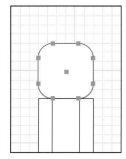

Select right edge of eraser shape. *Drag eraser to path on pencil body.* *Drag bottom of eraser to top of pencil body.* *Result.*

Next you'll create two shapes to represent the metal bands connecting the eraser to the pencil.

11 To create the first band, click once anywhere in the artwork to open the Rounded Rectangle dialog box again. Type **0.85** in the Width text box, **0.10** in the Height text box, and **0.05** in the Corner Radius text box. Click OK.

12 Using the Selection tool, click the band, select the bottom left anchor point, and move the band to the top of the pencil body. Release the mouse button. (Smart Guides snap the anchor point to the top corner of the pencil body.)

13 With the band still selected, hold down Alt (Windows) or Option (Mac OS), select the anchor point again, drag straight up to make a copy, and move it above the original band. Release the mouse button. (Smart Guides snap the anchor point of the new copy to the top of the original band.)

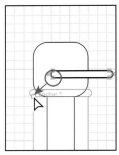 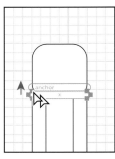 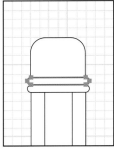

Move first metal band between eraser and pencil body. *Alt/Option+drag a copy above first metal band.* *Smart Guides snap objects into position.*

You've been working in Preview mode. This default view of a document lets you see how objects are painted (in this case, with a white fill and black stroke). If paint attributes seem distracting, you can work in Outline mode.

Now you'll draw two triangles to represent the pencil tip and its lead, using Outline mode.

14 Choose View > Outline to switch from Preview to Outline mode.

Illustrator lets you control the shape of polygons, stars, and ellipses by pressing certain keys as you draw. You'll draw a polygon and change it to a triangle.

15 Select the Polygon tool (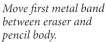), and position the pointer over the center point of the two rectangles.

16 Drag to begin drawing a polygon, but don't release the mouse button. Press the Down Arrow three times to reduce the number of sides on the polygon to a triangle, and move the mouse in an arc to rotate one side of the triangle to the top. Before you release the mouse button, hold down the spacebar and drag the triangle down to position it below the pencil body. Release the mouse button when the triangle is positioned.

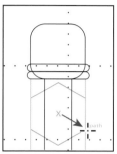
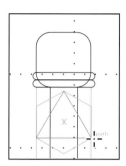
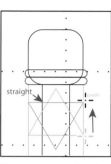
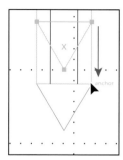

Drag to draw polygon; don't release mouse button.
Press Down Arrow key three times.
Drag to rotate triangle.
Hold down spacebar and move triangle.

Now you'll create the second triangle for the pencil's lead tip using the Scale tool.

17 Choose View > Show Bounding Box to turn the bounding box back on and switch to the Selection tool (▶). Make sure that the triangle is still selected. Notice how the bounding box is rotated. Choose Object > Transform > Reset Bounding Box. After rotating objects, you can reset the bounding box.

18 With the triangle still selected, choose Edit > Copy and Edit > Paste in Front to paste a copy directly on top. Select the Selection tool and holding the Shift key, resize from the top, middle point of the bounding box to the desired size for the pencil lead.

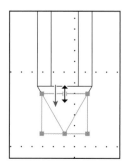

19 Choose Select > All to select the pencil shapes. Choose Object > Group to group.

20   With the group still selected, you will now rotate the pencil. In the Transform panel (Window > Transform) enter **-130** in the Rotate (△:) field and press Enter or Return to apply the rotation.

21   Choose View > Preview, and then choose File > Save to save your work.

Using the Pencil tool

The Pencil tool lets you draw open and closed paths as if you were drawing with a pencil on paper. Anchor points are created as you draw and are placed on the path where Illustrator deems necessary. However, you can adjust them once the path is complete. The number of anchor points set down is determined by the length and complexity of the path and by tolerance settings in the Pencil Tool Preferences dialog box, which we will discuss briefly.

1   With the pencil group rotated, select the Pencil tool (✏) in the Tools panel. In the Control panel, click Stroke color and select Black in the Swatches panel that appears, then click Fill color in the Control panel and select None (▱).

2   From the tip of the pencil group, click and drag to draw a curvy path with the Pencil tool. It's very similar to drawing with a regular pencil.

3   With the path still selected, position the Pencil tool on or near the end of the path located farthest from the large pencil tip you drew. When you're close enough to the path, the small x disappears from the tool. Click and drag from the end of the path to some point closer to the large pencil tip in the drawing, making sure to connect the end point of the new curve to the original squiggly line you drew. Illustrator will redraw the shape of the original squiggly line to match this new curve.

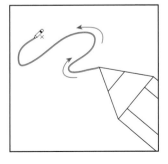
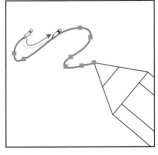

Click and drag with the   *Draw over the path with*
Pencil tool to create a shape.   *Pencil tool to redraw a portion.*

Pencil tool settings

The Pencil tool may behave differently than you would expect. The Pencil tool settings allow you to change how the tool works on paths you draw or edit, which gives you more control over how it functions.. Double-click the Pencil tool to set any of the following options.

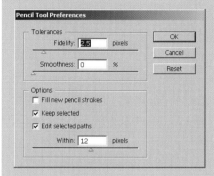

- **Fidelity** Controls how far you have to move your mouse or stylus before a new anchor point is added to the path. The higher the value, the smoother and less complex the path. The lower the value, the more the curves will match the pointer's movement, resulting in sharper angles. Fidelity can range from 0.5 to 20 pixels.

- **Smoothness** Controls the amount of smoothing applied when you use the tool. Smoothness can range from 0% to 100%. The higher the value, the smoother the path. The lower the value, the more anchor points are created, and the more the line's irregularities are preserved.

- **Fill New Pencil Strokes** Applies a fill to pencil strokes you draw after selecting this option, but not to existing pencil strokes. Remember to select a fill before you draw the pencil strokes.

- **Keep Selected** Determines whether to keep the path selected after you draw it. This option is selected by default.

- **Edit Selected Paths Determines whether or not you can change or merge an existing path when you are within a certain distance of it (specified with the next option).**

- **Within: _ pixels** Determines how close your mouse or stylus must be to an existing path in order to edit the path with the Pencil tool. This option is only available when the Edit Selected Paths option is selected.

—From Illustrator Help

Drawing the pencil can

Next you'll work with straight lines and line segments to create a can for holding pencils. Shapes can be created in many ways within illustrator, and usually simpler is better.

1   With **Pencil.ai** open, select the Hand tool (✋) in the Tools panel, and move to the upper right of the pencil to give yourself room to work.

2   Choose Window > Info to open the Info panel if it's not already open. Choose View > Smart Guides and make sure Smart Guides are still selected.

3   Select the Ellipse tool (⬭) from the same group as the Rectangle tool (▭) in the Tools panel. Draw an ellipse that has a width of **1"** and a height of **.25"**. (To see the size of the shape as you draw, reference the Info panel). In the Control panel, choose 1pt from the Stroke weight pop-up menu. Click the Fill color in the Control panel and select None (◻).

4   With the Direct Selection tool (k), drag across the lower part of the ellipse to select the bottom half (you may need to close the Swatches panel to make the selection). Choose Edit > Copy, Edit > Paste in Front to create a new path. Switch to the Selection tool and drag it down a few inches holding the Shift key down after you begin dragging.

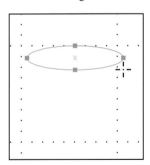
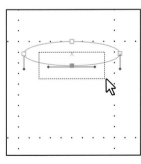
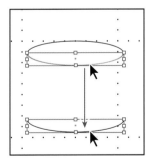

Draw an ellipse that has a width of 1" and height of .25".   *Select the line segment and copy/paste in front.*   *Shift+drag the copied line segment below.*

SALE!

(86th St. location only)

20% OFF DVDs

(All stores)

50% OFF
CLEARANCE

Thursday- Sunday
April 23-26

Offer not valid with other discounts or coupons.

SALE!

(86th St. location only)

20% OFF DVDs

(All stores)

50% OFF CLEARANCE

Thursday- Sunday
April 23-26

Offer not valid with other discounts or coupons.

5 Select the Line Segment tool (\) in the Tools panel. Hold down Shift while drawing a line from the left anchor point of the ellipse to the left anchor point of the new path. The anchor points highlight when the line snaps to them. Repeat on the right side of the ellipse. Select the Selection tool (▶) and drag across these shapes to select them, then choose Object > Group.

6 Select the Live Paint Bucket tool ( ) in the Tools panel. Click the Fill color in the Control panel and select Black in the Swatches panel that appears. With the grouped object still selected, click the center of the lower part of the can (see image below). That part of the can is now filled with black. You will learn more about the Live Paint Bucket tool in Lesson 6, "Color and Painting."

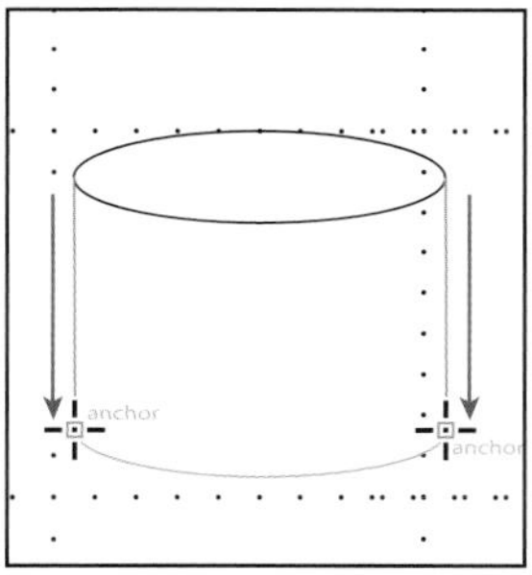

Draw 2 lines to create the pencil can sides.

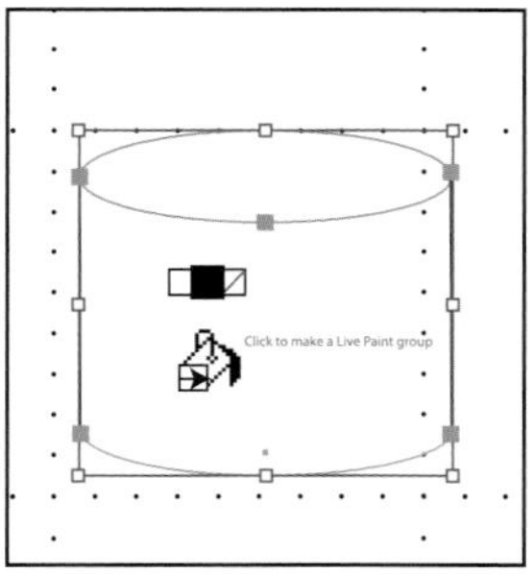

Click to paint the pencil can.

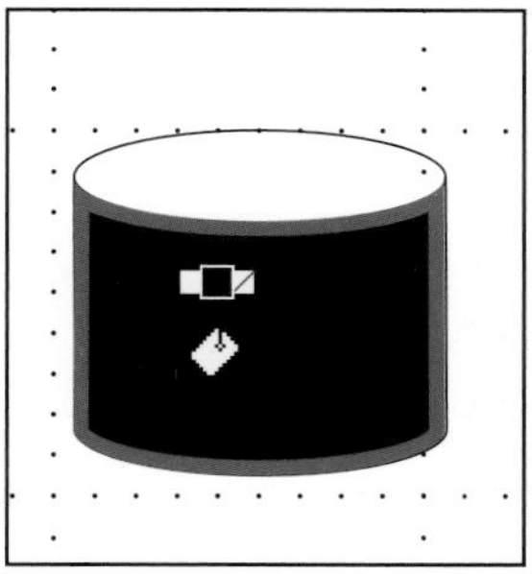
The result.

7 Choose File > Save and close the file.

Using Live Trace to create shapes

In this part of the lesson, you will review how to work with Live Trace. Live Trace will trace existing artwork, like a picture from another graphics program. You can then convert the drawing to vector paths or a Live Paint object

1 Choose File > Open, and open the L3start_02.ai file in the Lesson03 folder.

2 Choose File > Save As, name the file **snowboarding.ai**, and select the Lesson03 folder in the Save As window. Leave the file format set to Adobe Illustrator Document, and click Save. In the Illustrator Options dialog box, accept the default settings by clicking OK.

Note: *A missing profile dialog box may appear. Click OK to continue.*

3   With the Selection tool (k), select the snowboarder sketch.

Note that the Control panel options change when the scanned image is activated. It says Linked File on the left side of the Control panel and you can see the resolution (PPI: 150).

4   Click the Live Trace button (Live Trace) in the Control panel. This converts the image from raster to vector.

Choose the Live Trace button to recreate the artwork as vector.

Understand that the reason it is called Live Trace is that you can change the settings, or even the original placed image, and see immediate updates in Illustrator.

5   In this example, you selected the default trace setting, which worked fine for this image. To experiment with other presets and options, such as Comic Art, click the Tracing Options Dialog button (▦) in the Control panel, choose Comic Art from the Preset pop-up menu and check Preview. Leave the Tracing Options dialog box open.

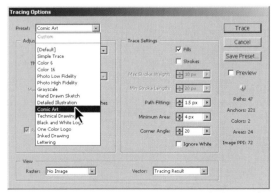

Change options using the Tracing Options dialog window.

Tracing options

Preset specifies a tracing preset.

Mode specifies a color mode for the tracing result.

Threshold specifies a value for generating a black and white tracing result from the original image. All pixels lighter than the Threshold value are converted to white, all pixels darker than the Threshold value are converted to black. (This option is available only when Mode is set to Black and White.)

Palette specifies a palette for generating a color or grayscale tracing from the original image. (This option is available only when Mode is set to Color or Grayscale.) To let Illustrator determine the colors in the tracing, select Automatic.

Max Colors specifies a maximum number of colors to use in a color or grayscale tracing result. (This option is available only when Mode is set to Color or Grayscale and when panel is set to Automatic.)

Output To Swatches creates a new swatch in the Swatches panel for each color in the tracing result.

Blur blurs the original image before generating the tracing result. Select this option to reduce small artifacts and to smooth jagged edges in the tracing result.

Resample resamples the original image to the specified resolution before generating the tracing result. This option is useful for speeding up the tracing process for large images but can yield degraded results. **Note:** The resample resolution is not saved when you create a preset.

Fills creates filled regions in the tracing result.

Strokes creates stroked paths in the tracing result.

Max Stroke Weight specifies the maximum width of features in the original image that can be stroked. Features larger than the maximum width become outlined areas in the tracing result.

Min Stroke Length specifies the minimum length of features in the original image that can be stroked. Features smaller than the minimum length are omitted from the tracing result.

Path Fitting controls the distance between the traced shape and the original pixel shape. Lower values create a tighter path fitting; higher values create a looser path fitting.

Minimum Area specifies the smallest feature in the original image that will be traced. For example, a value of 4 specifies that features smaller than 2 pixels wide by 2 pixels high will be omitted from the tracing result.

Corner Angle specifies the sharpness of a turn in the original image that is considered a corner anchor point in the tracing result.

Raster specifies how to display the bitmap component of the tracing object.

Vector specifies how to display the tracing result.

Select Preview in the Tracing Options dialog box to preview the result of the current settings.

—From Illustrator Help

As you see, the Live Trace feature can interpret black and white sketches as well as full-color images.

6 After experimenting with other settings in the Tracing Options dialog box, click Trace.

7 With the snowboarder still selected, click the Expand button (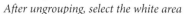) in the Control panel.

8 Choose Object > Ungroup to ungroup the shapes. Choose Select > Deselect All to deselect the shapes.

9 Select the Selection tool in the Tools panel, then click the white background surrounding the snowboarder. Press Delete to remove the white shape.

Note: If any unexpected white area is deleted, undo several steps by choosing Edit > Undo. Try tracing again and experimenting in the Tracing Options dialog box by raising the Threshold value to 210 or more.

After ungrouping, select the white area

Press Delete to remove the white area.

10 Choose File > Save and close the file.

For information on Live Trace, see "Tracing artwork" in Illustrator Help.

Tips for drawing polygons, spirals, and stars

You can control the shapes of polygons, spirals, and stars by pressing certain keys as you draw the shapes. As you drag the Polygon, Spiral, or Star tool, choose any of the following options to control the shape:

• To add or subtract sides on a polygon, points on a star, or number of segments on a spiral, hold down the Up Arrow or Down Arrow key while creating the shape. This only works if the mouse button is held down. Once the mouse is released, the tool remains set to the last specified value, and this will no longer work.

• To rotate the shape, move the mouse in an arc.

• To keep a side or point at the top, hold down Shift.

• To keep the inner radius constant, start creating a shape and then hold down Ctrl (Windows) or Command (Mac OS).

• To move a shape as you draw it, hold down the spacebar. This also works for rectangles and ellipses.

• To create multiple copies of a shape, hold down the ~ (tilde) key as you draw.

Exploring on your own

Experiment with shapes by creating a shape such as a circle, star or rectangle. Clone it several times using the Alt/Option key. Apply different colors and strokes to the shapes and reselect them using the Select Same menu item.

Review

▶ Review questions

1 What are the basic shape tools? Describe how to tear or separate a group of shape tools away from the Tools panel.

2 How do you select a shape with no fill?

3 How do you draw a square?

4 How do you change the number of sides on a polygon as you draw?

5 How can you convert a raster image to editable vector shapes?

▶ Review answers

1 There are six basic shape tools: Ellipse, Polygon, Star, Flare, Rectangle and Rounded Rectangle. To tear off a group of tools from the Tools panel, position the pointer over the tool that appears in the Tools panel and hold down the mouse button until the group of tools appears. Without releasing the mouse button, drag to the triangle at the bottom of the group, and then release the mouse button to tear off the group.

2 Items that have no fill must be selected by clicking the stroke.

3 To draw a square, select the Rectangle tool in the Tools panel. Hold down Shift and drag to draw the square, or click the artboard to enter equal dimensions for the width and height in the Rectangle dialog box.

4 To change the number of sides on a polygon as you draw, select the Polygon tool in the Tools panel. Start dragging to draw the shape and hold the Down Arrow key to reduce the number of sides and the Up Arrow key to increase the number of sides.

5 If you want to base a new drawing on an existing piece of artwork, you can trace it. To convert the tracing to paths, click Expand in the Control panel or choose Object > Live Trace > Expand. Use this method if you want to work with the components of the traced artwork as individual objects. The resulting paths are grouped together.

You can modify objects in many ways as you create artwork, including quickly and precisely controlling their size, shape, and orientation. In this lesson, you'll explore the various Transform commands, specialized tools and panel as you create three pieces of artwork.

4 | Transforming Objects

In this lesson, you'll learn how to do the following:

- Select individual objects, objects in a group, and parts of an object.

- Move, scale, and rotate objects using a variety of methods.

- Reflect, shear, and distort objects.

- Adjust the perspective of an object.

- Apply a distortion filter.

- Position objects precisely.

- Repeat transformations quickly and easily.

Getting started

In this lesson, you'll create a logo using partially completed files to use in three pieces of artwork to create a letterhead design, an envelope, and a business card template. Before you begin, you'll restore the default preferences for Adobe Illustrator CS3; then you'll open a file containing a composite of the finished artwork to see what you'll create.

1   To ensure that the tools and panels function exactly as described in this lesson, delete or deactivate (by renaming) the Adobe Illustrator CS3 preferences file. See "Restoring default preferences" on page 3.

2   Start Adobe Illustrator CS3.

Note: If you have not already copied the resource files for this lesson onto your hard disk from the Lesson04 folder from the Adobe Illustrator CS3 Classroom in a Book CD, do so now. See "Copying the Classroom in a Book files" on page 2.

3   Choose File > Open, and open the L4comp.ai file in the Lesson04 folder, located inside the Lessons folder within the AICIB folder on your hard drive.

This file contains a composite of the three pieces of finished artwork. The Stick surfboards logo in the upper-left corner of the letterhead is the basis for all of the modified objects. The logo has been resized differently for the letterhead, envelope, and business card.

Note: You can also view the individual pieces of finished artwork by opening the files L4end1.ai, L4end2.ai, and L4end3.ai in the Lesson04 folder.

4   Choose View > Zoom Out to reduce the view of the finished artwork, adjust the window size, and leave it on the screen as you work. (Select the Hand tool (✋) to move the artwork where you want it in the window.) If you don't want to leave the image open, choose File > Close.

To begin working, you'll open an existing art file set up for the letterhead artwork.

5   Choose File > Open to open the L4start1.ai file in the Lesson04 folder, located within the AICIB folder on your hard drive.

This start file has been saved with the rulers showing, custom swatches added to the Swatches panel, and blue guidelines for scaling objects used to create the logo.

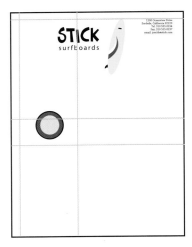

6   Choose File > Save As, name the file **Letterhead.ai**, in the Lesson04 folder. Leave the format set to Adobe Illustrator Document, and click Save. In the Illustrator Options dialog box, accept the default settings by clicking OK.

Scaling objects

Objects are scaled by enlarging or reducing them horizontally (along the x axis) and vertically (along the y axis) relative to a fixed reference point that you designate. If you don't designate an origin, the objects are scaled from their center points. You'll use three methods to scale the objects that will make up the complete logo.

First you'll set the preference to scale strokes and effects, then you'll scale the logo background by dragging its bounding box and align it to the guides provided.

1 Choose Edit > Preferences > General (Windows) or Illustrator > Preferences > General (Mac OS), and check Scale Strokes & Effects. This will scale the stroke width of any object scaled in this lesson. Click OK.

2 Choose View > Smart Guides to turn on the smart guides so that you can snap to the guides on the page.

3 Select the Selection tool (k) in the Tools panel, click the stroke (border) of the circle to select the group of objects that make up the logo's background.

4 While holding down the Shift key, click and drag the lower-right corner of the object's bounding box to snap to the aqua vertical guide. If you do not see the bounding box choose View > Show Bounding Box.

Next you'll resize the circles from the side.

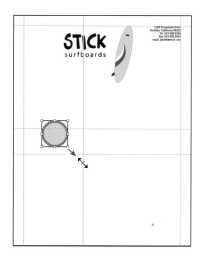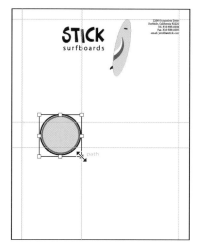

Note: *Holding down the Shift key constrains the object proportionally.*

5 With the logo background object still selected, click and drag from the bottom, middle bounding point holding down the Alt (Windows) or Option (Mac) as you drag. Drag to the lower horizontal guide. This doesn't have to be exact.

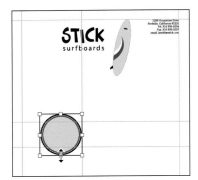
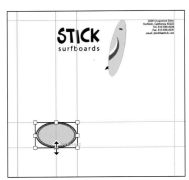

Opt/Alt click and drag.　　　　　　*Stop at bottom horizontal guide.*

6 With the logo background object still selected, choose Object > Lock > Selection to lock the object and deselect it. Locking the background object makes it easier to select other objects you'll add to the artwork. Once objects are locked, they cannot be selected or edited.

Next you'll use guides on another layer to position the group of outlined text objects. Then you'll use the Transform panel to scale up the logo text by entering new dimensions and designating the reference point from which the text will scale.

7 If the Layers panel is not visible, choose Window > Layers to display the Layers panel.

8 Click the box to the far left of the Text Guides layer to display the layer containing the guides. Scroll to the bottom of the list if the layer is not visible. Also, click the eye icon to the far left of the Page Guides layer to make those guides disappear.

9 Select the Selection tool in the Tools panel, and click the STICK surfboards text at the top of the page to select the group of outlined text objects.

10 Drag the grouped text objects over the logo background, and align the right edge of the K in STICK to the text guide. Try to center it horizontally as best as possible. Keep the text selected.

11 Choose Window > Transform to display the Transform panel if it's not already open.

The Transform panel contains a small square indicating the reference point of a selected object.

12 In the Transform panel, click the middle right reference point of the square to set the reference point from which the objects will scale. Click the Chain Link icon on the right side of the panel to turn on Constrain Width and Height Proportions and Type **57 pt** in the W text field, and then press Enter or Return to decrease the size of the text. The measurements are in inches. Typing pt tells Illustrator to convert the units to points.

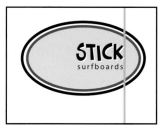

Next you'll position the surfboard and then use the Scale tool to resize the surfboard and set a fixed point for scaling.

13 Click the eye icon to the left of the Text Guides layer to turn off the visibility of the layer containing the guides used to align the text. Click the eye icon to the left of the Surfboard Guides layer to turn on the visibility of the surfboard guides.

14 Select the Selection tool in the Tools panel, and click the surfboard to select it. Drag the surfboard and align the left side and bottom of the surfboard with the guides.

15 Double-click the Scale tool (⬚) in the Tools panel.

16 In the Scale dialog box, type **26%** in the Scale text field and click OK to make the surfboard smaller.

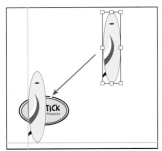
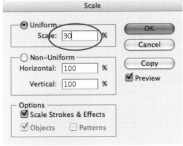
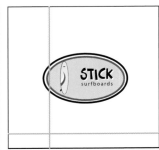

Move surfboard.   *Set reference point.*   *Scale dialog box.*

Reflecting objects

When an object is reflected, Illustrator creates a reflection of the object across an invisible vertical or horizontal axis. Copying objects while reflecting allows you to create a mirror image of the object based on a point. Similar to scaling and rotating, in reflecting you either designate the reference point from which an object will reflect or use the object's center point by default. You can also alter the position of a reflection by changing its angle.

Now you'll use the Reflect tool to flip and copy the surfboard object 90° across the vertical axis and then scale and rotate the copy into position.

1 Click the Selection tool (▶) to select the surfboard.

2 Select the Zoom tool in the Tools panel and click twice on the surfboard to zoom in. This will make it easier to see.

3 Select the Reflect tool (⬚) nested within the Rotate tool (⟲) in the Tools panel, then hold down Alt (Windows) or Option (Mac OS), and click the right edge of the surfboard.

4   In the Reflect dialog box, make sure that the Angle option is selected and **95°** is entered in the Angle text field. Then click Copy (not OK).

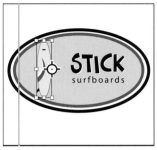
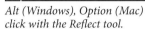
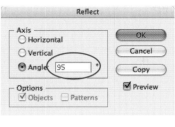
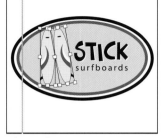

Alt (Windows), Option (Mac)   *Set reflect angle and copy.*   *The result.*
click with the Reflect tool.

Rotating objects

Objects are rotated by turning them around a designated reference point. You can rotate objects by displaying their bounding boxes and moving the cursor to an outside corner. Once the rotate cursor appears, click to rotate the object around its center point. You can also rotate objects using the Transform panel to set a reference point and a rotation angle.

You'll rotate both surfboards using the Rotate tool.

1   With the leftmost surfboard selected, select the Rotate tool (⟳) now nested within the Reflect tool (⊠) in the Tools panel. Double-click the Rotate tool (⟳) in the Tools panel. Notice that the surfboard's reference point (✥) is in the center of the surfboard.

2   In the Rotate dialog box, check Preview, and type **-10** in the Angle text field, then click OK to rotate the surfboard -10° around the reference point.

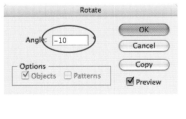

Note: *If you select an object, then select the Rotate tool, you can Alt (Windows) or Option (Mac OS) click anywhere on the object (or artboard) to set a reference point and open the Rotate dialog box.*

3 Select the Selection tool and click the surfboard to the right.

4 Select the Rotate tool. Click the bottom of the right surfboard to set the reference point (✥). Click and drag from the top of the selected surfboard. Notice how the movement is constrained to a circle rotating around the reference point. Continue dragging to the left until the surfboard is tilted a few more degrees to the left, and then release the mouse button.

5 Double-click the Scale tool in the Tools panel and enter **70** in the Uniform Scale text field and click OK.

6 Choose File > Save.

7 Click the eye icon (👁) next to the Surfboard Guides layer to turn the visibility off.

8 Choose Object > Unlock All to unlock the logo's background.

9 With the Selection tool, click and drag a marquee selection around the logo pieces only to select them.

10 Choose Object > Group to group the selected objects of the logo.

11 In the Layers panel, click the visibility column button to the left of lock icon in the Page Guides layer to show the layer guides.

12   Select the Selection tool ( ) in the Tools panel, and drag the logo to the upper, left corner of the page, positioning it where the upper-left blue page guides meet.

13   Click the eye icon next to the Page Guides layer to turn the visibility off for this layer and make sure that the address layer is visible.

14   Choose File > Save.

Distorting objects

Various tools and filters let you distort the original shapes of objects in different ways. Now you'll create a flower, first using the Twist distort filter to twirl the shape of a star, and then applying the Pucker & Bloat distort filter to transform another star in front of it.

To begin, you'll draw a star for part of the flower and use the Twist filter and Info panel to distort it.

1   Choose Window > Layers to open the Layers panel. Click the Flower layer to choose it.

2   Choose Window > Info to open the Info panel to help draw the star.

3 Select the Star tool (⭐) from the same group as the Rectangle tool (⬜) in the Tools panel, and position the cursor in the artwork in the lower right corner of the letterhead. Drag the tool to draw a five-pointed star that's about **150 pt** wide.

Your Tools panel may be a single column.

The star is painted with the paint attributes of the last selected object (in this case, the logo's background).

4 With the star still selected, click the Fill color in the Control panel and select the gradient swatch named Flower gradient. Leave the Stroke color set to None.

Now you'll distort the star using the Twist distort filter. This filter twists objects around their centers.

Twist distortion can be applied to objects two ways: applying it as a Filter permanently distorts the object; applying it as an Effect maintains the original shape and lets you remove or edit the effect at any time using the Appearance panel. You will be using both methods in the following exercise. Read more about using effects in Lesson 11, "Applying Effects."

5 Choose Filter > Distort > Twist. Type in the value of **45°** in the Twist dialog box and click OK.

Now you'll draw another star that's centered on top of the first star.

6 With the star selected, choose Window > Attributes to display the Attributes panel. Then click the Show Center button (⊡) to display the star's center point.

 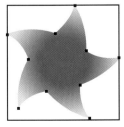

Display center point of star.

7 Select the Star tool again, and drag from the center point to draw another star, about the same size, over the center of the first one. Before you release the mouse button, drag the star in an arc to rotate it so the points appear between the points of the star behind it. Keep the star selected.

8 In the Attributes panel, click the Show Center button (▣) to display the second star's center point.

9 Shift+click the Fill color in the Control panel to link to the Color panel. Click the White color box at the right end of the color bar to paint the star's fill white.

By Shift+clicking the Fill color in the Control panel, you can choose the Color panel instead of the default link to the Swatches panel.

10 Click the Fill color in the Control panel again to hide the Color panel. Click once more on the Fill color to show the Swatches panel. Click the Stroke color in the Control panel, and select a color in the Swatches panel to paint the star's stroke. (We selected the Black color swatch).

Now you'll distort the frontmost star using the Pucker & Bloat effect. This effect distorts objects inward and outward from their anchor points.

11 With the white star selected, choose Effect > Distort & Transform > Pucker & Bloat. Applying it as an effect maintains the original shape and lets you remove or edit the effect at any time.

12 In the Pucker & Bloat dialog box, check the Preview option, and drag the slider to the right to distort the star (we selected 50%). Click OK.

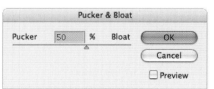

Draw star shape.   *Apply Pucker & Bloat effect.*   *Result.*

13 Keep the artwork selected, and choose File > Save.

Shearing objects

Now you'll complete the flower with an orange center, scale it, and shear it. Shearing an object slants, or skews, the sides of the object along the axis you specify, keeping opposite sides parallel and making the object asymmetrical.

1   Select the Ellipse tool (⬤) from the same group as the Star tool (☆) in the Tools panel.

2   With the stars still selected and their center points visible, press Alt (Windows) or Option (Mac OS), position the Ellipse tool's crosshairs over the stars' center points, and drag to draw an oval from the center.

3   Click the Fill box in the Tools panel to select the object's fill. In the Swatches panel, select the Orange swatch to paint the oval an orange color.

4   Choose Window > Color to open the Color panel. In the Color panel, drag the None icon (☑) and drop it on the Stroke color in the Color panel to remove the stroke.

Note: You may need to select Show Options from the Color panel menu to see these options.

Draw oval shape and paint fill.

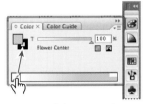

Drag and drop None button over Stroke box.

Now, you'll group and shear the flower.

5   Select the Selection tool (▸), Shift+click to select the three parts of the flower, and choose Object > Group to group them together.

6   In the Transform panel, type **10°** in the Shear text field, and press Enter or Return to apply the shearing effect on the flower.

Enter 10° shear angle.   Result.

7   Type **0.75 in** into the W text field to scale the flower down to three-quarters of an inch. Press Enter or Return.

Although the default unit of measure is set to points, when you type inches (or in) in the text fields, Illustrator calculates the equivalent measurement in points.

> You can have Illustrator convert unit values and perform mathematical operations in any text box that accepts numeric values. To automatically multiply or divide the size of an object by a number you specify, enter, respectively, an asterisk (*) or a slash (/) respectively, and a number after the value in either the W or the H text box, or in both text boxes, and press Enter or Return to scale the object. For example, enter /2 after the values in the W and H text boxes to scale the object by 50%.

8   Select the Selection tool and drag the flower to the lower-right corner of the page. Then Alt (Windows) or Option (Mac OS) click, and drag the flower two times to make a cluster of flowers in the corner.

9   Choose Select > Deselect to deselect the artwork.

10   Choose View > Guides > Hide Guides to hide guides, and then choose File > Save.

You've completed the letterhead artwork. Keep the file open so that you can use this artwork later in the lesson.

Positioning objects precisely

You can use the Transform panel to move objects to exact coordinates on the x and y axes of the page and to control the position of objects in relation to the trim edge.

[?] To learn how to produce crop marks for the trim edge, see "Printer's marks and bleed" in Illustrator Help.

You'll create the envelope by first pasting a copy of the logo into the envelope artwork, and then specifying its exact coordinates on the envelope.

1   Double-click the Hand tool ( ) in the Tools panel to fit the artwork in the window.

2   Using the Selection tool ( ), click the logo to select it. Make sure it is the only thing selected.

3   Choose Edit > Copy to copy the logo to the Clipboard.

Now you'll open the start file for the envelope artwork.

4   Choose File > Open to open the L4start2.ai file in the Lesson04 folder, located inside the Lessons folder within the AICIB folder on your hard drive.

5   Choose File > Save As, name the file **Envelope.ai**, and choose the Lesson04 folder. Leave the file format set to Adobe Illustrator Document, and click Save. In the Illustrator Options dialog box, accept the default settings by clicking OK.

6   Choose Edit > Paste.

You'll move the pasted logo to within 1/4-inch of the upper-left corner of the envelope by specifying the x and y coordinates in relation to the ruler origin. The ruler origin is the point where 0 appears on each ruler. We changed the ruler origin in this file to begin at the upper-left corner of the envelope, and the ruler units to inches.

For more information, see "Rulers, grids, and guides" in Illustrator Help.

7   In the Transform panel, click the upper-left reference point and then type **0.25 in** (18 pt) in the X text field and **–0.25 in** (a negative coordinate) in the Y text field. Press Enter or Return to apply the setting you typed.

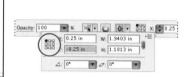

Copy the logo from the letterhead.   *Paste into the envelope.*   *Select top left reference point and enter x and y coordinates.*

8   With the logo still selected, hold down Shift and drag the lower-right corner of the bounding box to scale the logo and make it fit within the blue square guideline.

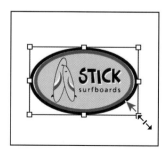

9   Click away from the artwork to deselect it, and then choose File > Save.

Changing the perspective

Now you'll use the Free Transform tool to change the perspective of the company name.

1   Select the Zoom tool (🔍) in the Tools panel and click twice on the logo to zoom in.

2   Select the Group Selection tool (📐) in the Tools panel, and click the word Stick three times to select the group.

3   Choose Edit > Copy and Edit > Paste to paste a copy With the Selection tool, click and drag the copied logo text into the center of the envelope. Double-click the Hand tool in the Tools panel to fit in window.

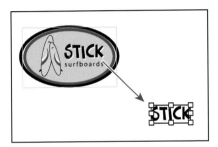

4   Select the Scale tool (📐) in the Tools panel, then Alt (Windows) or Option (Mac OS)-click the left side of the text to set the origin point, and open the Scale dialog box. Enter **500** in the Uniform Scale text field. Click OK.

5   With the text selected, select the Free Transform tool (📐) in the Tools panel.

6   Position the double-headed cursor (↔) over the lower-right corner of the object's bounding box. The next step will require a little coordination, so follow directions closely. Click and slowly drag the lower-right corner handle downward. While dragging,

press Shift+Alt+Ctrl (Windows) or Shift+Option+Command (Mac OS) to change the perspective of the object.

Note: If you were to use the modifier keys at the same time as clicking to select, the perspective feature would not work.

Holding down Shift as you drag scales an object proportionally. Holding down Alt/Option scales an object from its center point. Finally, holding down Ctrl/Command as you drag distorts an object from the anchor point or bounding box handle that you're dragging.

7   Choose Window > Transform to display the Transform panel.

You will use the Transform panel next to make the Stick text a certain width.

8   Select the Selection tool (➤). Click and begin dragging from the right edge of the text to change the width. While dragging press the Alt (Windows) or Option (Mac) to resize both sides. Then, in the Transform panel, type **4in** in the W Value field.

Change perspective.   Change transparency.   Make the logo wider.

9   Choose Select > Deselect.

10   Select the Group Selection tool (▷) in the Tools panel, and click the word Stick twice to select the group. In the Tools panel, make sure that the Fill box is in front. Select the yellow swatch from the Swatches panel to apply the fill.

11 Choose View > Outline to see the shapes as outlines. With the Group Selection tool, click the edge of the K farthest to the right. Click again to select the whole word. With the Fill box still up front in the Tools panel, select the Black swatch from the Swatches panel.

12 Click the Selection tool and select the entire Stick group. Choose Window > Transparency to open the Transparency panel and enter **20** in the Opacity field to fade the text into the background.

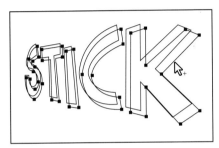

Select the text.   *Change transparency of group to 20%.*

13 Choose View > Preview. Choose File > Save. You can either minimize the file and leave it open on your desktop, or close the file.

Using the Free Transform tool

The Free Transform tool is a multi-purpose tool that, besides letting you change the perspective of an object, combines the functions of scaling, shearing, reflecting, and rotating.

Now you'll use the Free Transform tool to transform objects that you copy from the logo into a business card.

1 Choose File > Open, and open the L4start3.ai file in the Lesson04 folder, located inside the Lessons folder within the AICIB folder on your hard drive.

2 Choose File > Save As, name the file **Buscards.ai**, and save it inside the Lesson04 folder. Leave the file format set to Adobe Illustrator Document, and click Save. In the Illustrator Options dialog box, accept the default settings by clicking OK.

3 Choose Window > Navigator. In the Navigator panel, click the Zoom In button (⌃) a few times to zoom to 200%, and then move the red view box over the upper-left corner of the artwork.

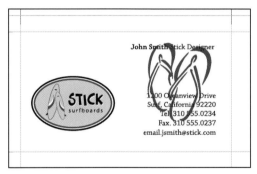

4 Select the Selection tool (▶)and click the blue sandals (be careful not to click on the text). With the sandals selected, select the Free Transform tool (⛶) in the Tools panel. Holding down Shift+Alt (Windows) or Shift+Option (Mac OS), drag the lower-left corner down to scale the object from its center and make the sandals bigger.

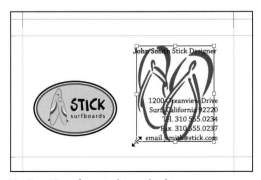

Use Free Transform tool to scale object.

Although you can scale objects using the Selection tool, scaling with the Free Transform tool lets you perform other transformations without switching tools.

5 To distort the sandals using the Free Transform tool, select the lower-right corner of the object's bounding box, but don't release the mouse button. Begin dragging, and then hold down Ctrl+Alt+Shift (Windows) or Command+Option+Shift (Mac OS) and slowly drag toward the lower- left corner of the object.

6 To slightly rotate the sandals, position the Free Transform tool just outside the lower-left corner of the object's bounding box, until you see the rotate cursor, and then drag in a counter-clockwise rotation to rotate the object.

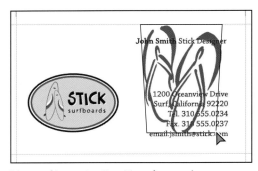
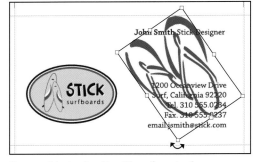

Distort object using Free Transform tool.   *Rotate object using Free Transform tool.*

7 In the Transparency panel, change the Opacity to 10%.

8 Select the Selection tool, and make sure that the sandals are still selected. Choose Object > Arrange > Send to Back, and move the sandals underneath the text.

Now you'll explore a slightly different way of distorting objects. Free Distort lets you distort a selection by moving any of its four corner points. It can be used either as a filter to apply a permanent change or as an effect to apply a change that can be removed.

9 With the sandals still selected, choose Filter > Distort > Free Distort.

Note: Choose the top Filter > Distort command. The lower Filter > Distort commands in the menu work only on bitmap images.

10 Drag one or more of the handles to distort the selection. Click OK. We dragged the upper-right anchor point to the left.

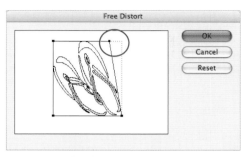

Previewing a free distortion.　　　　　*The result.*

11　Click outside the artwork to deselect it, and choose File > Save.

Making multiple transformations

Now you'll create multiple copies of the business card, and replicate the symbol instances in a few easy steps.

1　Double-click the Hand tool (✋) in the Tools panel to zoom out and fit the artwork in the window.

2　Choose Select > All to select all the objects on the business card.

3　Choose Object > Transform > Transform Each.

The Move options in the Transform Each dialog box let you move objects in a specified or random direction. Now you'll move a copy of the selected objects down two inches from the original objects.

4　In the Transform Each dialog box, enter **–2 in** in the Move Vertical text field, leave the other settings as they are, and click Copy (don't click OK).

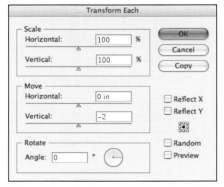

Move object -2 inches vertically and copy it.

5   Choose Object > Transform > Transform Again to create a third copy.

Now you'll use the keyboard shortcut to repeat the transformations.

6   Press Ctrl+D (Windows) or Command+D (Mac OS) twice to transform two additional times, creating a total of five cards in the column.

> 💡 *You can also apply multiple transformations as an effect, including scaling, moving, rotating, and reflecting an object. After selecting the objects, choose Effect > Distort & Transform > Transform. The dialog box looks the same as the Transform Each dialog box. Transforming as an effect has the advantage of letting you change or remove the transformation at any time.*

Next you'll use some shortcuts to make a copy of the column.

7   Press Ctrl+A (Windows) or Command+A (Mac OS) to select everything on the five business cards, and right-click (Windows) or Ctrl+click (Mac OS) in the window to display a shortcut menu. Choose Transform > Transform Each from the shortcut menu.

8   This time in the Transform Each dialog box, enter **3.5 in** in the Move Horizontal text field and **0 in** in the Move Vertical text field. Leave the other settings as they are, and click Copy (don't click OK).

9   To clear the window so that you can view the finished artwork, press Ctrl (Windows) or Command (Mac OS) and click outside the artwork to deselect it. Then choose View > Guides > Hide Guides to hide the blue guidelines, and press Tab to close the Tools panel and panels.

Pressing Tab toggles between hiding and showing the Tools panel and all the panels. Pressing Shift+Tab alternately hides or shows only the panels.

10   Choose File > Save and then choose File > Close.

Exploring on your own

In the letterhead project, off the page in the lower-right corner is a seahorse. Select the seahorse and use the Scallop tool (hidden under the Warp tool) to apply a scallop effect on the edge. Try other effects on the seahorse such as the Twirl tool (hidden under the Warp tool as well) on the tail.

Converting straight lines to zigzags

The Zig Zag filter transforms an object's path segments into a jagged or wavy array of uniformly sized peaks and valleys. Set the length between peaks and valleys using an absolute or relative size. Set the number of ridges per path segment and choose between wavy edges (Smooth) or jagged edges (Corner)

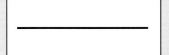  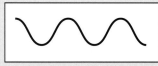

Original line.   *Line with four corner ridges applied.*   *Line with four smooth ridges applied.*

To convert straight lines to zigzags

1 Do one of the following:

- *To apply the distortion permanently, use any selection tool to select the line you want to convert. Then choose Filter > Distort > Zig Zag.*

- *To apply the distortion as an effect that can be removed, select an object or group, or target a group or layer in the Layers panel. (For more on targeting, see Lesson 8, "Working with Layers.") Then choose Effect > Distort & Transform > Zig Zag.*

2 Select how you wish to move points: either Relative by a percentage of the object's size, or Absolute by a specific amount.

3 For Size, enter the distance you want to move points on the line, or drag the slider.

4 For Ridges per Segment, enter the number of ridges per line segment you want, or drag the slider.

5 Select the type of line to create: Smooth to create smooth points for a wavy line, or Corner to create corner points for a jagged line.

6 Click Preview to preview the line.

7 Click OK.

Review

▶ Review questions

1   How can you select and manipulate individual objects in a group (as described in this chapter)?

2   How do you resize an object? Explain how you determine the point from which the object resizes. How do you resize a group of objects proportionally?

3   What transformations can you make using the Transform panel?

4   What does the square diagram indicate in the Transform panel, and how will it affect your transformations?

5   What's an easy way to change perspective? List three other types of transformations you can perform with the Free Transform tool.

▶ Review answers

1   You can use the Group Selection tool to select individual objects or subgroups of objects within a group and change them without affecting the rest of the group.

2   You can resize an object several ways: by selecting it and dragging handles on its bounding box, or by using the Scale tool, the Transform panel, or Object > Transform > Scale to specify exact dimensions. You can also scale by choosing Effect > Distort & Transform > Transform.

To determine the reference point from which an object scales, select a reference point from the reference point locator in the Transform panel or in the Transform Effect or Transform Each dialog box, or click in the artwork with the Scale tool. Holding down Alt (Windows) or Option (Mac OS) and dragging the bounding box or double-clicking the Scale tool will resize a selected object from its center point.

Shift+dragging a corner handle on the bounding box scales an object proportionally, as does specifying either a uniform scale value in the Scale dialog box or multiples of the dimensions in the Width and Height text fields in the Transform panel.

3   You use the Transform panel for making the following transformations:

- Moving or strategically placing objects in your artwork (by specifying the x and y coordinates and the reference point).

- Scaling (by specifying the width and height of selected objects).

- Rotating (by specifying the angle of rotation).

- Shearing (by specifying the angle of distortion).

- Reflecting (by flipping selected objects vertically or horizontally).

4   The square diagram in the Transform panel indicates the bounding box of the selected objects. Select a reference point in the square to indicate the reference point from which the objects as a group will move, scale, rotate, shear, or reflect.

5   An easy way to change the perspective of selected objects is to select the Free Transform tool, hold down Shift+Alt+Ctrl (Windows) or Shift+Option+Command (Mac OS), and drag a corner handle on the bounding box.

Other types of transformations you can perform with the Free Transform tool are distorting, scaling, shearing, rotating, and reflecting.

The Pen tool is a powerful tool for drawing straight lines, Bezier curves, and complex shapes. While the Pencil tool is easier for drawing and editing free form lines, the Pen tool is easier for drawing more precisely. You'll practice using the Pen tool on a blank artboard and then use the Pen tool to create an illustration of a pear.

5 | Drawing with the Pen tool

In this lesson, you'll learn how to do the following:

- Draw straight lines.
- Use Template layers.
- End path segments and split lines.
- Draw curved lines.
- Select and adjust curve segments.

Getting started

In the first part of this lesson, you will learn how to manipulate the Pen tool on a blank artboard.

1   To ensure that the tools and panels function exactly as described in this lesson, delete or deactivate (by renaming) the Adobe Illustrator CS3 preferences file. See "Restoring default preferences" on page 3.

Note: If you have not already copied the resource files for this lesson onto your hard disk from the Lesson05 folder from the Adobe Illustrator CS3 Classroom in a Book CD, do so now. See "Copying the Classroom in a Book files" on page 2.

2   Open the file named L5start_01.ai from the Lesson05 folder, located inside the Lessons folder within the AICIB folder on your hard drive. The top portion of the artboard shows the path that you will create. Use the bottom half of the artboard for this exercise.

3   Choose File > Save As. In the Save As dialog box, name the file **path1.ai**, and choose the Lesson05 folder. Leave the file format set to Illustrator (*.AI), and click Save. In the Illustrator Options window, leave the default settings and click OK.

4   Use Ctrl+0 (zero) (Windows) or Command+0 (Mac OS) to fit the entire page into the window and then close all the panels, except for the

Tool panel, by clicking their Close boxes or by holding down Shift and pressing Tab once. You won't need to use them for this lesson.

5   Select the Pen tool (🖋). Notice that when the Pen has not yet placed its first point, an "x" appears to the right of the pen icon. This indicates that you are starting a new path. Click and release once in the lower portion of the work area. As you move the mouse away from the original anchor point, the "x" disappears.

Note: If instead of the pen icon, you see a crosshair, the Caps Lock key is active. Caps Lock On turns tool icons into crosshairs, which indicates that the precise cursor is active.

6   Move the mouse to the right of the original point, and click once to create the next anchor point in the path.

Note: The first segment you draw will not be visible until you click a second anchor point. Also, if direction lines (handles) appear, you have accidentally dragged with the Pen tool; choose Edit > Undo, and click again. (Direction handles are used to reshape curved paths, and do not print.)

The first point connects to the new anchor point. Click back under the initial anchor point to create a zigzag pattern. The zigzag is complete when it has a total of six anchor points.

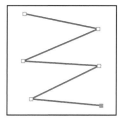

Click and release from point to point to create the zigzag.

One of the many benefits of using the Pen tool is that you can create custom paths and continue to edit the anchor points that make up the path. Next, see how the Selection tools relate to the Pen tool.

7   Select the Selection tool (▶) and click the zigzag path. Note how all the anchor points become solid, signifying that all anchor points are selected. Click and drag the path to a new location anywhere on the artboard, and notice that all the anchor points travel together, maintaining the zigzag path.

8 Deselect the zigzag path with any of these four ways:

• Select the Selection tool and click on an empty section of the artboard.

• Choose Select > Deselect from the menu.

• Select the Pen tool, hold down the Ctrl (Windows) or Command (Mac OS) key and click to deselect; this temporarily gives you the Selection tool. When the Control or Command key is released, you return to the Pen tool.

• Click the Pen tool once. Even though it looks like the path is still active, it will not connect to the next anchor point you create.

9 Select the Direct Selection tool (▸) and click on any one point in the zigzag. Clicking and dragging a marquee selection around an anchor point with the Direct Selection tool can make selecting individual anchor points easier. The selected anchor point turns solid, the unselected anchor points are hollow.

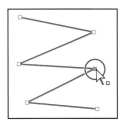

Only the active point appears solid.

10 With the anchor point selected, click and drag to reposition the anchor point. The anchor point is moving but the others are stationary. Use this technique to edit a path.

11 At times you will need to recreate just one line segment in a path. Choose Select > Deselect, then select the Direct Selection tool, click on any line segment that is between two anchor points and choose Edit > Cut.

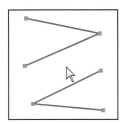

Select a segment of a path.

12 Select the Pen tool and position the cursor over one of the anchor points that was connected to the line segment. Note that the pen icon has a forward slash (/) to the right of it, signifying a continuation of an existing path. Click and release the mouse.

13 Position the cursor over the other point that was connected to the original line segment. An icon of a circle with a line through it (✏.) appears. This signifies that you are connecting to another path. Click the point to reconnect the paths.

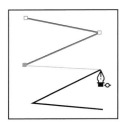

Reconnect the paths.

14 Choose File > Save and then File > Close.

Creating straight lines

In Lesson 4, "Transforming Objects," you discovered that using the Shift key in combination with shape tools constrains the shape of objects you create. This is also true with the Pen tool, except that the procedure constrains the paths you create in multiples of 45°.

In this part of the lesson, you will learn how to draw straight lines.

1 Open the file named L5start_02.ai from the Lesson05 folder, located inside the Lessons folder within the AICIB folder on the hard drive. The top portion of the artboard shows the path that you will create. Use the lower half of the page for this exercise.

2 Choose File > Save As. In the Save As window, name the file **path2.ai**, and navigate to the Lesson05 folder. Leave the file format set to Illustrator (*.AI), and click Save. In the Illustrator Options dialog box, leave the default settings and click OK.

3 Select the Pen tool (✏) and click once in the work area of the page.

4 Hold down the Shift key and click about an inch to the right of the original anchor point. Note that if you are not in the exact straight line position, you are snapped to that point.

5   While holding down the Shift key, click with the mouse and try to replicate the path in the exercise file.

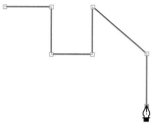

Hold down the Shift key while clicking to constrain the path.

6   Choose File > Save and close the file.

Creating curved paths

In this part of the lesson, you'll learn how to draw smooth, curved lines with the Pen tool. In vector-drawing programs such as Adobe Illustrator CS3, you draw a curve, called a Bezier curve, with control points. By setting anchor points and dragging direction handles (controls), you can define the shape of the curve. Although drawing curves this way can take some getting used to, it gives you the greatest control and flexibility in creating paths.

1   Before we get started with a lesson file, choose File > New to create a new letter-sized document in Adobe Illustrator, leaving the new document profile set at Print. Consider this page a "scratch" page for practicing the Bezier curve.

2   In the Control panel, click the Fill color and select the None swatch (⬜), then click the Stroke color and select the Black swatch.

3   Click the Stroke Weight pop-up menu in the Control panel and change the stroke weight to 1 pt.

4   Click and release the mouse anywhere on the page to create the initial anchor point. While holding the mouse down click in another location on the page, and drag to create a curved path.

Click and drag to create a curved path.

Continue clicking and dragging at various locations on the page. The goal for this exercise is not to create anything specific, but to get you accustomed to the feel of the Bezier curve.

Notice that as you click and drag, direction handles that end in round direction points appear. The angle and length of the direction handles determine the shape and size of the curved segments. Direction lines do not print and are not visible when the anchor is inactive.

5   Choose Select > Deselect.

6   Choose the Direct Selection tool (⬚) and select a curved segment to display the direction handles again. Moving the direction points reshapes the curves.

Note: Anchor points are square, and when selected, appear filled; unselected, they appear unfilled, like hollow squares. Direction points are round. These lines and points do not print with the artwork.

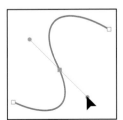

Select anchor points to access the direction handles.

7   Choose File > Close and do not save this file.

Components of a path

A smooth anchor point always has two direction handles that move together as a single, straight unit. When you drag the direction anchor point of either direction line on a smooth anchor point, both direction handles move simultaneously, maintaining a continuous curve at that anchor point.

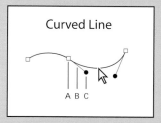

In comparison, a corner point can have two, one, or no direction handles, depending on whether it joins two, one, or no curved segments, respectively. Corner point direction handles maintain the corner by using different angles. When you drag a direction point on a corner point's direction line, the other direction line, if present, does not move.

*A. Anchor point. B. Direction line.
C. Direction point (or handle).*

Building a curve

In this part of the lesson, you will learn how to control the direction handles in order to control curves.

1   Open the file named L5start_03.ai from the Lesson05 folder. On this page you can see the paths that you will create. A template layer has been created in this file so that you can practice using the Pen tool (✎) by tracing. (See Lesson 8, "Working with Layers," for information about creating layers.) The work area below the path is for additional practice on your own.

2   Choose File > Save As. In the Save As dialog box, name the file **path3.ai**, and navigate to the Lesson05 folder. Leave the file format set to Illustrator (*.AI), and click Save. In the Illustrator Options dialog box, leave the default settings and click OK.

3 Press Z to switch to the Zoom tool (🔍) and drag a marquee around the first curve.

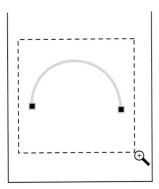

Zoom in to a specified area by dragging
a marquee when on the Zoom tool.

4 Select the Pen tool and click and hold at the base of the left side of the arch and drag up to create a direction line going the same direction as the arch. It helps to remember to always follow the direction of the curve. Release the mouse when the direction line is slightly above the arch.

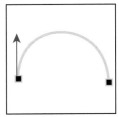

When a curve goes up, the
direction line should also go up.

Note: *The artboard may scroll as you drag the anchor point. If you lose visibility of the curve, choose View > Zoom Out until you see the curve and anchor point. Pressing the spacebar will temporarily give you the Hand tool and allow you to reposition the artwork.*

5   Click on the lower right base of the arch path and drag down. Release the mouse when the top direction line is slightly above the arch.

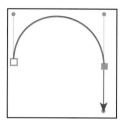

To control the path, pay attention to where the direction handles fall.

6   If the path you created is not aligned exactly with the template, return to the Direct Selection tool (⬉) and select the anchor points one at a time. Then adjust the direction handles until your path follows the template more accurately.

Note: *Pulling the direction handle longer makes a higher slope, while pulling it shorter makes the slope flatter.*

7   Use the Selection tool (▶) and click on the artboard anywhere there are no other objects, or choose Select > Deselect. If necessary, zoom out to see the next path on this page.

If you click with the Pen tool while the original path is still active, the path will connect to the next point. Deselecting the first path allows you to create a new path.

8   Save the file by choosing File > Save.

Note: *You can also hold down the Ctrl (Windows) or Command (Mac OS) key to temporarily switch you to the Selection or Direct Selection tool, whichever was last used. Hold down Ctrl/Command and click on the artboard where there are no objects to deselect.*

9   Select the Pen tool and click and drag at the left base of path "B," again in the direction of the arch. Click and drag down on the next square point, adjusting the arch with the direction handle before you release the mouse. Don't worry if it is not exact; you can correct this with the Direct Selection tool when the path is complete.

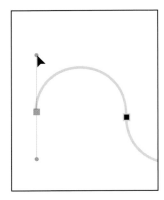

Click and drag up to create the
upward arch.

Continue along the path, alternating between clicking and dragging up and down. Put anchor points only where you see the square boxes. If you make a mistake as you draw, you can undo your work by choosing Edit > Undo. Adobe Illustrator CS3, by default, lets you undo a series of actions—limited only by your computer's memory—by repeatedly choosing Edit > Undo or Ctrl+Z (Windows) or Command+Z (Mac OS).

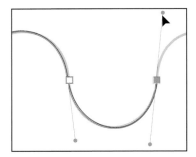

Alternate between dragging up and
down with the Pen tool.

10   When the path is complete, choose the Direct Selection tool and select an anchor point. When the anchor is selected, the direction handles reappear, and you can readjust the slope of the path.

11 Practice repeating these paths in the work area.

12 Choose File > Save and close the file.

Curves and corner anchor points

When creating curves, the directional handles help to determine the slope of the path. Returning to a corner point requires a little extra effort. In the next portion of the lesson, you will practice converting curve points to corners.

1 Open the file named L5start_04.ai from the Lesson05 folder. On this page you can see the path that you will create. Use the top section as a template for the exercise. Create your paths directly on top of those that you see on the page. The work area below is for additional practice on your own.

2 Choose File > Save As. In the Save As window, name the file **path4.ai,** and navigate to the Lesson05 folder. Leave the file format set to Illustrator (*.AI), and click Save. In the Illustrator Options dialog box, leave the default settings and choose OK.

3 Use the Zoom tool (🔍) and drag a marquee around the top path.

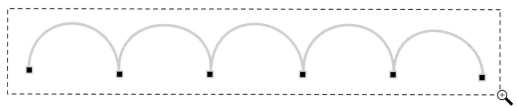

You will get a much more accurate path when you are zoomed in to an increased magnification.

4 Choose the Pen tool (✒), click on the first anchor point and drag up, then click on the second anchor point and drag down, just as you have been doing for previous exercises. Holding the Shift key when dragging constrains the angle of the handle to a straight line.

5 Hold down Alt (Windows) or Option (Mac OS) and position the mouse over either the last anchor point created or its direction handle. Look for the caret (^) symbol and click and drag up when it is visible.

An alert window will appear if you don't click exactly on the anchor point. If that appears, click OK and try again.

This alert will appear if you do not click on the anchor point.

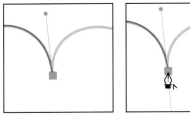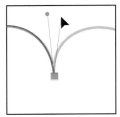

When the caret is visible, click and drag.

You can practice adjusting the direction handles with the Direct Selection tool (⟨⟩) when the path is completed.

6 Release the Alt/Option key and click on the next square point on the template path and drag down.

7 Hold down the Alt/Option key again and grab the last anchor point or direction line and pull it up for the next curve. Remember, you do not see the caret, you will create an additional loop.

8 Continue this pattern of clicking and dragging, using the Alt/Option key (to create corner points) until the path is completed. Use the Direct Selection tool to fine-tune the path, and then deselect the path.

9 Choose File > Save.

10 Choose View > Fit in Window. You can also use Ctrl+0 (zero) (Windows) or Command+0 (Mac OS). Use the Zoom tool (🔍) to drag a marquee around the second path and enlarge its view.

11 With the Pen tool, click on the first anchor point and drag up, then click and drag down on the second anchor point. This motion of creating an arch should be familiar to you by now. You will now go from the curve to a straight line. Simply pressing the Shift key and clicking will not produce a straight line, since this last point is a curved anchor point.

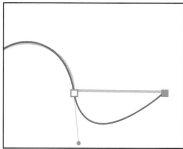

The path when a curved point is not turned into a corner point.

12 To create the next path as a straight line, click on the last point created to delete one handle from the path. Then hold down the Shift key and click to the next point.

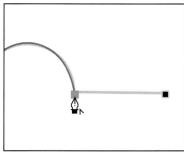

Click on the last anchor point created to force a straight path from it.

13 For the next arch, click and drag down (since the arch is going down) on the point you just created. This creates a directional handle.

14 Click on the next point and drag up to complete the downward arch.

15 Click and release on the last anchor point of the arch.

16 Shift+click to the next point.

17 Click and drag up, and then click and drag down on the last point, to create the final arch.

18 Practice repeating these paths in the lower portion. Use the Direct Selection tool to adjust your path if necessary.

19 Choose File > Save and then File > Close the file.

Creating the pear illustration

In this next part of the lesson, you'll create an illustration of a pear pierced by an arrow. This procedure will incorporate what you have learned in the previous exercises, and will also teach you some additional Pen tool techniques.

1 Choose File > Open, and open the L5end.ai file in the Lesson05 folder, located inside the Lessons folder within the AICIB folder on the hard drive.

2 Choose View > Zoom Out to make the finished artwork smaller and leave it on your screen as you work. (Use the Hand tool (🖐) to move the artwork to where you want it in the window.) If you don't want to leave the image open, choose File > Close.

3 Now you'll open the start file to begin the lesson. Choose File > Open, and open the L5start.ai file in the Lesson05 folder.

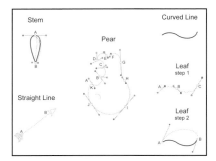

4 Choose File > Save As, name the file **Pear.ai**, and select the Lesson05 folder in the Save In menu. Leave the type of format set to Adobe Illustrator Document, and click Save. In the Illustrator Options dialog box, leave the options set at the defaults and click OK.

Creating the arrow

You'll begin by drawing the straight line for the arrow. The template layer allows you to follow along directly over the artwork.

1 Choose View > Straight Line to zoom into the left corner of the template.

Separate views that show different areas of the template at a higher magnification were created for this document and added to the View menu.

💡 *To create a custom view, choose View > New View. For information, see "To use multiple windows and views" in Illustrator Help.*

2 Choose View > Hide Bounding Box to hide the bounding boxes of selected objects. Select the Pen tool (✒) in the Tools panel, and move the cursor to the dashed line of the arrow in the artwork. Notice that the Pen tool cursor has a small "x" next to it. If you recall, this indicates that clicking will begin a new path.

3 Click point A at the left end of the line to create the starting anchor point—a small solid square.

Click point B at the right end of the line to create the ending anchor point.

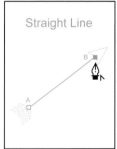

Click once to begin a straight line.   *Click again to end it.*

When you click a second time, a caret (^) appears next to the Pen tool. The caret indicates that you can drag out a direction line for a curve by clicking and dragging the Pen tool from this anchor point. The caret disappears when you move the Pen tool away from the anchor point.

4   Remember that you must end the path before you can draw other lines that aren't connected to this path. Choose Select > Deselect, or use any of the other methods discussed in the previous exercises.

Now you'll make the straight line thicker by changing its stroke weight.

5   With the Selection tool (‍) from the Tools panel, click the straight line to select it.

6   Choose Window > Stroke to display the Stroke panel.

7   In the Stroke panel, type **3 pt** in the Weight text field, and press Enter or Return to apply the change.

Splitting a path

To continue creating the arrow for this illustration, you'll split the path of the straight line using the Scissors tool, and adjust the segments.

1   With the straight line still selected, in the Tools panel, click and hold down on the Eraser tool (‍) to reveal the Scissors tool (‍) and click in the middle of the line to make a cut.

Cuts made with the Scissors tool must be on a line or a curve rather than on an endpoint.

Where you click with the Scissors tool, you will see a newly selected anchor point. The Scissors tool actually creates two anchor points each time you click, but because they are on top of each other, you can see only one.

2   Select the Direct Selection tool (‍) in the Tools panel and position it over the cut. The small hollow square on the cursor indicates that it's over the anchor point. Select the new anchor point, and drag it up to widen the gap between the two split segments.

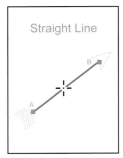

Click with the Scissors tool to cut the line.

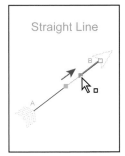

Drag to separate the new line segments.

Adding arrowheads

Adobe Illustrator lets you add pre-made arrowheads and tails to open paths by applying an Effect. The Add Arrowhead feature is available under the Filter menu as well as in the Effect menu. The benefit to using an Effect is that the arrow dynamically changes with the stroke to which it is applied. A filter, on the other hand, has no relationship to the stroke.

When a path with the Add Arrowhead Effect is changed, the arrowhead follows the path, whereas the Filter arrowhead remains in its original position. Read more about Effects and how to use them in Lesson 12 "Applying Appearance Attributes and Graphic Styles."

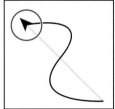

The Add Arrowhead Filter.

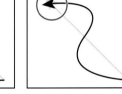

The Add Arrowhead Effect.

Now you'll add an arrowhead to the ending point of one line segment and a tail to the starting point of the other line segment.

1   With the top line segment selected, choose Effect > Stylize > Add Arrowheads.

Note: Choose the top, or first, Effect > Stylize command. The second Effect > Stylize command applies painted or impressionistic effects to RGB images.

2   In the Add Arrowheads dialog box, leave the Start section set to None. For the End section, click an arrow button to select the number 2 style of arrowhead (a thumbnail preview appears in the dialog box), and click OK.

Illustrator adds the arrowhead to the end of the line (the last anchor point created on the uncut line).

3   Using the Selection tool (⬉), select the bottom line segment, and choose Effect > Stylize > Add Arrowheads to open the dialog box again. Select the number 18 style of arrowhead from the Start section, select None for the End section, and click OK to add a tail to the starting point of the line.

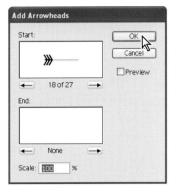

You can reapply the same arrowhead style to other selected objects by choosing Effect > Stylize > Add Arrowheads.

4   Choose Select > Deselect to deselect the artwork, and then choose File > Save.

Drawing curves

In this part of the lesson, you will review drawing curves by drawing the pear, its stem, and a leaf. You'll examine a single curve and then draw a series of curves together, using the template guidelines to help you.

Selecting a curve

1   Choose View > Curved Line to display a view of a curved line on the template.

2   Using the Direct Selection tool (⬉), click one of the segments of the curved line to view its anchor points and its direction handles, which extend from the points. The Direct Selection tool lets you select and edit individual segments in the curved line.

With a curve selected, you can also select the stroke and fill of the curve. When you do this, the next line you draw will have those same attributes. For more on these attributes, see Lesson 6, "Working with Color."

Drawing the leaf

Now you'll draw the first curve of the leaf.

1 Choose View > Leaf or scroll down to see the guides for Leaf step 1.

Instead of dragging the Pen tool (✒) to draw a curve, you will drag it to set the starting point and the direction of the line's curve. When you release the mouse button, the starting point is created and two direction handles are formed. Then, drag the Pen tool to the end of the first curve to set the starting point and direction of the next curve on the line.

2 Select the Pen tool and position it over point A on the template. Press the mouse button and drag from point A to the red dot. Then release the mouse button.

Next you'll set the second anchor point and its direction handles.

3 Press the mouse button and drag from point B to the next red dot. Release the mouse button. Illustrator connects the two anchor points with a curve that follows the direction handles you have created. Notice that if you vary the angle of dragging, you change the degree of the curve.

4 To complete the curved line, drag the Pen tool from point C on the template to the last red dot and release the mouse button.

5 Control+click (Windows) or Command+click (Mac OS) away from the line to indicate the end of the path. (You must do this to indicate when you have finished drawing a path. You can also do this by clicking the Pen tool in the Tools panel, or by choosing Select > Deselect.)

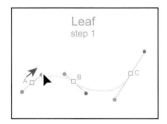

Drag to start the line and set direction of first curve.

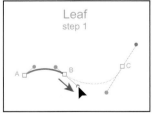

Drag to end first curve and set direction of second curve.

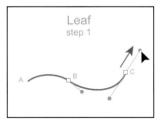

Drag to end second curve and adjust its direction.

Drawing different kinds of curves

Now you'll finish drawing the leaf by adding to an existing curved segment. Even after ending a path, you can return to the curve and add to it. The Alt (Windows) or Option (Mac OS) key lets you control the type of curve you draw.

Before starting this lesson, choose the arrow to the right of the status bar in the lower left corner of the Illustrator workspace and select Show > Current Tool.

1   Scroll down to the instructions on the template for Leaf step 2.

You'll add a corner point to the path. A corner point lets you change the direction of the curve. A smooth point lets you draw a continuous curve.

2   Position the Pen tool (✎) over the end of the line at point A. The slash next to the Pen tool indicates that you'll continue the path of the existing line, rather than start a new line.

3   Hold down Alt (Windows) or Option (Mac OS) and notice that the status bar in the lower left corner of the window displays "Pen: Make Corner." Now Alt/Option+drag the Pen tool from anchor point A to the red dot. Then release the mouse button.

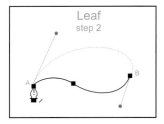 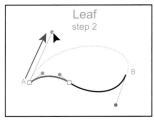

A slash indicates the Pen tool is aligned with anchor.   *Alt/Option+dragging creates corner point.*

So far, all the curves you have drawn have been open paths. Now you'll draw a closed path, in which the final anchor point is drawn on the first anchor point of the path. (Examples of closed paths include ovals and rectangles.) You'll close the path using a smooth point.

4   Position the cursor over anchor point B on the template. A small, open circle appears next to the Pen tool, indicating that clicking will close the path. Press the mouse button and drag from this point to the second red dot.

Notice the direction handles where you close the path. The direction handles on both sides of a smooth point are aligned along the same angle.

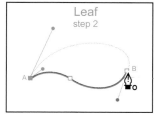

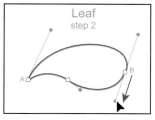

A small circle indicates that clicking with the Pen tool closes the path.

Drag to red dot to lengthen curved line.

5   Control+click (Windows) or Command+click (Mac OS) away from the line, and choose File > Save.

Convert between smooth points and corner points

Now you'll create the leaf stem by adjusting a curved path. You'll be converting a smooth point on the curve to a corner point and a corner point to a smooth point.

1   Choose View > Stem to display a magnified view of the stem.

2   Select the Direct Selection tool (⬚) in the Tools panel, position the cursor over point A at the top of the curve to display a hollow square on the cursor, and then click the anchor point to select it and display its red direction handles for the smooth point.

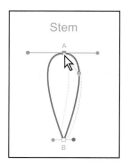

3   Select the Convert Anchor Point tool (⋏) from the same group as the Pen tool (✎) in the Tools panel, or use the shortcut for Convert Anchor Point tool by pressing the Alt (Windows) or Option (Mac OS) key while the Pen tool is selected.-

4   Using the Convert Anchor Point tool, select the left direction point (on top of the red dot) on the direction line, drag it to the gold dot on the template, and then release the mouse button.

Dragging with the Convert Anchor Point tool converts the smooth anchor point to a corner point and adjusts the angle of the left direction line.

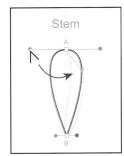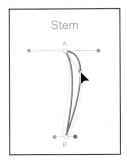

Use Convert Anchor Point tool to convert curves to corners.

Converting points

Smooth anchor points can now easily be converted to corner points and vice-versa by clicking on the Convert selected anchor points to corner button (⊤) or the Convert selected anchor points to smooth button (⊓) in the Control panel. After Selecting a point or points with the Direct Selection tool (⬚), you can access these buttons in the Control panel.

5   Using the Convert Anchor Point tool, select the bottom anchor point and drag from point B to the red dot to convert the corner point to a smooth point, rounding out the curve, and then release the mouse button. Two direction handles emerge from the anchor point, indicating that it is now a smooth point

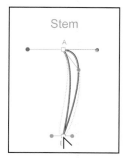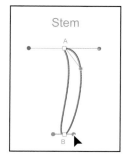

Use Convert Anchor Point tool to convert corners to curves.

Next you'll edit the shape of the stem some more.

6   With the Direct Selection tool (❧), click the top point or click and drag a marquee around the top point to select it. From the Control panel, choose Cut path at selected anchor points (✂). Drag the selected anchor point to the left.

7   Shift + click on the two points at the top. From the Control panel, choose Connect selected end points ( ). This should create a straight line across the top of the stem.

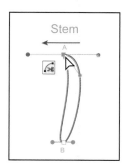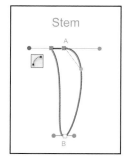

8   Choose File > Save.

Drawing the pear shape

Now you'll draw a single, continuous object that consists of smooth points and corner points. Each time you want to change the direction of a curve at a specific point, you'll hold down Alt (Windows) or Option (Mac OS) to create a corner point.

1   Choose View > Pear to display a magnified view of the pear.

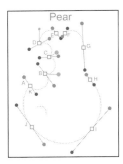

First you'll draw the bite marks on the pear by creating corner points and changing the direction of the curve segments.

2   Select the Pen tool (✒) from the same group as the Convert Anchor Point tool (⏷). Drag the Pen tool from point A on the template to the red dot to set the starting anchor point and direction of the first curve. Release the mouse button.

3   While holding down the mouse button, drag the Pen tool from point B to the red dot and, while holding down Alt (Windows) or Option (Mac OS), drag the direction handle from the red dot to the gold dot. Release the mouse button.

4   Continue drawing to points C and D by first dragging from the anchor point to the red dot and then Alt/Option+dragging the direction handle from the red dot to the gold dot.

At the corner points B, C, and D, you first drag to continue the current segment, and then Alt/Option+drag to set the direction of the next curved segment.

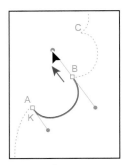   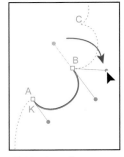

Drag to adjust curve.   *Alt/Option+drag direction point to set corner point.*

Next, you'll complete the drawing of the pear by creating smooth points.

5   Drag each of the points from E through J to their red dots, and then click anchor point K to close the pear shape. Notice that when you hold the cursor over anchor point K, a small open circle appears next to the pen, indicating that the path will close when you click.

6   Hold down Control (Windows) or Command (Mac OS) and click away from the path to deselect it, and then choose File > Save.

Editing curves

To adjust the curves you've drawn, you can drag either the curve's anchor points or its direction handles. You can also edit a curve by moving the line.

1   Select the Direct Selection tool (⬉) and click the outline of the pear.

Clicking with the Direct Selection tool displays the curve's direction handles and lets you adjust the shape of individual curved segments. Clicking with the Selection tool (⬈) selects the entire path.

2   Click the anchor point G at the top right of the pear to select it, and adjust the segment by dragging the top direction handle as shown in the illustration. Shift + click on points F and G to select them. Using the arrow keys, press the right arrow to nudge the points to the right. Notice that with both points selected that the handles disappear. In the Control panel, click on Show handles for multiple selected anchor points (▣) to see the direction lines to be able to edit them.

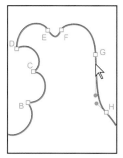
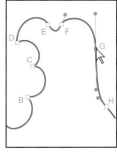
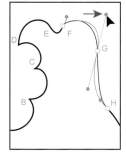

Use Direct Selection tool to select individual segments.   *Select anchor point.*   *Adjust anchor point.*

3   Make sure the fill is set to none. If not, click the Fill color in the Control panel. When the Swatches panel appears click the None box.

4   Now select the Pen tool (✐) and drag to draw the small curve on the pear where the arrow pierces it. (Use the dashed line on the template as a guide.)

Note: If you can't see the dashed, curved line on the template, make sure that the Fill in the Tools panel is set to None and that the Stroke is set to black.

5   Choose File > Save.

Finishing the pear illustration

To complete the illustration, you'll make some minor modifications and assemble and paint the objects. Then you will position parts of the arrow to create the illusion of the pear being pierced.

Assembling the parts

1   Double-click the Zoom tool (🔍) to zoom to 100%.

2   Choose Window > Layers to display the Layers panel.

3   In the Layers panel, click the template icon (◳), next to the Template layer name, to hide the template.

4   Choose View > Show Bounding Box so that you can see the bounding boxes of selected objects as you transform them.

5   Choose the Selection tool (▶) in the Tools panel, and Shift+click to select the two single curved lines that you no longer need for the leaf. Press Backspace (Windows) or Delete (Mac OS) to delete them.

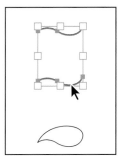

Select and delete extra lines.

Now you'll make the stem and leaf smaller, and rotate them slightly using the Transform commands.

6 Select the stem and choose Object > Transform > Scale. Select Uniform and enter **50%** in the Scale text field. Select the Scale Strokes & Effects Option, and click OK.

The Scale Strokes & Effects Option scales stroke weights and effects automatically. You can also set this Option as a preference, choose Edit > Preferences > General (Windows) or choose Illustrator > Preferences > General (Mac OS).

7 Choose Object > Transform > Rotate. Enter **45** in the Angle text field, and click OK.

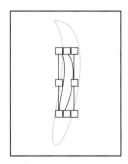
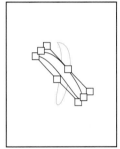

Scale stem 50%.   *Rotate stem 45°.*

Now you'll repeat the scaling and rotation on the leaf.

8 Select the leaf and choose Object > Transform > Scale. Leave the settings as they are, and click OK to scale the leaf by 50%. Then choose Object > Transform > Rotate, enter **15** in the Angle text field, and click OK.

You can also scale and rotate objects by using the Scale and Rotate tools, respectively, or by using the Free Transform tool to do either. For information, see Lesson 4, "Transforming Objects."

9 Select the Selection tool, and move the stem and the leaf to the top of the pear.

10 Move the parts of the arrow over the pear to make it look as if the arrow is entering the front of the pear and exiting the back.

Objects are arranged in the order in which they are created, with the most recent in front.

The Finished Pear

11 Select the bottom part of the arrow, and Shift+click to select the curve where the arrow pierces the pear. Then choose Object > Arrange > Bring to Front to arrange them in front of the pear.

Painting the artwork

Now paint the objects as you like. In the color illustration, you have removed the stroke on the leaf, the stem, and the pear, and we've painted the fills with custom-made gradients called Pear leaf, Pear stem, and Pear body, which are provided in the Swatches panel. We painted the arrow with a dark blue color, and then we added some detail lines to the leaf, the stem, and the round part of the pear using the Paintbrush tool (✐) and the Pen tool (✐). We also stroked the curve where the arrow pierces the pear.

1 Select an object, and then click the Fill color in the Control panel to view the Swatches panel. Use the named swatches: Pear leaf, Pear stem, and Pear body for the appropriate parts and Dark Blue for the arrow.

2 Choose File > Save to save your work, then File > Close.

To learn how to create your own gradients, see Lesson 9, "Blending Shapes and Colors." To learn more about painting options in Illustrator, see Lesson 6, "Color and Painting." For additional practice with the Pen tool, try tracing over images with it. As you practice with the Pen tool, you'll become more adept at drawing the kinds of curves and shapes you want.

Exploring on your own

Experiment by placing your own images and recreating them using a template. Find an image, logo, or other simple artwork that you would like to create save it as any number of image file formats that Illustrator CS3 can accept, including: .pdf, .psd, .tiff, .eps, .jpg and more.

1 Create a new Illustrator document, choose the size and color mode based upon your needs, or simply leave the defaults settings unchanged.

2 Choose File > Place. Browse to locate the artwork you wish to recreate, select it and check the Template checkbox. Choose OK. The image is placed on a locked template with a clean layer at the top of the stacking order.

3 Select your Pen tool (✐) and start using the techniques you learned throughout this lesson to help recreate the graphic.

Review

▶ **Review questions**

1 Describe how to draw straight vertical, horizontal, or diagonal lines using the Pen tool.

2 How do you draw a curved line using the Pen tool?

3 How do you draw a corner point on a curved line?

4 Name two ways to convert a smooth point on a curve to a corner point?

5 Which tool would you use to edit a segment on a curved line?

▶ **Review answers**

1 To draw a straight line, click twice with the Pen tool. The first click sets the starting anchor point, and the second click sets the ending anchor point of the line. To constrain the straight line vertically, horizontally, or along a 45° diagonal, hold down the Shift key as you click with the Pen tool.

2 To draw a curved line using the Pen tool, hold down the mouse button and drag to create the starting anchor point and set the direction of the curve, and then click to end the curve.

3 To draw a corner point on a curved line, hold down Alt (Windows) or Option (Mac OS) and drag the direction handle on the endpoint of the curve to change the direction of the path, and then continue dragging to draw the next curved segment on the path.

4 Use the Direct Selection tool to select the anchor point, and then use the Convert Anchor Point tool to drag a direction handle to change the direction. Also, choose a point or points with the Direct Selection tool and choose the Convert selected anchor points to corner button from the Control panel.

5 To edit a segment on a curved line, select the Direct Selection tool and drag the segment to move it, or drag a direction handle on an anchor point to adjust the length and shape of the segment.

MAKE YOUR DAY GO FROM
BLAHHH TO AHHH!!!!

AQUO life

Spice up your illustration with colors by taking advantage of color controls available in Illustrator CS3. Discover how to use the Color Guide and color groups, Live Paint, as well as how to traditionally create and paint fills and strokes in this information packed lesson.

6 | Color and Painting

In this lesson, you'll learn how to do the following:

- Paint with, create, and edit colors using the Control panel and shortcuts.

- Name and save colors, create color groups and build a color palette.

- Use the Color Guide panel and Live Color features.

- Copy paint and appearance attributes from one object to another.

- Paint with gradients, patterns, and brushes.

- Use the Live Paint features.

- Save your file as a PDF.

Getting started

In this lesson, you will learn about the fundamentals of color and create and edit colors using the Color panel and the Swatches panel:

1   To ensure that the tools and panels function exactly as described in this lesson, delete or deactivate (by renaming) the Adobe Illustrator CS3 preferences file. See "Restoring default preferences" on page 3.

2   Start Adobe Illustrator CS3.

Note: If you have not already copied the resource files for this lesson onto your hard disk from the Lesson06 folder from the Adobe Illustrator CS3 Classroom in a Book CD, do so now. See "Copying the Classroom in a Book files" on page 2.

Color Mode

First, before starting a new illustration, you must determine if the image should use CMYK colors or RGB.

CMYK—Cyan, Magenta, Yellow, and Black colors are part of the four-color process. These four colors are combined and overlapped in a screen pattern to create what appears to be a multitude of other colors. You will select this mode when printing.

RGB—Red, Green, Blue is the natural method of viewing color using light. Select this mode if using images for screen presentations or the Internet.

The color mode is selected when you choose File > New and pick the appropriate New Document Profile such as Print, which chooses CMYK for the color mode. The Color Mode can be changed by toggling the arrow to the left of Advanced to see the Advanced options.

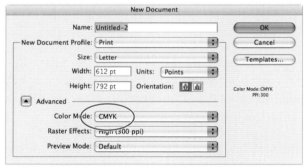

Select the New Document Profile when creating a new Illustrator document to select the color mode.

When a Color Mode is selected, Adobe Illustrator CS3 opens the applicable panels built with colors in either the CMYK or RGB mode. A document's color mode can be changed after the file is created by using File > Document Color Mode > CMYK Color or RGB Color.

Understanding the color controls

In this lesson, you will discover the traditional method of coloring objects in Adobe Illustrator CS3. This includes painting objects with colors, gradients, or patterns, and is done using a combination of panels and tools—the Control panel, Color panel, Swatches panel, Gradient panel, Stroke panel, Color Guide panel, and the paint buttons in the

Tools panel—that let you select and change an object's paint and line attributes. You'll begin by looking at finished artwork to which color has already been applied.

1 Choose File > Open and open L6end.ai in the Lesson06 folder to open a poster.

2 Choose the Selection tool (⬉) in the Tools panel, then click the blue shape in the Aquo logo off of the left edge of the artboard (you may need to scroll over).

In the Tools panel, notice that the Fill box appears in the foreground, indicating that it is selected. (This is the default.) The box has a fill of a blue color. Behind the Fill box, the Stroke box has no outline, represented by a red slash (⊘). As a rule, the color of the box in the background is not in the current selection.

The Fill and Stroke attributes of the selected object also appear in Window > Appearance panel. Appearance attributes can be edited, deleted, or saved as Graphic Styles, and applied to other objects, layers, and groups. You'll use this panel later in this lesson.

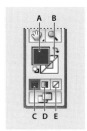
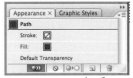

*A. Fill. **B.** Stroke. **C.** Color.*
*D. Gradient. **E.** None.*

Appearance panel reflects
selected object's paint attributes.

Note: *Your Tools panel may look different. Due to screen size, some monitors may display the Tools panel as a double column rather than the default single column Tools panel.*

3   Choose Window > Color to open the Color panel. The Color panel displays the current color for the fill and stroke, and its CMYK sliders show the percentages of cyan, magenta, yellow, and black. At the bottom of the Color panel is the color spectrum bar.

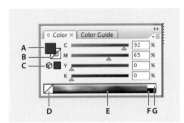

A. Fill box. B. Stroke box. C. Out of Web Color Warning.
D. None box. E. Color spectrum bar.
F. Black color box. G. White color box.

The color spectrum bar lets you quickly and visually select a fill or stroke color from a spectrum of colors. You can also choose white or black by clicking the appropriate color box at the right end of the color bar.

> *Shift-click on the Color spectrum bar at the bottom of the Color panel to rotate through the different color modes.*

4   Open the Color Guide panel by choosing Window > Color Guide or clicking on its tab. Click on the blue swatch in the upper left corner of the panel to set the base color as the red of the selected object (labeled A in the diagram below). Click on the Harmony Rules menu and choose Complementary 2. The Color Guide helps to pick color tints, analogous colors and much more. From this panel you can also access the Live Color feature which allows you to edit and create colors.

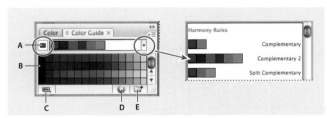

A. Set base color. B. Swatches. C. Color Libraries.
D. Edit or apply colors. E. Save Color Group to Swatches panel.

5 Open the Color panel by clicking on the Color tab. Using the Selection tool (), click on various shapes in the file to see how their paint attributes are reflected in the various panels.

6 You will work with an unfinished version of this illustration later in the lesson. You can choose to leave it open at this time, or choose File > Close.

Color fundamentals

Before opening the project file for this lesson, you'll open a basic document to gain a better understanding of how color is applied in Adobe Illustrator CS3.

1 Choose File > Open and select the file named color.ai in the Lesson06 folder inside the AICIB folder.

2 Choose File > Save As. In the Save As dialog box, name the file **color_practice.ai**, and navigate to the Lesson06 folder. Leave the file format set to Illustrator (*.AI), and click Save. In the Illustrator Options dialog box, accept the default settings by clicking OK.

3 Using the Selection tool (), select some of the objects and note that they have a white fill and a black stroke.

4 Choose any one of the stars, and click once on Fill color in the Control panel. Choose the Pure Yellow swatch from the Swatches panel that appears.

5 With the same star selected, choose the color box to the left of the word Stroke in the Control panel and select the Pumpkin swatch.

6 Using the Stroke Weight menu, choose 4 pt.

7 With the same star still selected, click on the word Stroke in the Control panel to open the Stroke panel. Note that you can choose to have the stroke of an object centered on the path or on the inside or outside. For this exercise, put the stroke on the outside of the path.

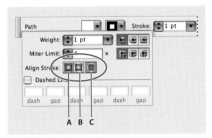

A. Align Stroke to Center.
B. Align Stroke to Inside.
C. Align Stroke to Outside.

8 If the Stroke panel is not visible, choose Window > Stroke. Click on the panel menu icon ( ) and choose Show Options.

9 In the Stroke panel, select Dashed Line, the path defaults to 12 pt dashes.

Select Dashed Line.

Change the stroke to a dashed line.

10 Choose File > Save.

Copying attributes

1 Using the Selection tool ( ), select one of the stars that has not yet been colored, then Shift-click to add all other unpainted stars to the selection.

2 Using the Eyedropper tool ( ), click on the star you painted. All stars that are unpainted pick up the attributes from the painted star.

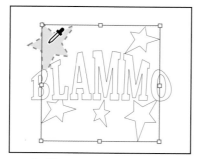

Sample fill and stroke attributes using the Eyedropper tool.

All selected stars pick up the painted star's attributes.

Using the Appearance panel for fills and strokes

Up to this point you have mostly used the Control panel to paint Fills and Strokes, but you can also use the Appearance panel to paint and apply other attributes specific to the Fill or Stroke.

1 Using the Selection tool (↖), select the "Blammo" text.

2 If the Appearance panel is not open, choose Window > Appearance. Notice that the selected text is listed as a group in the Appearance panel. Double-click the word Contents in the Appearance panel to show the Fill and Stroke attributes for the text.

3 Click on Fill in the Appearance panel. Click on the Fill color in the Control panel to open the Swatches panel, then select the Pantone 187 swatch (▨). The text fill is now red.

4 Click the word Stroke in the Appearance panel, and choose the same Pantone 187 swatch (▨) from the Stroke color in the Control panel.

5 With Stroke still selected in the Appearance panel, from the Control panel click on the Stroke Weight menu, and select **5 pt**.

6 Select Opacity from the Control panel; enter **50** into the Opacity text field.

Notice that because only the Stroke was selected in the Appearance panel, the Fill is still at 100% Opacity.

7 Choose File > Save and close the file.

Building and saving your own custom color

The illustration you are about to work on is in the CMYK color mode, which means that you can create your own color from any combination of Cyan, Magenta, Yellow, and Black.

1   Choose File > Open and select the file named L6start1.ai in the Lesson06 folder inside the AICIB folder.

2   Choose File > Save As, name the file **aquo_poster.ai**, and save it into the Lesson06 folder. Leave the type of format set to Adobe Illustrator Document, and click Save. In the Illustrator Options dialog box, accept the default settings by clicking OK.

3   If the Color panel is not visible, choose Window > Color. If the CMYK sliders are not visible, choose CMYK from the Color panel menu.

4   Enter this combination in the CMYK text fields: C = **92**, M = **65**, Y = **0**, K = **0**.

5   Open the Swatches panel by clicking on it's icon and choose New Swatch from the Swatches panel menu ( ).

6   Name the color **logo background,** and click OK.

💡 *To save the color you made in the Color panel, you can also click on the New Swatch button in the Swatches panel to open up the New Swatch dialog box.*

Note: The Swatches panel stores the colors, gradients, and patterns that have been preloaded into Adobe Illustrator CS3, as well as those you create and save for reuse. New colors added to the Swatches panel are saved with the current file. Opening a new artwork file displays the default set of swatches that comes with Adobe Illustrator CS3. If you want to load a Swatches panel from one saved document into another, click the Swatch Libraries Menu button and choose Other Library, then locate the document with the Swatches panel you wish to import.

7   Off the left side of the artboard is the Aquo logo. With the Selection tool (➤), click the stroke of the outer shape to select it. Click on the Fill box in the Control panel. When the Swatches panel appears, choose the logo background swatch.

8   Click Stroke color in the Control panel and choose None (▨).

9   Choose Select > Deselect to make sure no objects are selected.

Using Illustrator swatch libraries

Perhaps the Aquo company always uses yellow/orange for the text in their company logo. When this color of yellow/orange is defined, it could be a warm, dark, or light yellow/orange. This is why most printers and designers rely on a color matching system, like the Pantone® system, to help maintain color consistency and to give a wider range of colors in some cases.

Creating a spot color

In this section, you will see how to load a color library, such as the Pantone color system, and how to add a Pantone (PMS) color to the Swatches panel.

1   From the Swatches panel, click on the Swatch Libraries menu button (▤⌄), and then scroll down until you can find Color Books. Hover over Color Books and choose the Pantone solid coated library. The Pantone solid coated library appears in its own panel.

2   Using the Pantone solid coated panel menu icon (), choose Show Find Field. Type the value **116** into the Find field. Pantone 116 C is highlighted. Click on the highlighted swatch to add it to the Swatches panel.

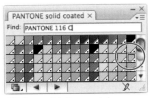

Click to add the swatch
to the Swatches panel.

The color appears in the
Swatches panel.

Note: All of the libraries you see when clicking on the Swatch Libraries Menu button come with Adobe Illustrator by Default. Most, but not all, of the libraries listed are CMYK colors. The libraries supplied by third party vendors are located under Color Books. Explore the libraries such as Forest or Jeweltones and you will see a whole collection of colors that share some association. These can be an excellent place to start when creating colors for a project.

3   With the Selection tool (➤), Shift-click the tail of the q in the "Aquo" text and "NATURAL ENERGY" to select them both. From the Fill color in the Control panel, choose the Pantone 116 C color to fill the text. Make sure that the Stroke color is None (▱).

4   Choose Select > Deselect.

5   Choose File > Save to save the file. Keep it open.

Why does my Pantone Swatch look different from the other swatches?

When you add the Pantone solid coated swatch, you should notice a black spot and triangle in the lower right corner of the swatch.

As a default, the Pantone solid coated swatch is defined as a Spot color; hence, the black dot. A spot color is not created from a combination of Cyan, Magenta, Yellow, and Black (CMYK) inks but is its own solid ink color. A press operator uses a pre-mixed PMS (Pantone Matching System) color in the press, offering consistency and better color accuracy.

The triangle indicates that this color is Global. If this color is edited, all color references used in the illustration are updated. Any color can be Global, not only Pantone colors.

To learn more about spot colors, visit the Help by choosing Help > Illustrator Help and searching for "spot colors."

Creating color groups

Adobe Illustrator CS3 has the ability to save colors into color groups. A color group is an organization tool that lets you group related color swatches together in the Swatches panel. We organize our colors by what they are used for, such as grouping all of the colors for the logo. Groups have much more functionality, such as editing the color group as a whole using Live Color, but you'll focus on grouping right now.

1   With the Swatches panel showing, Shift-click on the logo background swatch and the Pantone 116 C swatch created earlier to select both.

2   Click on the New Color Group button (⬛⁺) at the bottom of the Swatches panel to group the colors together and open the New Color Group dialog box. Type in Logo and click OK to name the group.

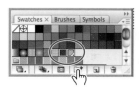
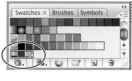

Shift-select swatches   *The result.*
and create a color group.

Note: *If you have artwork selected when you click on the New Color Group button, an expanded New Color Group dialog box appears. Adobe Illustrator CS3 allows you to create a color group from the colors in the artwork, even allowing you to convert the artwork colors to global colors if they aren't already.*

Next you'll edit a color in the group and add a color.

3   With the Selection tool (➤), click on any color in the top of the Swatches panel to ensure that the color group is no longer selected in the Swatches panel.

4   Click on the blue background shape of the Aquo Natural Energy logo to select it. Click on the Fill box in the Tools panel.

5   In the Swatches panel, double-click on the logo background color in the Logo color group to open the Swatch Options dialog box. Check the Global option and change the K slider to **20** to make the blue a little darker. Click OK and notice the white triangle in the corner of the color swatch indicating it's a global color (▣).

Note: If you double-click to edit a color and the color is not Global, then any edits to the color won't affect objects on the page that were using that swatch. That is why we selected the blue shape first, so that the edits would apply to it.

6   The swatch named K=90 in the Swatches panel group above the Logo group is one that needs to be added to the Logo group. Click on the K=90 swatch and drag it between the blue and yellow colors in the Logo group. Notice that after you drag and drop that you can reorder the swatches within the group by dragging them. Drag the K=90 swatch to the right of the Pantone 116 C (yellow) swatch.

The colors for the logo have now been saved with this document as a color group. You can always refer back to them later on.

💡 *Colors can be created using a variety of methods including the Color panel and Swatches panel and dragged into a group.*

7   Choose File > Save.

🔢 To learn more about working with color groups see "Working with color groups" in Illustrator Help.

Next you'll work with the logo and the Live Color option.

Editing color with Live Color

Adobe Illustrator CS3 has many tools for working with color including the Color Guide panel and the Live Color feature. Use the Color Guide panel (Window > Color Guide) as a tool for color inspiration while you create your artwork. The Color Guide panel suggests harmonious colors based on the current color in the Tools panel. You can use these colors to color artwork or you can save them as swatches.

In this section you will see how to edit colors using the Live Color dialog box. You will make a copy of the Aquo logo and test colors.

1   With the Selection tool (▶), click and drag a marquee selection around the Aquo Natural Energy logo and choose Edit > Copy, Edit > Paste. Move the copy down below the original logo and keep it selected.

2   Choose Edit > Edit Colors > Convert to CMYK. This way the yellow PMS color in the copied logo has been converted to CMYK.

3   Choose Edit > Edit Colors > Recolor Artwork. This will open the Live Color dialog box and allow you to edit the colors in the logo.

The Live Color dialog box should appear, so keep it open for the next steps.

You use the Live Color dialog box to create and edit color groups, as well as reassign or reduce the colors in your artwork. All of the color groups that you create for a particular document appear in the Color Groups storage area of the Live Color dialog box (as well as the Swatches panel). You can select and use these color groups at anytime.

💡 *To access the Live Color dialog box, you can also double-click on a group folder icon in the Swatches panel. The Live Color dialog box can also be opened from the Color Guide panel.*

4 In the Live color dialog box, click on the Hide Color Group Storage icon (◀) on the right side of the dialog box. This will hide the color groups storage area for now.

5 Click on the Edit tab to edit the colors in the artwork using a color wheel.

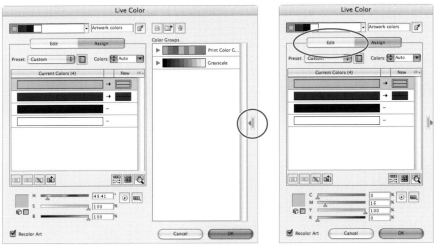

Hide Color Groups storage area.

6 Click on the Color Mode button (⊙) and choose CMYK from the menu (if the CMYK sliders are not already visible.)

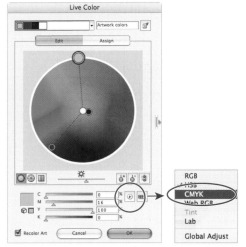

Choose CMYK from the color mode drop down menu.

7   While still in the Live Color dialog box, click on the Link Harmony Colors icon
( ) to link all of the colors together (if you see a link icon ( ), then they are already
linked). This way if you make an edit to one color, it will affect the others. These are
called Harmony colors.

8   Holding the Shift key, click and drag the yellow color circle to the left into the
green area of the color wheel. Drag the Brightness slider to the right to make the colors
brighter overall. This will perform a global adjustment. Keep the Live Color dialog box
open.

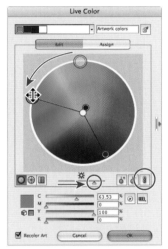

*Link the colors, adjust the
yellow color, change the brightness.*

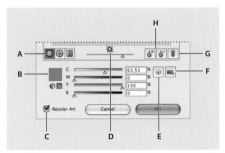

A. Color display options. B. Color of selected color marker or color bar.
C. Recolors selected artwork when checked. D. Show saturation and hue on Wheel.
E. Color Mode button. F. Color Group To Colors In A Swatch Library button.
G. Unlink harmony colors. H. Add and subtract color marker tools.

Live Color Overview

You use the Live Color dialog box to create and edit color groups, as well as reassign or reduce the colors in your artwork. All of the color groups that you create for a particular document appear in the Color Groups storage area of the Live Color dialog box (as well as the Swatches panel). You can select and use these color groups at anytime.

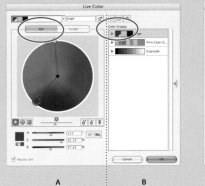

A   B   C

Create or edit color groups, and assign colors using the Live Color dialog box.
A. Create and edit a color group in the Edit tab. B. Select a color group from the Color Groups list.
C. Assign colors in the Assign tab.

The Recolor Art option at the bottom of the dialog box lets you preview colors on selected artwork, and specifies whether or not artwork is recolored when you close the Live Color dialog box.

The main areas of the Live Color dialog box are:

• **Edit:** Use the Edit tab to create new color groups or edit existing color groups. Use the harmony rule menu and the color wheel to experiment with color harmonies. The color wheel shows you how colors in a harmony are related, while the color bars let you see and manipulate individual color values. In addition, you can adjust brightness, add and remove colors, save color groups, and preview the colors on selected artwork.

• **Assign:** Use the Assign tab to view and control how colors from a color group replace original colors in your artwork. You can assign colors only if you have artwork selected in the document. You can specify which new colors replace which current colors, whether spots are preserved, and how colors are replaced (for example, you can replace colors entirely or replace hue while retaining brightness). Use Assign to control how artwork is recolored with the current color group or to reduce the number of colors in the current artwork.

• **Color Groups** lists all saved color groups for the open document (these same color groups appear in the Swatches panel). While in the Live Color dialog box, you can edit, delete, and create new color groups using the Color Groups list. All your changes are reflected in the Swatches panel. The selected color group denotes which color group is currently being edited. You can select any color group and edit it or use it to recolor selected artwork. Saving a color group adds the group to this list.

—From Illustrator Help

Creating a color group using Live Color

You can create a color group in the Live Color dialog box by choosing a base color and a harmony rule. The harmony rule uses the base color as the basis for generating the colors in the color group. For example, if you choose a blue base color and the Complementary harmony rule, a color group is created using the base color, blue, and its compliment, red.

Next you will create a color group from the colors you edited in the Live Color dialog box.

1 Click on the Show Color Group Storage icon ( ) on the right side of the Live Color dialog box to show the Color Groups list. Click on the New Color Group icon ( ) to create a color group from the colors you edited. A new color group will appear in the Color Groups list.

2 Double-click on the new color group name to open the Edit Name dialog box. Change the name of the group to Logo2 and click OK.

3 Click on the Hide Color Group Storage icon ( ) on the right side of the Live Color dialog box to hide the Color Groups area.

4 Click OK to close the Live Color dialog box.

Note: If a dialog box appears, click Yes to save changes to the color group.

5 Look in the Swatches panel to see the new Logo2 color group appear. You may need to scroll down in the Swatches panel top see it.

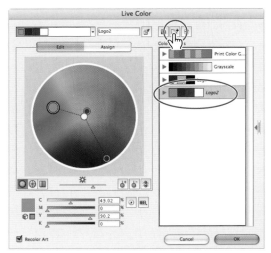

Create a new color group from the edited logo colors and rename to Logo2.

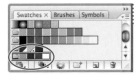

The result in the Swatches panel.

6 The copied logo should have the purple and green colors of the new color group you created.

Original copied logo.

The result.

Assign colors to your artwork

The Assign tab of the Live Color dialog box lets you assign colors from a color group to your artwork. You can assign colors in several ways, including using a new color group chosen from the Harmony Rule menu. In this next section of the lesson, we will practice assigning new colors to the color bar and "Aquo Life" text at the bottom of the poster.

1 Choose View > Fit in Window.

2 Choose Select > Deselect and with the Selection tool (⬏), click and drag to select the blue bar and "Aquo Life" text at the bottom of the poster.

3 Choose Edit > Edit Colors > Recolor Artwork to open the Live Color dialog box.

4   From the Harmony Rule menu, choose the Complimentary harmony rule. This will pick a set of colors that is complimentary to the green color. Leave the Live Color dialog box open.

Notice in the Live Color dialog box that the green color has a new green color assigned and the blue color has a new purple color assigned. The white color has no new color assigned because the complimentary color group that was chosen only had two colors.

Artwork selected.

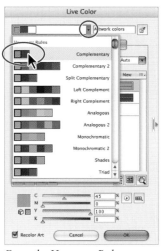

From the Harmony Rules menu choose Complimentary.

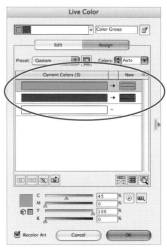

The result.

Assign new colors to selected artwork

After selecting the artwork you want to recolor and choosing Edit > Edit Colors > Recolor Artwork, you can assign new colors to the artwork on the Assign tab of the Live Color dialog box.

If you want to assign colors from a color group, do one of the following:

- Choose a color group from the Color Groups list.

- Create a new color group by selecting a new harmony rule from the menu from the Harmony Rules menu.

Note: If you create a new color group, you can click Edit to fine tune the colors, and then click Assign. Or, if you want to adjust a few colors in the selected artwork, select the color you want to adjust and edit it with the color sliders.

—From Illustrator Help

5   With the Live Color dialog box still open, click and drag the purple color on top of the green color in the New column. This will swap the green and purple colors. Leave the Live color dialog box open.

Note: *If you accidentally double-click on the new purple color the Color Picker will appear. Click cancel to close and try again.*

Drag to swap the new colors.

The result.

Reassigning colors in selected artwork.

Do any of the following to reassign colors:

- To assign a current color to a different color, drag the current color up or down in the Current Colors column until it's adjacent to the new color you want.

Note: If a row contains multiple colors and you want to move them all, click the selector bar at the left of the row and drag up or down.

- To assign a new color to a different row of current colors, drag the new color up or down in the New column.

- To exclude a row of current colors from being reassigned, click the arrow between the columns. To include it again, click the dash.

- To exclude a single current color from being reassigned, select the color and click Excludes Selected Colors So They Will Not Be Recolored.

- To randomly reassign colors, click the Randomly Change Color Order button . The New colors move randomly to different rows of current colors.

- To add a row to the Current Colors column, click Add A Row.

—From Illustrator Help

6   From the Colors menu, choose **1**.

Notice that in the Colors menu, some of the numbers are dimmed. You can select up to the number of colors originally found in the object. In this case it is three (green, blue, and white).

7   At the bottom of the Live Color dialog box, make sure that the HSB sliders are showing. If they are not, select HSB from the Color Mode menu by clicking on the Color Mode button (⊙) to the right of the sliders.

8   Change the HSB values to H=360, S=87, and B=84. This will edit the purple color to a red.

Notice how the new purple color has changed to red. Also notice how the blue and green colors are merged in the Current Colors column. The red color in the New column is split into 3 different sections (■■) (The 3 sections are subtle because one section is a tint of the red). This indicates the new red color (the top half) and the tints of the new red beneath it. The darkest color in the row (the blue) is replaced with the specified new color (the red). Other current colors in the row (the green) are replaced with a proportionally lighter tint of the red because you chose to use 1 color.

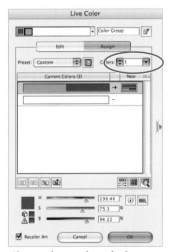
Change the number of colors to 1.

Change the HSB values to red.

The result.

9   Click on the Show Color Group Storage icon (▶) on the right side of the Live Color dialog box to show the Color Groups list if it isn't already showing. Click New Color Group (▣) to create a color group from the colors you edited. The color group called Color Group will appear in the Color Groups list.

10   Double-click on the new color group name in the Color Groups list to open the Edit Name dialog box. Change the name of the group to LogoBar and click OK.

11   Click OK in the Live Color dialog box and click Yes if a save dialog appears. The new color group should appear in the Swatches panel.

🔲 To learn more about how to work with Live Color, see "Live Color overview" in Illustrator Help.

Painting with gradients and patterns

In addition to process and spot colors, the Swatches panel can also contain pattern and gradient swatches. Adobe Illustrator CS3 provides sample swatches of each type in the default panel and lets you create your own patterns and gradients. Click on the buttons at the bottom of the panel to see all swatches or specific types of swatches.

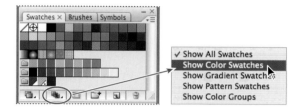

1   Choose Window > Workspace > [Panel].

2   Choose Select > Deselect.

3   Choose Window > Gradient if your Gradient panel is not visible. Choose Show Options from the panel menu. Click once below the gradient slider at the bottom of the panel to make the color stops visible.

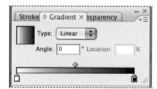

*The Gradient Ramp with a
color stop at either end.*

You can create your own gradient by activating the color stops on the gradient slider, or by dragging existing swatches directly on top of the existing gradient color stops.

4   In the Swatches panel, click and hold down on the color Dark Orange, don't release. Then drag the swatch on top of the black color stop on the right side of the gradient slider. If you miss the color stop, another stop may appear below the gradient slider. Choose Edit > Undo Gradient and try again.

5   Select the CMYK Yellow swatch and drag it onto the white color stop on the left side of the gradient slider.

6   Choose Radial from the Type menu in the Gradient panel.

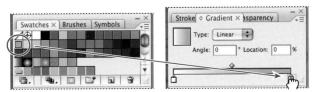
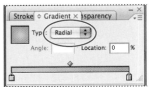

Drag the swatch onto the color stop.   *Change to radial.*

Note: To delete any extra colors in a Gradient you can also click and drag the color stops off the gradient slider.

💡 *If dragging the swatches isn't your thing, you can click a color stop then Alt (Windows) or Option (Mac) click on a swatch to replace gradient stop colors.*

7   Click on the New Swatch button (⬜) at the bottom of the Swatches panel, and name this **background gradient** in the New Swatch dialog box. You could also drag the swatch from the Gradient panel (in the upper left corner of the panel) directly into the Swatches panel.

8   Click the Layers panel tab to reveal the layers panel. Click in the Visibility column to the left of the Background layer to display the contents.

9   With the Selection tool, click the stroke of the large rectangle in the background (it is larger than the artboard). Click the Fill color in the Control panel and choose your new background gradient. The gradient has been applied.

10   Select one of the stars in the center of the artboard. Since these are part of a group, all become selected.

11   Click on the Fill box in the Control panel, and apply the background gradient to the stars. Change the Stroke color in the Control panel to None (⬜).

Now you will reverse the colors of the gradient, swapping the orange and the yellow.

12 In the Gradient panel, Alt (Windows) or Option (Mac) drag the left color stop (the yellow color) to the right until you are over the orange color stop on the right and release.

The gradient ramp should reverse. If it doesn't reverse, choose Edit > Undo and try again. From the Swatches panel, try dragging a darker orange onto the orange swatch onto the orange color stop on the left of the gradient ramp.

13 Select the Gradient tool (▣) and position the pointer in the center of the stars. Click and drag from the center of the artboard to the outer edge of the group of stars.

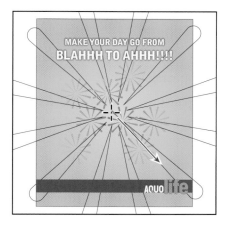

Notice that the Gradient is now smoothly transitioned through all stars, as though they are one object.

14 Choose Select > Deselect.

15 Choose File > Save.

Using patterns

You can use preset patterns that load with Adobe Illustrator CS3, or create your own. In this section, you will do both.

1 If the Swatches panel is not open, choose Window > Swatches. Click on the Swatch Libraries menu button (▤.) at the bottom of the panel and choose Patterns > Basic

Graphics > Basic Graphics_Dots to open the pattern library. A separate panel appears with supplied patterns.

2   Choose View > Outline to view the artwork as outlines. You should see a group of shapes radiating from the center of the artboard.

3   Using the Selection tool (➤), select the edge of the shape, then choose View > Preview to see the artwork again.

4   Click on the Stroke color in the Control panel and choose None (☐).

5   If the Appearance panel is not visible, choose Window > Appearance. Double-click on the word Contents to edit the object stroke and fill.

Since the pattern you are going to be using has a clear background, you will give this object two separate fills.

6   Select the word Fill in the Appearance panel. From the Appearance panel menu, choose Duplicate Item. Two fills appear in the Appearance panel.

7   With the top fill selected in the Appearance panel, choose the pattern named 10 dpi 60% from the Basic Graphics_Dots panel. Close the Basic Graphics_Dots panel.

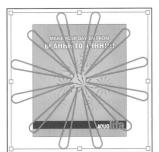 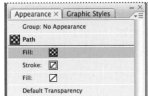 

Choose the 10 dpi 60% texture for the top Fill of the object.

8   Double-click on the Scale tool (⬚) in the Tools panel to make the pattern larger without affecting the shape. Deselect Objects, and Patterns becomes checked. Type **160** in the Uniform Scale text field, click OK. Only the pattern is enlarged.

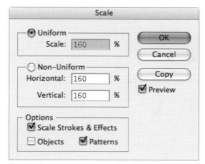

Before scaling the pattern.   *Scale the pattern, not the object, using the Scale tool options.*   *After scaling the pattern.*

9   Select the bottom fill attribute in the Appearance panel (you may need to scroll in the Appearance panel), and from the Swatches panel, select the Swatch named Dark Orange. The object now has a solid yellow/orange fill, as well as a pattern fill.

10   In the Appearance panel, click on the word Path to select the path for editing.

11   If the Transparency panel is not open, choose Window > Transparency. Click on the Blending Mode menu and choose Overlay. Change the opacity to 70% and see what you think.

The result.

12   To get rid of the shapes hanging off of the page, you can create a quick mask. With the Selection tool (▶), select the rectangle in the background with the gradient applied and choose Edit > Copy and Edit > Paste in Front to paste a copy directly on top of the copied shape.

13 With the shape still selected, choose Object > Arrange > Bring to Front. Shift click on the star shape hanging off the artboard and choose Object > Clipping Mask > Make to hide the extra.

14 Choose Select > Deselect.

15 Choose File > Save.

Creating your own pattern

In this section of the lesson you will create your own custom pattern and add it to the Swatches panel. You will then discover how to edit an existing pattern and update it in the Swatches panel. If your Swatches panel is not visible, choose Window > Swatches.

For this section, you will assign colors using the Tools panel.

1 Click the Fill box at the bottom of the Tools panel to make sure it is forward. It does not matter if it shows the last used color.

Make sure Fill box is selected before applying color.

2 With the Fill box selected, choose the CMYK Red swatch from the Swatches panel.

3 Press the "X" key to swap the Fill and Stroke in the Tools panel. When the Stroke box is selected, choose None by clicking the None button (⊘) at the bottom of the Tools panel.

4 In the Tools panel, click on the Rectangle tool, hold down the mouse button to view the hidden tools, and then select the Rounded Rectangle tool (▱). Click once off of the right edge of the Artboard (do not click and drag!). In the Rounded Rectangle dialog box, enter **.7 in** in the Width text field, **.7 in** in the Height text field, and **.3 in** in the Corner Radius text field and click OK.

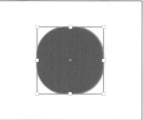

Enter values in the
Rounded Rectangle dialog box.

The result.

A red rounded corner square appears. Using the Selection tool (▶), position it off the artwork if it is touching any of your existing illustration.

5   Click on the Swatches panel tab to reveal the Swatches panel. With the Selection tool, click and drag the selected rounded rectangle into the Swatches panel. You have created a new pattern.

Note: *A pattern swatch can be composed of more than one shape. For instance, to create a flannel pattern for a shirt, you could create three overlapping rectangles or lines each with varying colors. Then select all three shapes and drag them as one into the Swatches panel.*

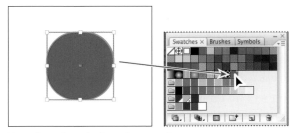

Drag shape into the Swatches panel.

6   Double-click on the pattern swatch you added to assign the name **dots**. Click OK.

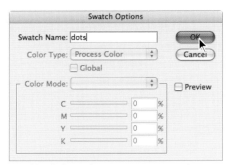

Double-click on the new pattern swatch
to name it.

Applying the pattern

1   With the Selection tool, select the red rectangle beneath the "Aquo Life" text in the poster.

You can assign the pattern using a number of different methods. In this instance you will use the Swatches panel to apply the pattern. You could also apply the pattern using the Fill color in the Control panel.

2   Click on the Fill box in the Tools panel, then in the Swatches panel, click on the dots pattern swatch you created.

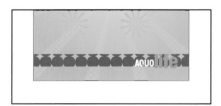

*The pattern is applied to the fill
of the red rectangle.*

💡 *As you add more custom swatches, it may be beneficial to view the Swatches panel by the Swatch names. You can change the view by choosing List View from the Swatches panel menu.*

3   Select the rounded rectangle used to create the pattern (off the right edge of the artboard), and press Delete, as you will no longer need the original.

4   Using the Selection tool (↖), select the red rectangle and choose **2 pt** from the Stroke Weight menu in the Control panel.

5   Click the Stroke color in the Control panel and choose CMYK Red from the Swatches panel.

6   Click the word Stroke in the Control panel and change the stroke to apply to the inside of the path.

7 Choose File > Save.

The result.

Editing the pattern

Perhaps you have used a pattern several times in an illustration and want to update its contents. Not a problem, just follow these steps:

1 Using the Selection tool (➤), click and drag the dots pattern swatch you created from the Swatches panel to an empty location on the artboard. The rounded rectangle returns to your artboard.

2 Choose Select > Deselect, and choose the Direct Selection tool (➤). Select the rounded rectangle.

3 Click the Stroke color in the Control panel, and select CMYK Red for the rounded rectangle. You will create a tint of the CMYK Red using the Color panel.

4 Choose Window > Color if the Color panel is not visible, and make sure the Stroke color is selected in the Color panel. With the rounded rectangle still selected, hold down the Shift key, and drag either the Yellow or Magenta slider to create a "tint" of this color. Notice that when you hold down the Shift key, the sliders move relative to each other. Use this method to create a lighter red color; an exact tint is not necessary.

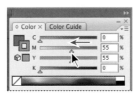

5   Using the Selection tool, select the rounded rectangle and hold down the Alt (Windows) or Option (Mac OS) key while dragging it back on top of the existing pattern Swatch called dots. The pattern is updated.

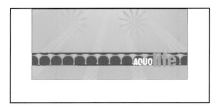

6   Select the rounded rectangle that you edited to create the updated pattern and delete it.

7   Choose File > Save.

Applying Live Paint

Live Paint lets you paint vector graphics intuitively by automatically detecting and correcting gaps that previously would have affected how fills and strokes were applied. Instead of having to plan every detail of an illustration, you can work more as you would coloring by hand on paper.

1   Choose File > Open and open the file in the Lesson06 folder named L6start2.ai.

2   Choose File > Save As. In the Save As dialog box, name the file **snowboarder.ai** and navigate to the Lesson06 folder. Leave the file format set to Illustrator (*.AI), and click Save. In the Illustrator Options dialog box, accept the default settings by clicking OK.

3   Use the Selection tool (➤) to select the snowboarder traced image and choose Object > Live Paint > Make. This creates a Live Paint group which can now be easily painted.

There are some gap issues to work with before painting. Gaps are the little spaces that leave openings in shapes that allow for paint to leak from one shape to another. Before starting the paint work on the snowboarder, choose Object > Live Paint > Gap Options. The Gap Options window appears.

4   The Gap Detection checkbox should be selected (if not select it). The Gap Preview Color is set to highlight in red.

5   Change Paint stops at to Medium Gaps. This will stop paint from leaking through some of the larger gaps as you apply paint. Change the Gap Preview Color to Green and have a look at the artwork, moving the Gap Options dialog box out of the way if necessary. Any gaps it finds will be green. Click OK.

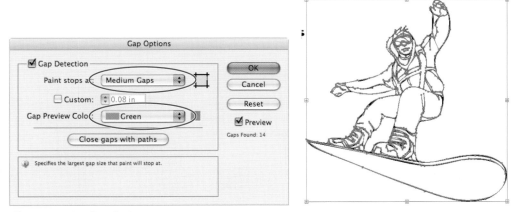

Close gaps using Gap Options.

6   Select the Live Paint Bucket tool (🪣) from the Tools panel. Before painting, click the Fill color in the Control panel and select the snowboarder swatch from the Swatches panel.

7 If the Color Guide panel is not visible, choose Window > Color Guide or click on its tab. From the Color Guide panel, choose Left Complement to choose complementary colors to use. Then click on the Save color group to Swatch panel button (⊡⁺) in the Color Guide panel. The color group should appear in the Swatches panel. You may have to scroll down to see it.

8 In the Swatches panel, click on the red color (color farthest to the left) in the color group to select it.

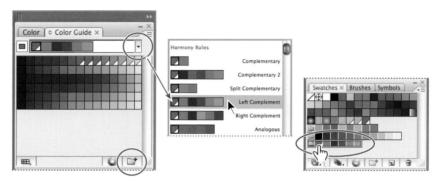

Select Left Complement, then save the color group.

The color group in the Swatches panel.

9 Move the mouse over the snowboarder's left leg. As you move over Live Paint objects in the traced image they highlight and three color swatches appear above the cursor. The three swatches represent the three swatches next to each other in the Swatches panel group you just made (the group is selected in the swatches panel after you make it). Click when part of the leg becomes highlighted. Click on the other leg to paint it as well.

10 Move the cursor over the snowboard. Click the left arrow key to cycle to the light green color in the Swatches panel group. Click to apply to the snowboard.

Note: You can also watch the Swatches panel to see what color in the group is selected and click on a color in the Swatches panel to paint with another color.

Coloring a shape using the Live Paint Bucket tool.

Use the left arrow to cycle through swatches.

11 From the Swatches panel, choose the Black swatch. Click to fill in the top edge of the snowboard.

12 With the Selection tool (➤) click and drag across the snow trail to the left of the snowboarder making sure to encompass all of the pieces. Choose Object > Live Paint > Make.

13 Choose a light blue from the Fill color in the Control panel to fill.

If you were to have selected the Live Paint Bucket and started clicking to fill the snow trail with color, you would soon realize that each piece is a separate object. To make it easier to select a series of objects in a live paint object, you can use the Live Paint Selection tool. You can either Shift-click to select multiple objects to colorize or drag across.

14 Select the Live Paint Selection tool (▨) and click and drag across the left half of the snow trail. Choose a lighter blue from the Swatches panel to paint the selection.

15 Choose Select > Deselect.

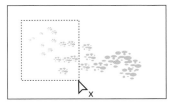

Select with the Live Paint Selection tool.

Part of artwork selected.

Result with color change.

16 Referencing the L6_end2.ai illustration, complete the painting of this illustration. You can use the colors in the example, or create your own interpretation. Also, move the snow trail to the left side of the snowboard where it belongs.

It is helpful to zoom in to see details. Don't worry if you fill a region with the wrong color, just choose the right color and fill again.

17 When completed, choose File > Save, and close the file.

Editing Live Paint regions

Once you've made a Live Paint group, each path remains fully editable. When you move or adjust a path's shape, the colors that had been previously applied don't just stay where they were, like they do in natural media paintings or image editing programs. Instead, Illustrator automatically reapplies them to the new regions that are formed by the edited paths.

To experience this feature further, create a blank new file on which you will create a simple illustration.

1 Using File > New, create a new letter-sized document. Leave at the default settings, and choose OK.

2 On the blank document, use the Ellipse tool (⬤) to create a circle anywhere on the artboard. The size of the circle shape is not important.

3 Using the Selection tool (▶), hold down the Alt (Windows) or Option (Mac OS) key to clone the circle shape, drag it so the duplicated circle is overlapping the initial circle shape.

4 Choose Select > All. Choose None from Fill in the Control panel, and then choose None from Stroke color in the Control panel.

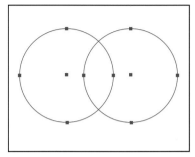

Create two overlapping circle shapes. Paint both the Fill and Stroke None.

5	Select the Live Paint Bucket tool (🪣), and cross over the center overlapping area; when it becomes highlighted, click once to activate the center shape as a Live Paint group

6	Select a color from the Swatches panel and click on the center Live Paint object to color it.

7	Select a color. Then using the Live Paint Bucket tool, click the left Live Paint object and click inside of it. Repeat this with a different color for the right Live Paint object.

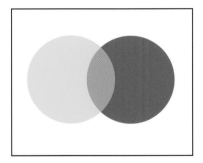

Assign different colors to the Live Paint objects.

8	Choose Select > Deselect. Choose the Direct Selection tool (▸). Select and reposition one of the circles, keeping some of the overlap. Notice that the intersecting area is dynamic. It changes the fill based upon the relationship of the two circles.

Note: *The Selection tool selects an entire Live Paint group; the Direct Select tool selects the individual paths inside a Live Paint group. For instance, clicking once*

with the Selection tool selects the entire Live Paint group, and clicking once with the Direct Selection tool or the Group Selection tool selects individual paths that make up the Live Paint group.

You can use the different selection tools depending on what you want to select and affect in a Live Paint group. For instance, use the Live Paint Selection tool (▧) to apply different gradients across different faces in a Live Paint group, and use the Selection tool to apply the same gradient across the entire Live Paint group.

9   Choose File > Close. Choose to not save the file.

▣ To learn more about working with Live Paint see "Live Paint groups" in Illustrator Help.

Create a PDF from your artwork

Adobe Portable Document Format (PDF) is a universal file format that preserves the fonts, images, and layout of source documents created on a wide range of applications and platforms. PDF is the standard for the secure, reliable distribution and exchange of electronic documents and forms around the world. Adobe PDF files are compact and complete, and can be shared, viewed, and printed by anyone with free Adobe Reader® software. In addition, Adobe PDF can preserve all Adobe Illustrator data, which means that you can reopen the file in Adobe Illustrator without any loss of data.

Adobe PDF is highly effective in print publishing workflows. By saving a composite of your artwork in Adobe PDF, you create a compact, reliable file that you or your service provider can view, edit, organize, and proof. Then, at the appropriate time in the workflow, your service provider can either output the Adobe PDF file directly, or process it using tools from various sources for such post-processing tasks as preflight checks, trapping, imposition, and color separation.

1   Choose File > Save As and change the type of format to Adobe PDF (*.PDF).

2   In the Save Adobe PDF dialog box, keep the [Illustrator Default] Adobe PDF Preset selected and click Save PDF.

Exploring on your own

When you select groups or other objects, you may not see the individual attributes of the Fill and Stroke in the Appearance panel. Follow these steps to discover how to separately apply Fill and Stroke attributes to groups.

Choose File > Open and select the file named L6end.ai in the Lesson06 folder inside the AICIB folder. Using the Selection tool (➤), select the stars in the center of the poster, and notice that it appears as a Group in the Appearance panel. In the Appearance panel, double-click on Contents to reveal the text objects Fill and Stroke attributes.

Using the techniques you learned in this lesson, apply a 2-point white stroke to this text, and change the opacity of the fill only to 50% white.

Review

▶ Review questions

1 Describe at least three ways to fill an object with color.

2 How can you save a color?

3 How do you name a color?

4 How do you assign an object a transparent color?

5 Name two things that the Live Color feature allows you to do.

6 How do you add pattern swatches to the Swatches panel?

▶ Review answers

1   To fill an object with color, select the object and the Fill box in the Tools panel. Then do one of the following:

* Click on the Fill box in the Control panel.

* Drag the color sliders, or type in values in the text boxes in the Color panel.

* Click a color swatch in the Swatches panel.

* Select the Eyedropper tool, and click a color in the artwork.

* Choose Window > Swatch Libraries to open another color library, and click a color swatch in the Color Library panel.

2   You can save a color for painting other objects in your artwork by adding it to the Swatches panel. Select the color, and do one of the following:

* Drag it from the Fill box and drop it over the Swatches panel.

* Click the New Swatch button at the bottom of the Swatches panel.

* Choose New Swatch from the Swatches panel menu.

You can also add colors from other color libraries by selecting them in the Color Library panel and choosing Add to Swatches from the panel menu.

3   To name a color, double-click the color swatch in the Swatches panel, or select it and choose Swatch Options from the panel menu. Type the name for the color in the Swatch Options dialog box.

4   To paint a shape with a transparent color, select the shape and fill it with any color. Then adjust the opacity percentage in the Transparency panel or Control panel to less than 100%.

5   You use the Live Color dialog box to create and edit color groups, as well as reassign or reduce the colors in your artwork and much more.

6   Create a pattern (patterns cannot contain patterns themselves), and drag it into the Swatches panel.

KICK IT UP!

Don't just stand there...

WALK! RUN! DANCE!

SAMMY'S SHOEWORLD

Create a statement with your shoes

Nothing makes you look more put together than a new clean pair of polished shoes. **Sammy's ShoeWorld** can help you make the statement you want by providing you an enormous selection of boots, high heels, sneakers, walking and running shoes in wall-high displays that span over a mile. There is no style, no size that we can't provide for you. *(Special order the size and size you want at no extra charge.)* Come and see for yourself, we are not pulling your leg, we just want to fit your leg with an incredible shoe deal!

Throw away your old tired shoes

With this sale, there is no reason to run around in unfashionable and tired shoes. *Check out the two for one sale going on from July 17th to August 1st.* Buy any one pair of shoes and get the second, lesser priced. Shoe for free. This sale is good on all shoes in stock. Sale not valid for special orders or sizes.

We are all over the place!

That's right, just about everywhere you look, you'll find a **Sammy's ShoeWorld**. Find us at the Shaw Plaza, North Mall, and the Loop Center. Browse our entire selection of shoes online at **sshoeworld.com**.

Text as a design element plays a major role in your illustrations. Like other objects, type can be painted, scaled, rotated, and so on. In this lesson discover how to create basic text and interesting text effects in Illustrator CS3.

7 | Working with type

In this lesson on type, you'll learn how to do the following:

- Import text.
- Create columns of type.
- Change text attributes.
- Use and Save Styles.
- Sample type.
- Wrap type around a graphic.
- Reshape text with a warp.
- Create text on paths and shapes.
- Create type outlines.

Getting started

You'll be working in one art file during this lesson, but before you begin, restore the default preferences for Adobe Illustrator CS3. Then open the finished art file for this lesson to see the illustration.

1   To ensure that the tools and panels function exactly as described in this lesson, delete or deactivate (by renaming) the Adobe Illustrator CS3 preferences file. See "Restoring default preferences" on page 3.

2   Launch Adobe Illustrator CS3.

Note: If you have not already copied the resource files for this lesson onto your hard disk from the Lesson07 folder from the Adobe Illustrator CS3 Classroom in a Book CD, do so now. See "Copying the Classroom in a Book files" on page 2.

3   Choose File > Open. Locate the file named L7end.ai in the Lesson07 folder inside the AICIB folder that you copied onto your hard drive. This art is a poster for Sammy's ShoeWorld, and you will create the text in this lesson.

4   If the Font Problems dialog box appear, click Open. If this were a file that we were to print, those font problems would need to be fixed. Leave it open for reference, or choose File > Close.

For information on missing fonts, search for "Find and replace fonts" in Illustrator Help.

The finished Type Poster.

5   Choose File > Open. From the Open window, navigate to the Lesson07 folder inside the AICIB folder. Open the file named L7start.ai.

This file has some non-text components already in it; you will build all text elements necessary to complete the poster.

6   Choose File > Save As. In the Save As dialog box, name the file **shoe_poster.ai,** and choose the Lesson07 folder. Leave the file format set to Illustrator (*.AI), and click Save. In the Illustrator Options window, leave at the default and choose OK.

Importing a text file

You can import text into artwork from a file that was created in another application. Illustrator supports the following formats for importing text:

• Microsoft Word for Windows 97, 98, 2000, 2002, 2003, and 2007.

• Microsoft Word for Mac OS X and 2004.

• RTF (Rich Text Format).

- Plain text (ASCII) with ANSI, Unicode, Shift JIS, GB2312, Chinese Big 5, Cyrillic, GB18030, Greek, Turkish, Baltic, and Central European encoding.

You can also copy and paste text, but formatting can be lost when text is pasted. One of the advantages of importing text from a file, rather than copying and pasting it, is that imported text retains its character and paragraph formatting. For example, text from an RTF file retains its font and style specifications in Illustrator.

1 Before importing text, create a text area by selecting the Type tool (T) and clicking and dragging from the upper left corner of the provided guide box to the lower right corner.

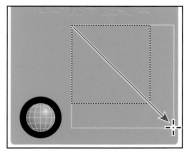

Using the Type tool, click and drag from the upper left to the lower right.

2 Choose File > Place. Navigate to the Lesson07 folder inside the AICIB folder, select the file named L7copy.txt, and choose Place.

Fonts on the Illustrator CS3 CD

The following fonts and accompanying documentation are not installed, but are included in the Documentation folder on the Illustrator CS3 product DVD, or in the packaged download file (if you downloaded Illustrator CS3 from Adobe Store). For trial customers, this additional content is only available after purchase.

* Adobe® Caslon® Pro	* Bernhard Modern	* Caflisch Script® Pro
* Kozuka Gothic® Std	* Kozuka Mincho® Std	* News Gothic
* Wood Type Ornaments Std	* Ryo Display	* Ryo Gothic
* Ryo Text	* Adobe Fansong	* Adobe Heiti Std

You will also find the fonts listed in the installed set above, but with a number of additional font faces not included in the installation. Anyone who cares about getting all of the available fonts should definitely take the time to install the additional set.

3   The Text Import Options window offers additional options that you can set prior to importing text. For this example, leave the default settings and choose OK.

The text is now placed in the text area. Don't be concerned about formatting the text. You will discover how to apply attributes later in this lesson.

4   Choose File > Save and leave this file open.

Creating columns of text

Create columns and rows of text easily in Illustrator by using the Area Type options.

1   If the text area is no longer selected, use the Selection tool (↖) to select it now.

2   Choose Type > Area Type Options. When the Area Type Options dialog box appears, you see many choices that include settings for rows and columns.

3   For this example, check Preview and change the Number text field under the heading of Columns to **2**, and click OK.

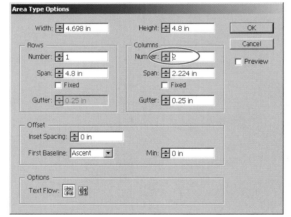

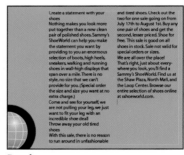

Creating columns of text.   *Result.*

4   Choose File > Save. Leave this document open.

What are the other Area Type options?

You can use the Area Type options to create rows and columns of text. Read about additional options below:

• **Number** specifies the number of rows and columns you want the object to contain.

• **Span** specifies the height of individual rows and the width of individual columns.

• **Fixed** determines what happens to the span of rows and columns if you resize the type area. When this option is selected, resizing the area can change the number of rows and columns, but not their width. Leave this option deselected if you want row and column widths to change when you resize the type area.

Create a statement with your shoes Nothing makes you look more put together than a new clean pair of polished shoes. Sammy's ShoeWorld can help you make the statement you want by providing to you an enor-	mous selection of boots, high heels, sneakers, walk-ing and running shoes in wall-high displays that span over a mile. There is no style, no size that we can't provide for you. (Special order the size and size you want at no extra charge.)

Original columns.

Create a statement with your shoes Nothing makes you look more put together than a new clean pair of polished shoes. Sammy's ShoeWorld can help you make the statement you want by providing to you an enor-	mous selection of boots, high heels, sneakers, walk-ing and running shoes in wall-high displays that span over a mile. There is no style, no size that we can't provide for you. (Special order the size and size you want at no extra charge.)	Come and see for yourself, we are not pulling your leg, we just want to fit your leg with an incredible shoe deal! Throw away your old tired shoes With this sale, there is no reason to run around in

Columns resized with Fixed selected.

Create a statement with your shoes Nothing makes you look more put together than a new clean pair of polished shoes. Sammy's ShoeWorld can help you make the statement you want by providing to you an enormous selection of boots, high heels, sneakers, walking and running shoes in wall-high displays that span over a mile. There is no style, no size that we can't provide for you.	(Special order the size and size you want at no extra charge.) Come and see for yourself, we are not pulling your leg, we just want to fit your leg with an incredible shoe deal! Throw away your old tired shoes With this sale, there is no reason to run around in unfashionable and tired shoes. Check out the two for one sale going on from July 17th

Columns resized with Fixed deselected.

• **Gutter** specifies the distance between rows or columns.

• **Inset** controls the margin between the text and the bounding path. This margin is referred to as the inset spacing.

• **First Baseline** controls the alignment of the first line of text with the top of the object.

• **Text Flow** determines how text flows between rows and columns.

–From Illustrator Help

Understanding text flow

For this next section, you will keep the shoe_poster.ai file open, but create a new blank document in addition to it. The purpose is to find out more details about flowing text in Adobe Illustrator CS3.

1   Choose File > New. In the Document Setup, choose Inches for Units, and keep other defaults the same. Click OK.

2   Create a fixed type area by selecting the Rectangle tool (▭) and clicking once on the page...do not click and drag! The Rectangle dialog window appears.

3   Type **2 inches** into both the Width and Height text fields. Click OK.

A square appears. It may have a fill or stroke color. Both fill and stroke will change to None when the shape is converted into a type area.

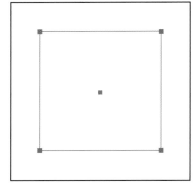

Setting the dimensions   Result.

Note: If you inadvertently dragged the cursor, you now have a small rectangle. Delete this using Edit > Undo, or Ctrl+Z (Windows)/Command+Z (Mac OS). You can also delete by pressing the Delete or Backspace key.

4   Select the Type tool (T) and cross it over the edge of the square. The text insertion point swells, or becomes curved, indicating that when you click, the text cursor will appear inside this shape.

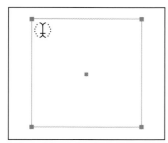 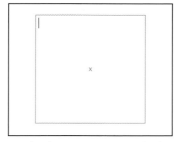

The text insertion point when crossed over an edge of a shape.

Result. The text cursor is inside the shape, strokes and fills are changed to none.

Note: Even though there is a hidden Area Type tool in the Tools panel, it is not necessary to switch to this tool.

5   With the cursor still active in the square, choose File > Place and navigate to the Lesson07 folder inside the AICIB folder on your hard drive. Select the file order_copy.doc, and then click Place. You are placing a native Microsoft Word document, so you will have additional options to choose from.

6   In the Microsoft Word Options dialog window, leave the default settings and click OK.

The text appears in the square. Text remembers the last used settings, so the type may appear slightly different from that in our example; this is not a problem.

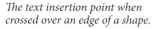

Order your shoes today!
At Sammy's ShoeWorld you
can place an order with total
confidence.
Free shipping and free
returns are standard policy.
You won't pay sales tax*, and
our price guarantee means
you'll never find a better
deal. Also, your transactions

Working with overflow text and text reflow

Each area type object contains an in port and an out port, which enable you to link to other objects and create a linked copy of the type object. An empty port indicates that all the text is visible and that the object isn't linked or overflowing. A red plus sign (⊞) in an out port indicates that the object contains additional text. This remaining unseen text is called overflow text.

Order your shoes today!
At Sammy's ShoeWorld you
can place an order with total
confidence.
Free shipping and free
returns are standard policy.
You won't pay sales tax*, and
our price guarantee means
you'll never find a better
deal. Also, your transactions

Note that since the text area created is too small, there is a plus sign in the out port.

There are two main methods for remedying overflow text.

- Thread the text to another text area.
- Re-size the text area.

Threading text

Thread, or connect, one text area to another to create a dynamic connection between the areas by following these steps:

1 Use the Selection tool (↖) to select the type area.

2 With the Selection tool, click the out port of the selected type area. The cursor changes to the loaded text icon (▦).

3 Click and drag on an empty part of the artboard.

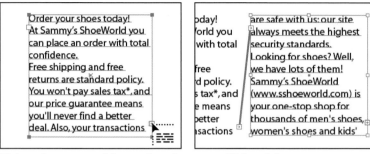

*Click on the out port of the overflowed text area. Click and drag to create
a threaded text area.*

💡 *Click off the existing type area to create an object of the same size and shape as the
original text area.*

Note: *Another method for threading text between objects is to select an area type object,
select the object (or objects) you want to link to, and then choose Type > Threaded Text >
Create.*

Threading text between objects

You can break threads and have the text flow into either the first or the next object, or you can remove
all threads and have the text stay in place.

• To break the thread between two objects, double-click the port on either end of the thread. The text
flows into the first object.

• To release an object from a text thread, choose Type > Threaded Text > Release Selection. The text
flows into the next object.

• To remove all threads, choose Type > Threaded Text > Remove Threading. The text stays in place.

—From Illustrator Help

Resizing the text area

For this next lesson, you will see how to re-size the text area to make room for additional text.

1   If you have created additional text areas using the threading method, switch to the Selection tool (⬉) and click to select and delete all but the original text area. Make sure the overflow text icon is still visible.

2   Use the Selection tool to drag a handle on the bounding box. Drag the handle on the middle of the right side so that the text area changes in size only horizontally. Click and drag to make the text area larger.

Resizing the text using a middle handle.

3   Grab the lower right corner handle to see how dragging a corner handle will increase the size of the area both horizontally and vertically.

Resizing the text area using a corner handle.

Create unique text area shapes by deselecting the text area and selecting the Direct Selection tool. Click and drag the edge or corner of the type to adjust the shape of the path. This method is easier to use when View > Hide Bounding Box is selected.

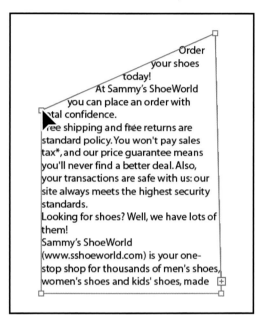

Adjusting the type path using the Direct Selection tool is easiest when you're in Outline view.

4 You have completed the text flow section of this lesson. Choose File > Close. In the Adobe Illustrator alert window, choose not to save this file. This returns you to your original project shoe_poster.ai.

Changing text attributes

In this section, you'll discover how to change text attributes, such as size, font, and style. Fortunately, with this version most attributes can be changed quickly and easily in the Control panel.

1 With the project shoe_poster.ai open, select the Type tool (T) and insert the cursor anywhere in the text area created earlier.

2 Choose Select > All, or Ctrl+A (Windows) or Command+A (Mac OS). All text becomes selected.

In this next section, you will discover two different methods for font selection, both using the Control panel.

3   Change the font of selected text from the Font menu in the Control panel. Click the arrow to the right of the menu and scroll until you find the font Times, or Times New Roman.

Choose fonts using the Control panel.

4   With the text still selected, choose from the menu items Type > Font to see the font display to the right of the font name. This may take a little more time because of the display, but scroll to change the selected font to Arial Regular or Helvetica.

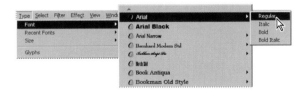

5   This next method is the most dynamic method for selecting a font. Make sure the text is still selected and then follow these instructions:

• Click and drag over the Font Name in the Font text field in the Control panel.

Select the font name in the Control panel.

• Now, begin typing the name, "Myriad Pro," an OpenType font. Illustrator will filter through the list.

6   Font styles are specific to each font family. Though you may have the Myriad Pro font family on your system, you may not have condensed and italic styles of that family. Find the available styles by choosing them from the Font Style pop-up menu.

What is OpenType?

If you frequently send files back and forth between platforms, you should be designing your text files using the OpenType format.

OpenType is a cross-platform font file format developed jointly by Adobe and Microsoft. Adobe has converted the entire Adobe Type Library into this format and now offers thousands of OpenType fonts.

The two main benefits of the OpenType format are its cross-platform compatibility (the same font file works on Macintosh and Windows computers), and its ability to support widely expanded character sets and layout features, which provide richer linguistic support and advanced typographic control.

OpenType fonts can include an expanded character set and layout features, providing broader linguistic support and more precise typographic control. Feature-rich Adobe OpenType fonts can be distinguished by the word "Pro," which is part of the font name and appears in application font menus. OpenType fonts can be installed and used alongside PostScript Type 1 and TrueType fonts.

—From Adobe.com/type/opentype

Changing font size

1   If the text is not active, use the Type tool (**T**) to insert the cursor in the text area and choose Select > All.

2   In the Control panel, choose a preset size from the Font Size pop-up menu, or click and drag over the present size and enter a value in points. If the font size is not 12, choose **12** now.

Changing the font size in the Control panel.

Change selected text font size dynamically by using the keyboard shortcut Ctrl+Shift+> (Windows), Command+Shift+> (Mac OS) to make the font size larger, or Ctrl+Shift+< (Windows), Command+Shift+< (Mac OS) to make the font size smaller by increments of 2.

Changing font color

In this next section, you'll change the font color; you can change both the fill and/or the stroke of selected text. In this example you will change the fill.

1   Click and drag to select the first paragraph in the text area, or click three times.

Click twice to select a word, three times to select an entire paragraph. The end of a paragraph is defined as where a return has been entered.

2   Click the Fill color in the Control panel. When the Swatches panel appears choose White. The text fill changes to white.

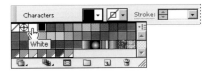

3   While you still have the first line of text selected, change the font size by selecting **14** from the Font size pop-up menu in the Control panel.

4   Change the font style for the selected text by selecting the Font Style pop-up menu in the Control panel and choosing Bold.

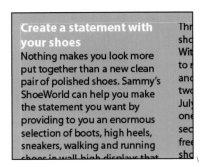

Changing additional text attributes

By clicking the Character panel link in the Control panel you can change many other attributes that are worth investigating but not covered in this particular exercise.

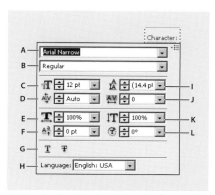

A. Set the font family. B. Set the font style.
C. Font size. D. Kerning. E. Horizontal Scale.
F. Baseline Shift. G. Underline and Strikethrough.
H. Language. I. Leading. J. Tracking.
K. Vertical Scale. L. Rotation.

Changing paragraph attributes

Just like with character attributes, you can set paragraph attributes (such as alignment or indenting) before you enter new type, or reset them to change the appearance of existing, selected type. If you select several type paths and type containers, you can set attributes for them all at the same time.

Now you'll add more space before all the paragraphs in the column text.

1   With the Type tool (T), insert the cursor anywhere in the text area and choose Select > All.

2   Click the word Paragraph in the Control panel. This links you to the Paragraph panel.

3   Type **6** in the Space Before Paragraph text field (in the bottom left corner) and press Enter. Spacing before paragraphs, rather than pressing the Return key, is recommended when creating large text areas.

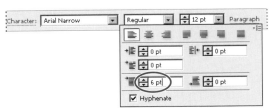

Enter a space before the paragraphs.

Saving and using styles

In Illustrator, you can save and use styles. This keeps text consistent and is helpful when text attributes need to be updated. Once a style is created, a change needs to be made only to the saved style. Then, all text with that style applied is updated.

There are two types of styles in Adobe Illustrator CS3:

• Paragraph—This retains text and paragraph attributes and applies them to an entire paragraph.

• Character—This retains the text attributes and applies them to selected text only.

Creating and using a Paragraph style

1   Click the Text tool (T) and insert the cursor in the first line of text. No text needs to be selected to create a Paragraph Style, but you do have to have the text insertion point in the line of text containing the attributes you wish to store.

2   Choose Window > Type > Paragraph Styles, click the panel menu (⊡≣)and choose New Paragraph Style from the panel menu.

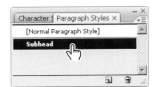

Use the panel menu to create Paragraph Styles.

3   In the New Paragraph Style window, type **subhead** for the Style Name, click OK. The text attributes used in the paragraph have been saved in a Paragraph style named subhead.

4   Apply the new paragraph style by selecting the text: "Throw away your old tired shoes." Then, select the named subhead style in the Paragraph Styles panel.
The text attributes are applied to the selected text.

5   Select the text: "We are all over the place!" and apply the subhead style by holding down the Alt (Windows) or Option (Mac OS) key while you select the subhead style name in the Paragraph Styles panel.

Note: If you see a plus (+) to the right of the style name, another attribute that is not part of the named style is applied to the selected text. Holding down the Alt (Windows) or Option (Mac OS) key when you select the style name overwrites any existing attributes.

Creating and using Character styles

Whereas Paragraph styles apply attributes to an entire paragraph, Character styles can be applied to selected text only.

1   With the Type tool (T), select "Sammy's ShoeWorld" in the first column of the paragraph text.

2   Change the font style to Bold using the Font Style menu in the Control panel.

3   Click the Fill color in the Control panel and select the Red swatch in the Swatches panel that appears.

The selected text is now bold and red.

Now save these attributes as a Character Style, and apply it to other instances in the text.

4   Choose Window > Type > Character Styles.

5   Alt+click (Windows) or Option+click (Mac OS) the Create New Style button at the bottom of the Character Styles panel. Alt/Option+clicking on the New Style button allows you to name the style as it is added to the panel. You can also double-click a style to name and edit it.

6   Name the style **Bold** and click OK. The style records the attributes applied to your selected text.

Now you will apply that Character Style to other text.

7   With the Sammy's ShoeWorld text still selected, Alt+click (Windows) or Option+click (Mac OS) the style named Bold in the Character Styles panel to assign the style to that text. Remember, the Alt/Option+click is used to clear any attributes from the text that are not part of the Character Style.

8   Select the text "sshoeworld.com" and assign it the Bold style as well.

9   Choose Select > Deselect.

Perhaps you decide that the color isn't working and you want to change it. Using styles, you have to change the color only once, and all instances are updated.

10   Choose Character Style Options from the Character Styles panel menu. Select a type attribute option from the window on the left, and then assign specific attributes by selecting characteristics on the right.

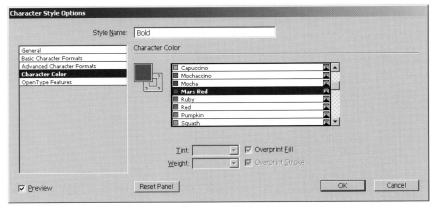

Update Styles using the Character Style Options Dialog box.

11   For this exercise, click on Character Color. In the window that appears on the right, choose the swatch named Mars Red.

12   Click OK. The text that was assigned the Character style is all updated to the new color.

13   Choose File > Save. Leave the file open.

Sampling text

Perhaps you just want to quickly sample text to retrieve its attributes without creating a style. Use the Eyedropper tool to pick-up type attributes and apply them to selected text.

1   With the Type tool (T) select the text: "Special order the style and size you want at no extra charge." in the first paragraph.

2   In the Control panel, change the font Fill color to White and the Font Style to Italic.

3   Now select the text: "Check out the two for one sale going on from July 17th to August 1st."

4   Select the Eyedropper tool (✐) and click on any of the text in the line of text, Special order the size...the attributes are immediately applied to your selected text.

and running shoes in wall-high displays that span over a mile. There is no style, no size that we can't provide for you. *(Special order the size and size you want at no extra charge.)* Come and see for yourself, we are not pulling your leg, we just want to fit your leg with an incredible shoe deal!

to run around in unfashionable and tired shoes. *Check out the two for one sale going on from July 17th to August 1st.* Buy any one pair of shoes and get the second, lesser priced. Shoe for free. This sale is good on all shoes in stock. Sale not valid for special orders or sizes. **We are all over the place!**

Use the Eyedropper tool to sample and apply text attributes.

5   Choose File > Save. Leave the file open.

Wrapping text around a graphic

Create interesting and creative results by wrapping text around a graphic.

1   With the file shoe_poster.ai still open, choose File > Open. In the Open dialog window, choose shoe.ai.

2   With the Selection tool (↖), select the shoe on the page and choose Edit > Copy, then File > Close.

3   Return to the shoe_poster.ai file, and choose Edit > Paste. The shoe graphic is placed on the page.

4   Position the Shoe graphic so it is in the middle of the two columns.

5   With the shoe graphic still selected, click the Fill color in the Control panel. When the Swatches panel appears choose the White swatch.

6   Using the Opacity text field in the Control panel, change the opacity to **30%**.

The Shoe Graphic positioned between the columns.

7   With the shoe graphic still selected, choose Object > Text Wrap > Make. The text wraps around the graphic.

Note: Objects that are to be used to create a text wrap must be above the text area.

8   If you still have text flowing in areas that you would rather close off, choose Object > Text Wrap > Text Wrap Options. In the Text Wrap Options window, change the Offset to **16**. Click OK.

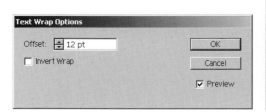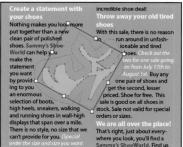

You can increase or decrease the Offset in the Text Wrap Options window.

9   With the Selection tool, reposition the shoe graphic to create a better text flow. For this example, it is OK if some of your text overflows out of the text area.

10   Choose File > Save. Keep the file open.

Reshaping text with a warp

Warping text is fun because it allows you to use an effect on your text to give it a more interesting shape, while also giving you the ability to edit the text and warped shape at any time.

1   Choose Select > Deselect and select the Type tool (T). Before typing, change the Font in the Control panel to Myriad Pro (if it is not already selected), the Font Style to Bold and the Font Size to **85**.

2   Use the Selection tool (▸) to select the silhouette of the people and choose Object > Lock > Selection. Reselect the Type tool and then click once on the poster art slightly above the silhouette of the people. Exact placement is not important. A text cursor appears.

3 Type the words **KICK IT UP!** Then select the Selection tool again and reposition the text so it is centered over the silhouette art.

💡 *With the Type tool, you can temporarily switch to the Selection tool by holding down Ctrl (Windows) or Command (Mac OS).*

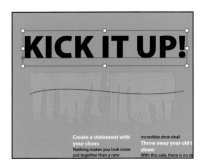

4 With the text still selected, choose Effect > Warp > Arc Upper. The Warp Options window appears. Check the Preview checkbox. The Text stays flat on the bottom and arcs only in the upper part.

Using the Settings and Style pop-up menu, you can experiment with many different combinations. Click OK when you have finished with this window. Use the Selection tool to reposition your text if necessary.

Note: *Illustrator CS3 has the Make Envelope button (🗐) in the Control panel. This will not apply as an effect, but will turn the text into an envelope object. The same visual result will be achieved using the Make Envelope button as choosing Effect > Warp > Arc Upper. For more information about the envelopes, see "Reshape using envelopes" in Illustrator Help.*

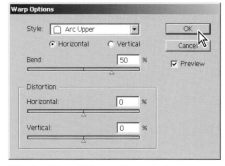

The Arc Upper Effect options window.

Result.

5   With the Type tool, click and drag to select the words "KICK IT UP!".

6   In the Control panel, click Fill color and choose White from the Swatches panel.

7   Click Stroke Color and choose Pumpkin.

8   Choose **2 pt** from the Stroke Weight pop-up menu in the Control panel.

Notice that additional attributes are applied easily to the warped text.

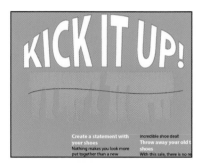

Easily apply new text attributes to text
warped with an Effect.

Next you will add a Drop Shadow Effect to the warped text.

9   Click the Selection tool and select "KICK IT UP!"

10   Choose Effects > Stylize > Drop Shadow. In the Drop Shadow Options window, leave the defaults and choose OK. Read more about applying and editing effects in Lesson 12, "Applying Appearance Attributes and Graphic Styles."

11   Choose Select > Deselect and File > Save. Leave the file open.

Creating text on paths and shapes

With the Type tools in Illustrator CS3, you can type on paths and on shapes.

1   With the Selection tool (➤), select the wavy path crossing the silhouette artwork.

💡 *To quickly switch to the Selection tool and back to the Type tool, hold down Ctrl (Windows) or Command (Mac OS).*

2   With the Type tool (T), cross the cursor over the left side of the path to see an insertion point with an intersecting wavy path (𝒥). Click when this cursor appears. The stroke attributes of the stroke change to None and a cursor appears. Don't type yet.

3   In the Font Size text field in the Control panel, type **36** and press the Enter key.

4   Type **Don't just stand there...** Note that the newly typed text follows the path.

Type on a path.

5   With the Type tool, click and drag over the text you just entered (or click three times on the text). Click the Fill color in the Control panel to link to the Swatches panel. Then choose the White swatch.

Now you will put text on a closed path.

6   With the Selection tool, select the small black circle in the lower left corner of the poster.

7   Switch to the Type tool. Holding down the Alt (Windows) or Opt (Mac OS) key, cross over the left side of the circle. The type on a path icon (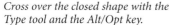) appears. Click, but don't type.

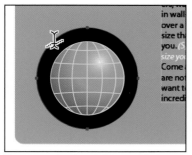

Cross over the closed shape with the Type tool and the Alt/Opt key.

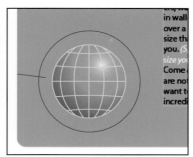

After clicking, the text cursor appears.

The fill and stroke attributes of the circle are changed to None, and you have a cursor on the path.

Note: *If you do not want to use the keyboard shortcut (Alt/Opt), you can choose to use the Type on a Path tool hidden in the Text tool.*

8   From the Font Size pop-up menu in the Control panel, change the text size to **24**. From the Font menu choose Myriad Pro (or Myriad), and from the Font Style menu choose Bold.

9   Click the Align Center button to the right of Paragraph in the Control panel.

10   Type **SAMMY'S SHOEWORLD** in capital letters. The text flows on the circular path.

11   To adjust the placement on the path, select the Selection tool. The type object is selected. A bracket appears at the beginning of the type, at the end of the path, and at the midpoint between the start and end brackets. These brackets look like lines.

For information on type on a path and brackets, search for "Move or flip text along a path" in Illustrator Help.

12 Position the cursor over the type's center bracket until a small icon (⌐) appears next to the cursor, and drag the center bracket along the path. Hold down Ctrl (Windows) or Command (Mac OS) to prevent the type from flipping to the other side of the path. Position the text so it is centered across the top of the circle.

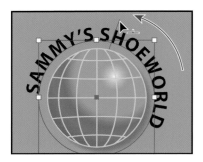

💡 *To flip the direction of text along a path, drag the bracket across the path. Alternatively, choose Type > Type On A Path > Type On A Path Options, select Flip, and click OK.*

Creating text outlines

When creating artwork for multiple purposes, it is wise to create outlines of text so the recipient doesn't need your fonts to create, open, and use the file correctly. Note that you will want to keep an original of your artwork, as you cannot change outline text back to editable text.

1 Select the Type tool (T). Click off to the left in the scratch area (away from the poster art).

2 Type **WALK! RUN! DANCE!**

3 Double-click the Rotate tool (⟳). The Rotate Options window appears, type **90**. Click OK. The text is rotated 90 degrees counterclockwise.

Rotate text 90 degrees   Result.

4   With the Selection tool (➤), position the text so it is in the lower left corner of the poster art.

5   Select the Selection tool. While holding down the Shift key, click and drag the upper right handle of the text's bounding box. This enlarges the text proportionally to the height of the poster.

6   With the Selection tool (➤), Shift-click to select the world and the Sammy's World text. Choose Object > Arrange > Bring to Front.

*Enlarge a text area using
the bounding box.*

7   With the Selection tool (▶) select the "Walk! Run! Dance!" text again, click the Fill color in the Control panel and select White in the Swatches panel.

8   Click once on the word Opacity in the Control panel to link to the Transparency panel. From the Blend Mode pop-up menu choose Soft Light. Change the Opacity to **75%** in the Opacity text field.

9   With the text area still selected, choose Type > Create Outlines. The text is no longer linked to a particular font, but has become artwork, much like any other vector art in your illustration.

> 💡 *One of the benefits of creating outlines from text is that it allows you to fill the text with a gradient. If a gradient fill is what you wish to achieve, but you still want to maintain text editing control, select the text with the Selection tool and choose Effect > Path > Outline Object.*

10   Choose File > Save.

Congratulations! You have completed the lesson.

Exploring on your own

Experiment with Illustrator CS3 text features by integrating paths with illustrations. Use the clip art provided in the Lesson07 folder and try some of these type techniques:

• pizza.ai—Using the Pen tool, create paths representing steam rising from the slice. Create text on a the wavy paths and apply varying levels of opacity.

• airplane.ai—Complete a banner following the airplane with text of your own.

Take the project further by using your graphic in a one-page sales flyer that has the following text elements on the page:

• Using the placeholder.txt found in the Lesson07 folder, create a three-column text area.

• Use the graphic of the pizza or plane for a text wrap.

• Create a masthead across the top of your page that has text on a curve.

• Create a Paragraph Style.

Review

▶ **Review questions**

1   Name two methods for creating text area in Adobe Illustrator CS3.

2   What are two benefits of using an OpenType font?

3   What is the difference between a Character and Paragraph Style?

4   What are the advantages and disadvantages of converting text to outlines?

▶ **Review answers**

1   There are several methods for creating text areas; you can choose from any of these three:

• With the Type tool, click on the artboard. A cursor appears; start typing. After typing, note that a text area has been created to accommodate the text.

• Select the Type tool, click and drag to create a text area. A cursor appears in the text area; start typing.

• With the Type tool, click on a path or closed shape to convert it to text on a path or a text area. Alt/Opt+Click when crossing over the stroke of a closed path creates text around the shape.

2   The two main benefits of the OpenType format are its cross-platform compatibility (the same font file works on Macintosh and Windows computers), and its ability to support widely expanded character sets and layout features, which provide richer linguistic support and advanced typographic control.

3   A Character Style can be applied to selected text only. A Paragraph style is applied to an entire paragraph. Paragraph styles are best when indents, margins, and line spacing attributes need to be saved.

4   A benefit of converting type to outlines is that doing so eliminates the need to send the font along with the file when sharing with others. You can also fill the type with a gradient and create interesting effects on individual letters.

However, when you create outlines from text, you must consider:

- Text is no longer editable. The content and font cannot be changed on outlined text. It is best to save a layer with the original text, or use the Outline Object Effect.

- You cannot convert bitmap fonts or outline-protected fonts to outlines.

- Outlining text that is less than 10 points in size is not recommended. When you convert type to outlines, the type loses its hints—instructions built into outline fonts to adjust their shape so that your system displays or prints them optimally at a wide range of sizes. Therefore, if you plan to scale the type, do so by adjusting its point size before converting it to outlines.

- You must convert all the type in a selection to outlines; you cannot convert a single letter within a string of type. To convert a single letter into an outline, create a separate type area containing only that letter.

Layers let you organize your work into distinct levels that can be edited and viewed as individual units. Every Adobe Illustrator CS3 document contains at least one layer. Creating multiple layers in your artwork lets you easily control how artwork is printed, displayed, and edited.

8 | Working with Layers

In this lesson, you'll learn how to do the following:

- Work with the Layers panel.

- Create, rearrange, and lock layers, nested layers, and groups.

- Move objects between layers.

- Paste layers of objects from one file to another.

- Merge layers into a single layer.

- Apply a drop shadow to a layer.

- Make a layer clipping mask.

- Apply an appearance attribute to objects and layers.

Getting started

In this lesson, you'll finish the artwork of a wall clock as you explore the various ways to use the Layers panel. Before you begin, you must restore the default preferences for Adobe Illustrator and then you will open the finished art file for this lesson to see what you'll create.

1 To ensure that the tools and panels function exactly as described in this lesson, delete or deactivate (by renaming) the Adobe Illustrator CS3 preferences file. See "Restoring default preferences" on page 3.

2 Start Adobe Illustrator CS3.

Note: If you have not already copied the resource files for this lesson onto your hard disk from the Lesson08 folder from the Adobe Illustrator CS3 Classroom in a Book CD, do so now. See "Copying the Classroom in a Book files" on page 2.

3 Choose File > Open, and open the L8end.ai file in the Lesson08 folder, located inside the Lessons folder within the AICIB folder on your hard drive.

Separate layers are used for the objects that make up the clock's frame, striped clock face, hands, and numbers—as indicated by their layer names in the Layers panel.

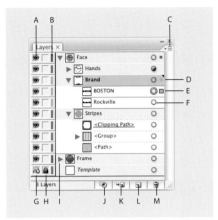

A. *Visibility column (Hide/Show)*
B. *Layer color*
C. *Layers panel menu*
D. *Selected-art indicator*
E. *Selection column*
F. *Target column*
G. *Template Layer icon*
H. *Edit column (Lock/Unlock)*
I. *Expand/Collapse toggle arrow*
J. *Make/Release Clipping Mask*
K. *Create New Sublayer button*
L. *Create New Layer button*
M. *Delete button*

4   If you like, you may leave the file open as a visual reference. Do this by reducing the size of your window then choose View > Fit in Window. If you don't want to leave the image open, choose, File > Close.

To begin working, you'll open an existing art file.

Note: You may receive missing profile dialog boxes when opening the files for this lesson. Click OK and continue.

5　Choose File > Open, and open the L8start.ai file in the Lesson08 folder, located inside the Lessons folder within the AICIB folder on your hard drive.

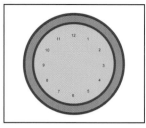

The artwork contains some of the basic objects for the clock illustration.

6　Choose File > Save As. In the Save As dialog box, name the file **Clock.ai**, and choose the Lesson08 folder. Leave the file format set to Illustrator (*.AI), and click Save. In the Illustrator Options dialog box, leave at the defaults and click OK.

Using layers

You can use the Layers panel to create multiple levels of artwork that reside on separate, overlapping layers, sublayers, and groups in the same file. Layers act like individual, clear sheets containing one or more objects. Where no filled (or nontransparent) objects overlap, you can see through any layer to the layer below.

You can create and edit objects on any layer without affecting the artwork on any other layer. You can also display, print, lock, and reorder layers as distinct units.

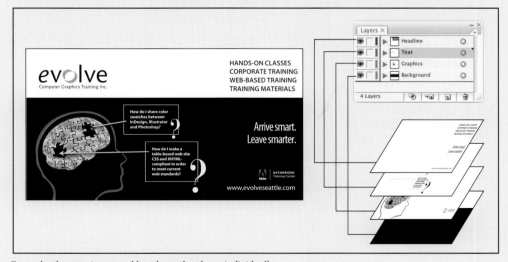

Example of composite art and how layers break out individually.

Creating layers

By default, all items are organized in a single, parent layer. You can rename the layer and add more layers at any time as you create the artwork. Placing objects on separate layers lets you easily select and edit them. For example, by placing type on a separate layer, you can change the type all at once without affecting the rest of the artwork.

You'll change the layer name to "Clock," and then you'll create another layer.

1   If the Layers panel isn't visible, choose Window > Layers.

Layer 1 (the default name for the first layer) is highlighted, indicating that it is active. The layer also has a triangle (▾), indicating that objects on the layer can be edited when you use the tools.

2   In the Layers panel, double-click the layer name to open the Layer Options dialog box. Type **Clock** in the Name text field, and then click OK.

Double-click layer name.   *Change layer name to Clock.*

Now you'll create a sublayer for the clock numbers.

3   Click once on the named layer, Clock, in the Layers panel and then Alt+click (Windows) or Option+click (Mac OS) the Create New Sublayer button (⬏⬜) at the bottom of the Layers panel to create a new sublayer and display the Layer Options dialog box. Creating a new sublayer also opens the layer to show existing sublayers.

(If you want to create a new sublayer without setting any options or naming the layer, you can click the Create New Sublayer button. New sublayers created without Alt+clicking are numbered in sequence, for example, Layer 2.)

Create sublayer named Numbers.

4   In the Layer Options dialog box, type **Numbers** in the Name text field, and click OK. The new sublayer appears directly beneath its main layer name (Clock) and is selected.

Layers and color

By default, Illustrator assigns a unique color (up to nine colors) to each layer in the Layers panel. The color displays next to the layer name in the panel. The same color displays in the illustration window in the bounding box, path, anchor points, and center point of a selected object. You can use this color to quickly locate an object's corresponding layer in the Layers panel, and you can change the layer color to suit your needs.

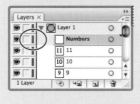

—From Illustrator Help

Moving objects and layers

By rearranging the layers in the Layers panel, you can reorder layered objects in your artwork. You can also move selected objects from one layer or sublayer to another.

First you'll move the clock numbers into their own sublayer.

1   In the Layers panel, grab the thumbnail for the 11 object and drag it over the thumbnail for the Numbers layer. Release the mouse button when you see the large black triangles at either end of the Numbers layer in the panel. (The large triangles indicate that you are adding something to that layer.)

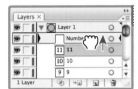 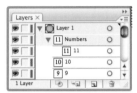

Grab thumbnail and move it onto sublayer thumbnail.

💡 *To select multiple layers or sublayers quickly, select a layer and then Shift-click additional layers.*

2   Repeat step 1 for each of the twelve numbers in the Layers panel.

3   Choose Select > Deselect. Then choose File > Save.

Now you'll move the face of the clock to a new layer to use later when you add the stripes, hands, and brand name of the clock. You'll also rename the Clock layer to reflect the new organization of the artwork.

4   With the Selection tool (↖), click behind the numbers in the artwork to select the clock face. In the Layers panel, the object named <Path> becomes active (as indicated by the square selection color box (■) in the far-right selection column.)

5   Alt+click (Windows) or Option+click (Mac OS) the Create New Layer button at the bottom of the Layers panel, or choose New Layer from the Layers panel menu.

6   In the Layer Options dialog box, enter **Face** in the Name text field, select a different layer color from the pop-up menu (such as Orange), and click OK.

The new Face layer is added above the Clock layer and becomes active.

7 In the Layers panel, select the square selection color box in the selection column of the <Path> layer, and drag it up and to the right of the round target indicator (○) of the new Face layer.

Drag selection indicator up to move object to another layer.

This action moves the selected object to the new layer. The color of the selection lines in the artwork changes to the color of the new Face layer (such as Orange in this case).

Now that the Face layer is on top of the Clock layer and the Numbers sublayer, the clock numbers are covered up. You'll move the Numbers sublayer into a different layer and rename the Clock layer to reflect the new organization of the artwork.

8 In the Layers panel, drag the Numbers sublayer thumbnail over the Face layer thumbnail. Release the mouse button when you see the indicator bar with large black triangles at either end of the Face layer in the panel.

Now you can see the numbers again.

9 Double-click the Clock layer to display the Layer Options dialog box, and change the layer name to **Frame**. Then click OK.

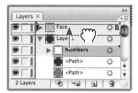

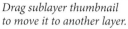
Drag sublayer thumbnail to move it to another layer.
Change layer name.

10 Choose Select > Deselect to deselect all active objects, and then choose File > Save.

Locking layers

As you edit objects in a layer, use the Layers panel to lock other layers and prevent selecting or changing the rest of the artwork.

Now you'll lock all the layers except the Numbers sublayer so that you can easily edit the clock numbers without affecting objects on other layers. Locked layers cannot be selected or edited in any way.

1   To simplify your work, click the toggle arrow to the left of the Frame layer to collapse the layer view.

2   Click the edit column to the right of the eye icon on the Frame layer to lock the layer. The padlock icon (🔒) indicates that a layer and all its objects are locked.

3   Click the edit column to the right of the eye icon next to the <Path> sublayer, below the Numbers layer.

Click the edit column to lock a layer.

You can unlock individual layers by clicking the lock icon to make it disappear from the edit column. Clicking again in the edit column will lock the layer again. Holding down Alt (Windows) or Option (Mac OS) as you click the edit column alternately locks and unlocks all other layers.

Now you'll change the type size and font of the numbers.

4   In the Layers panel, click the selection column to the right of the Numbers layer to select all objects on that layer.

A quick way to select all the type or objects in a layer is to click the selection column—the blank area to the right of the target indicators—in the Layers panel.

The Numbers layer now has a square selection color box (red, in this case), indicating that everything in the layer is selected.

5   Click Character in the Control panel to display the Character panel.

6   In the Character panel, choose another font or font size for the group of numbers. (We used Myriad Pro Bold, size 28 points.)

Note: Myriad Pro is an OpenType font included with Illustrator CS3.

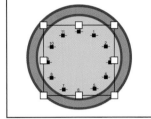
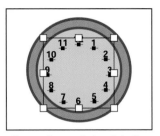

Click the selection column.   *All type is selected.*   *Change font and size globally.*

7   If you wish, use the Color panel or Swatches panel to change the color of the selected numbers.

8   In the Layers panel, click the lock icons (🔒) next to the <Path> and the Frame layers to unlock them.

Viewing layers

The Layers panel lets you hide layers, sublayers, or individual objects. When a layer is hidden, objects in the layer are also locked and cannot be selected or printed. You can also use the Layers panel to display layers or objects in either Preview or Outline mode independent of other layers or objects in the artwork.

Now you'll edit the frame on the clock, using a painting technique to create a three-dimensional effect on the frame.

1 In the Layers panel, if the Frame layer is not already selected, click the Frame layer to select it, then Alt+click (Windows) or Option+click (Mac OS) the eye icon (👁) next to the Frame layer name to hide the other layers.

> 💡 *Alt/Option+clicking the layer eye icon alternately hides and shows a layer. Hiding layers also locks them and prevents them from being changed.*

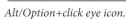
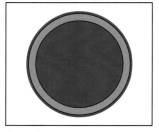

Alt/Option+click eye icon.   *Only objects on Frame layer appear.*

2 With the Selection tool (➤), click the inside circle of the frame to select it. Then holding down the Shift key, click the next largest circle to add it to the selection.

3 With the two inner circles selected, click the Fill color in the Control panel, and then click the Clock.frame swatch in the Swatches panel to paint the circles with a custom gradient.

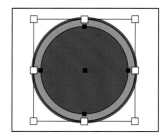
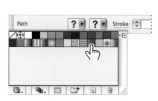

Select two inner circles.   *Paint with gradient fill.*   *The result.*

4   Shift-click the second largest circle to deselect it and keep the inside circle selected.

5   Select the Gradient tool (▣) in the Tools panel. Drag the tool in a vertical line from the top of the circle straight down to the bottom to change the direction of the gradient.

The Gradient tool works only on selected objects that are filled with gradients. To learn more about using the Gradient tool, see Lesson 9, "Blending Shapes and Colors."

Drag over selected object   The result.
with the Gradient tool.

6   Choose Select > Deselect to deselect the artwork, and then choose File > Save.

7   In the Layers panel, choose Show All Layers from the panel menu.

As you edit objects in layered artwork, you can display individual layers in Outline mode, keeping the other layers in Preview mode.

8   Ctrl-click (Windows) or Command-click (Mac OS) the eye icon next to the Face layer to switch to Outline mode for that layer.

This action lets you see the gradient-filled circle behind the clock face. Displaying a layer in Outline mode is also useful for viewing the anchor points or center points on objects without selecting them.

White fill in eye icon   Preview view of other layers shows
indicates Outline view.   through Face layer in Outline view.

9   Ctrl/Command+click the eye icon next to the Face layer to view that layer in Preview mode again.

Pasting layers

To complete the clock, you'll copy and paste the finishing parts of artwork from another file. You can paste layered files into another file and keep all of the layers intact.

1   Choose File > Open, and open the Details.ai file, located in the Lesson08 folder, inside the Lessons folder within the AICIB folder on your hard drive.

Note: You may receive missing profile dialog boxes when opening the files for this lesson. Click OK and continue.

Clock.ai file.

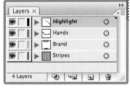
Details.ai file.   *Layers panel for Details.ai file.*

2   If you want to see how the objects are organized in the layers, Alt/Option+click the eye icons in the Layers panel to alternately display each layer and hide the others. You can also click the toggle arrows (▸) to the left of the layer names to expand and collapse the layers for further inspection. When you've finished, make sure that all the layers are showing and that they are fully collapsed.

If a layer is hidden, its objects are locked and cannot be selected or copied.

3   Choose Select > All and then Edit > Copy to select and copy the clock details to the Clipboard.

4   Choose File > Close. If an Adobe Illustrator alert window appears, choose not to save changes.

5   In the Clock.ai file, choose Paste Remembers Layers from the Layers panel menu to select the option. (A check mark next to the option indicates that it's selected.)

Selecting the Paste Remembers Layers option indicates that when multiple layers from another file are pasted into the artwork, they're added as individual layers in the Layers panel. If the option is not selected, all objects are pasted into the active layer.

6 Choose Edit > Paste In Front to paste the details into the clock.

The Paste In Front command pastes the objects from the Clipboard to a position relative to the original position in the Details.ai file. The Paste Remembers Layers option causes the Details.ai layers to be pasted as four separate layers at the top of the Layers panel (Highlight, Hands, Brand, Stripes). Some of the layers need to be repositioned.

7 Close any open layers by clicking the toggle arrow to the left of layer names then you may need to scroll down in the Layers panel. Move the Frame layer above the Highlight layer and then the Face layer above Frame.

Release the mouse button when the indicator bar with large black triangles extends the full column width above the Highlight and Frame layer. (You want to create a separate layer, not a sublayer.)

Paste artwork from Details.ai file. *Drag Face and Frame layers to the top of the layer stack.* *The result.*

Now you'll move the brand and hands into the Face layer and the Highlight layer in front of the Frame layer.

8 Select the Selection tool (▶), and click away from the artwork to deselect it.

9 In the Layers panel, click the Highlight layer, and drag it up between the Face and Frame layers.

Move Highlight layer above the Frame layer.

10 Click the toggle arrow to the left of the Face layer to show the sublayers.

11 Click the Hands layer and Shift-click the Brand layers in the Layers panel.

12 Drag the selected layers up between the Numbers and <Path> sublayers; when the insertion bar appears between those sublayers, release the mouse button to make the Hands and Brand layers sublayers of the Face layer.

Note: You may want to resize the Layers panel by clicking and dragging the bottom of the Layers panel down so it is easier to see the layers.

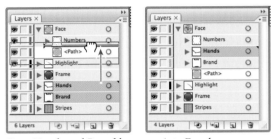

Drag Hands and Brand layers up into Face layer.

13 Choose File > Save to save the changes.

Creating clipping masks

The Layers panel lets you create clipping masks to control how artwork in a layer (or in a group) is hidden or revealed. A *clipping mask* is an object or group of objects whose shape masks artwork below it so that only artwork within the shape is visible.

Now you'll create a clipping mask with the circle shape in the Face layer. You'll group it with the Stripes sublayer so that only the stripes show through the circle shape.

1   If necessary, drag the bottom of the Layers panel down to reveal all of the layers.

2   In the Layers panel, drag the Stripes layer up until the insertion bar's double lines are highlighted above the <Path> layer within the Face layer. Release the mouse button when the indicator bar appears.

Drag the Stripes layer up   *The result.*
above the <Path> sublayer.

A masking object must reside above the objects it will mask in the Layers panel. Since you want to mask only the stripes, you'll move the circular <Path> object to the top of the Stripes sublayer before you create the clipping mask.

3   Drag the <Path> sublayer with the circle color fill onto the Stripes thumbnail to add it to that layer as the top sublayer.

Drag <Path> on top of the Stripes layer.

4   In the Layers panel, click the toggle arrow (▷) to the left of the Stripes layer to expand the layer view.

5   Make sure that the <Path> with the circle color fill is the topmost sublayer in the Stripes layer, moving it if necessary. (Clipping masks are always the first object in a layer or group.)

6   Select the Stripes layer to highlight it.

7   Click the Make/Release Clipping Mask button at the bottom of the Layers panel. Notice that all the layer dividing lines are now dotted. The name of the first path has also changed to <Clipping Path>. The clipping path name is also underlined to indicate that it is the masking shape.

Before the clipping mask.

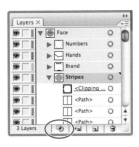

Click Make/Release
Clipping Mask button.

The result.

8   Click the toggle arrow next to the Stripes layer name to collapse the layers.

9   Choose Select > Deselect. Then choose File > Save.

Merging layers

To streamline your artwork, you can merge layers. Merging layers consolidates the contents of all selected layers into one layer.

1   In the Layers panel, click the Numbers layer, and then Shift-click the Hands layer. Notice the selected-art indicator (▾) shows the last highlighted layer as the active layer. The last layer you select will determine the name and color of the merged layer.

2 Choose Merge Selected from the Layers panel menu ( ) to merge the objects from the Numbers layer into the Hands layer.

The objects in the merged layers retain their original stacking order, and are added above the objects in the destination layer.

3 Now click the Highlight layer, and then Shift-click the Frame layer.

4 Choose Merge Selected from the Layers panel menu to merge the objects from the Highlight layer into the Frame layer.

5 Choose File > Save.

Applying appearance attributes to layers

You can apply appearance attributes such as styles, effects, and transparency to layers, groups, and objects in the Layers panel. When an appearance attribute is applied to a layer, all objects in that layer are targeted, and will take on that attribute. If an appearance attribute is applied only to a specific object in a layer, it targets only that object, not the entire layer.

First you will target an object in one layer and apply an effect to it. Then you'll copy that effect to a layer to target all of the objects in that layer.

1   In the Layers panel, collapse the Face layer and expand the Frame layer to reveal all its objects.

2   Select the lower <Path> in the Frame layer.

3   Click the target icon (◎) to the right of the lower <Path> name to target that object. Clicking the target icon indicates that you want to apply an effect, style, or transparency change.

*Click the target indicator
to target the bottom path.*

4   Choose Effect > Stylize > Drop Shadow. Leave the settings at the default values and click OK. A drop shadow appears on the outer edge of the clock.

Note: Choose the first Stylize option from the Effect submenu. Effect > Stylize > Drop Shadow command.

Notice that the target icon (◉) is now a shaded double-ring, indicating that the object has appearance attributes applied to it.

5   Click the Appearance icon (◉) in the dock of panels collapsed on the right side of the workspace to reveal the Appearance panel. (If the Appearance panel isn't visible, choose Window > Appearance.) Notice that Drop Shadow has been added to the list of appearance attributes for the selected shape.

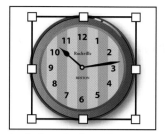

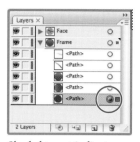

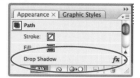

Apply drop shadow effect to clock edge.

Shaded target indicates appearance attributes.

Appearance panel lists selection's attributes.

You will now use the Layers panel to copy an appearance attribute onto a layer and then edit it.

6   Click the Layers panel icon (on the right side of the workspace) to reveal the Layers panel. Expand the Face layer to reveal its contents. If you need to, drag the bottom of the Layers panel down to display the entire list.

7   With the Selection tool (⬉), click on the clock hands on the page to select them.

8   Choose Locate Object in the Layers panel menu. This will select and scroll to the hands group in the Layers panel for you. You may need to scroll the Layers panel for the next step.

9   Hold down Alt (Windows) or Option (Mac OS) and drag the shaded target indicator of the <Path> sublayer to the target indicator of the Hands layer, without releasing the mouse button. The hand cursor with a plus sign indicates that the appearance is being copied.

10   When the target indicator of the Hands layer turns light gray, release the mouse button. The drop shadow is now applied to the entire Hands layer, as indicated by the shaded target indicator.

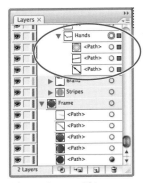
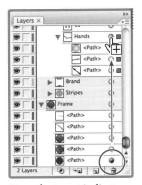
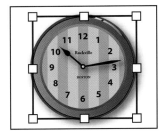

Choose Locate Object
to copy effect.

Drag the target indicator

The result.

Now you'll edit the drop shadow attribute for the type and clock hands, to tone down
the effect.

11 In the Layers panel, click the target indicator for the Hands layer. This automatically
selects the objects on the Hands layer and deselects the object on the Frame layer.

12 In the Appearance panel, double-click the Drop Shadow attribute. In the Drop
Shadow dialog box, enter **3 pt** for the X and Y offsets and the Blur amount. Click OK.

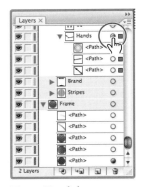
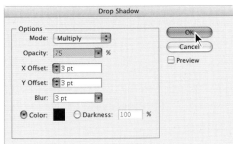

Target Hands layer.

Edit Drop Shadow effect.

The result.

For more information on appearance attributes, see Lesson 12, "Applying
Appearance Attributes and Graphic Styles."

13 Choose Select > Deselect.

14 Choose File > Save. Choose File > Close.

You have finished building a layered file.

In some cases after the artwork is complete, you may want to place all the layers of art into a single layer and delete the empty layers. This is called flattening artwork. Delivering finished artwork in a single layer file can prevent accidents, such as hiding layers and not printing parts of the artwork.

To flatten specific layers without deleting hidden layers, select the layers you want to flatten, and then choose Merge Selected from the Layers panel menu.

To consolidate layers and groups

Merging and flattening layers are similar in that they both let you consolidate objects, groups, and sublayers into a single layer or group. With merging, you can select which items you want to consolidate; with flattening, all visible items in the artwork are consolidated in a single layer. With either option, the stacking order of the artwork remains the same, but other layer-level attributes, such as clipping masks, aren't preserved.

• *To merge items into a single layer or group, hold down Ctrl (Windows) or Command (Mac OS) and click the names of the layers or groups that you want to merge. Alternatively, hold down Shift to select all listings in between the layer or group names you click. Then, select Merge Selected from the Layers panel menu. Note that items will be merged into the layer or group that you selected last.*

• *Layers can only merge with other layers that are on the same hierarchical level in the Layers panel. Likewise, sublayers can only merge with other sublayers that are within the same layer and at the same hierarchical level. Objects can't be merged with other objects.*

• *To flatten layers, click the name of the layer into which you want to consolidate the artwork. Then select Flatten Artwork from the Layers panel menu.*

—From Illustrator Help

For information on opening layered Photoshop files in Illustrator and working with layered Illustrator files in Photoshop, see Lesson 14, "Combining Illustrator CS3 Graphics with the Creative Suite."

For a complete list of shortcuts that you can use with the Layers panel, see "Keyboard Shortcuts" in Illustrator Help.

Exploring on your own

When you print a layered file, only the visible layers print in the same order in which they appear in the Layers panel—with the exception of template layers, which do not print even if they're visible. Template layers are locked, dimmed, and previewed. Objects in template layers neither print nor export.

Now that you've learned how to work with layers, try creating layered artwork by tracing an image on a template layer. We've provided a bitmap photo image of a goldfish that you can use to practice, or use your own artwork or photo images.

1   Choose File > New to create a new file for your artwork.

2   Choose File > Place. In the dialog box, select the Goldfish.eps file, located in the Lesson08 folder, inside the Lessons folder within the AICIB folder on your hard drive; or locate your file containing the artwork or image you want to use as a template and click Place to add the placed file to Layer 1.

3   Create the template layer by choosing Template from the Layers panel menu or choosing Options for Layer 1 and selecting Template in the Layer Options dialog box.

4   Click the Create New Layer button to create a new layer on which to draw.

5   With Layer 2 active, use any drawing tool to trace over the template, creating new artwork.

6   Create additional layers to separate and edit various components of the new artwork.

7   If you wish, delete the template when you've finished, to reduce the size of the file.

You can create custom views of your artwork with some layers hidden and other layers showing, and display each view in a separate window. To create a custom view, choose View > New View. To display each view in a separate window, choose Window > New Window.

For information on custom views, search for "To use multiple windows and views" in Illustrator Help.

Review

▶ **Review questions**

1   Name two benefits of using layers when creating artwork.

2   How do you hide layers? Display individual layers?

3   Describe how to reorder layers in a file.

4   How can you lock layers?

5   What is the purpose of changing the selection color on a layer?

6   What happens if you paste a layered file into another file? Why is the Paste Remembers Layers option useful?

7   How do you move objects from one layer to another?

8   How do you create a layer clipping mask?

9   How do you apply an effect to a layer? How can you edit that effect?

▶ **Review answers**

1   Benefits of using layers when creating artwork include: You can protect artwork that you don't want to change, you can hide artwork that you aren't working with so that it's not distracting, and you can control what prints.

2   To hide a layer, you click the eye icon to the left of the layer name; you click in the blank, leftmost column to redisplay a layer.

3   You reorder layers by selecting a layer name in the Layers panel and dragging the layer to its new location. The order of layers in the Layers panel controls the document's layer order—topmost in the panel is frontmost in the artwork.

4   You can lock layers several different ways:

•   You can click in the column to the left of the layer name; a padlock icon appears, indicating that the layer is locked.

•   You can choose Lock Others from the Layers panel menu to lock all layers but the active layer.

•   You can hide a layer to protect it.

5   The selection color controls how selected anchor points and direction lines are displayed in a layer, and helps you identify the different layers in your document.

6   The Paste commands paste layered files or objects copied from different layers into the active layer by default. The Paste Remembers Layers option keeps the original layers intact when the objects are pasted.

7   Select the objects you want to move and drag the square selection color box (to the right of the target indicator) to another layer in the Layers panel.

8   Create a clipping mask for a layer by selecting the layer and clicking the Make/Release Clipping Mask button. The topmost object in the layer will become the clipping mask.

9   Click the target icon of the layer you want to target to apply an effect. Then choose an effect from the Effect menu. To edit the effect, make sure that the layer is targeted; then double-click the name of the effect in the Appearance panel. The effect's dialog box will open, and then you can change the values.

Gradient fills are graduated blends of two or more colors. You use the Gradient panel to create or modify a gradient fill. The Blend tool blends the shapes and colors of objects together into a new blended object or a series of intermediate shapes.

9 | Blending Shapes and Colors

In this lesson, you'll learn how to do the following:

- Create and save gradients.
- Add colors to a gradient.
- Adjust the direction of a gradient blend.
- Create smooth-color blends between objects.
- Blend the shapes of objects in intermediate steps.
- Modify a blend, its path, shape and color.

Getting started

You'll explore various ways to create your own color gradients, and blend colors and shapes together using the Gradient panel and the Blend tool.

Before you begin, you'll restore the default preferences for Adobe Illustrator. Then you'll open the finished art file for this lesson to see what you'll create.

1 To ensure that the tools and panels function exactly as described in this lesson, delete or deactivate (by renaming) the Adobe Illustrator CS3 preferences file. See "Restoring default preferences" on page 3.

2 Start Adobe Illustrator CS3.

Note: If you have not already copied the resource files for this lesson onto your hard disk from the Lesson09 folder from the Adobe Illustrator CS3 Classroom in a Book CD, do so now. See "Copying the Classroom in a Book files" on page 2.

3 Choose File > Open, and open the L9end.ai file in the Lesson09 folder, located within the AICIB folder on your hard drive.

4   The necklace, background, Evening News type, and anchorwoman are all filled with gradients. The objects that make up the necklace, the squares in the background, and the anchorwoman's hair have all been blended to create new objects.

5   If you like, choose View > Zoom Out to make the finished artwork smaller, adjust the window size, and leave it on your screen as you work. (Use the Hand tool (🖐) to move the artwork where you want it in the window.) If you don't want to leave the image open, choose File > Close.

To begin working, you'll open an existing art file.

6   Choose File > Open, and open the L9start.ai file in the Lesson09 folder, located within the AICIB folder on your hard drive.

7   Choose File > Save As. In the Save As dialog box, name the file **News.ai**, and navigate to the Lesson09 folder. Leave the file format set to Illustrator (*.AI), and click Save. In the Illustrator Options dialog box, leave at the default settings and click OK.

8   Choose Window > Workspace > [Panel] to expand the panels.

Creating a gradient fill

Gradients can be used very much like colors to fill objects that you create. A gradient fill is a graduated blend between two or more colors. You can easily create your own gradients, or you can use the gradients provided with Adobe Illustrator CS3 and edit them for the desired effect.

To begin the lesson, you'll create a gradient fill for the background.

1 Using the Selection tool (▶), click to select the box in the background.

The background is painted with a white color fill and a black stroke, as indicated in the Fill and Stroke boxes in the Tools panel. The Gradient button below the Fill and Stroke boxes indicates the current gradient fill (which is by default a black-and-white gradient until you select a gradient-filled object or a gradient swatch in the Swatches panel).

2 Click the Gradient button (▢) in the Tools panel to select it.

The default, black-and-white gradient appears in the Fill box in the Tools panel and is applied to the selected background.

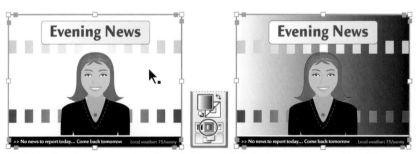

Click Gradient button to paint selected object with default or current gradient fill.

Note: Your Tools panel may look different. Due to screen size, some monitors may display the Tools panel as a double column rather than the default single column Tools panel.

3 Choose Window > Gradient if the Gradient panel is not visible. You use the Gradient panel to create your own gradients and to modify the colors of existing gradients.

4   Now click the Gradient tab on the panel. From the Gradient panel menu (▾≡),
choose Show Options. In the Gradient panel, click on the Gradient Fill box.

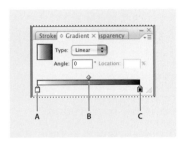

A. *Starting gradient color.*
B. *Midpoint between blended colors.*
C. *Ending gradient color.*

In the Gradient panel, the left gradient square, or stop, under the gradient bar marks the
gradient's starting color; the right gradient stop marks the ending color. A gradient stop
is the point at which a gradient changes from one color to the next. A diamond above
the bar, called a gradient slider, marks the midpoint where two colors blend equally.

5   Click the left gradient stop to select the starting color of the gradient. The tip of the
gradient stop appears darker to indicate that it's selected.

6   Click on the Color tab to view the Color panel. In the Color panel, choose Show
Options from the panel menu (▾≡). A gradient stop appears beneath the Fill box,
indicating which color in the gradient is currently selected. Now you'll paint the selected
color in the gradient with a new color.

7   In the Color panel, choose CMYK from the panel menu button (▾≡) to switch
from the Grayscale palette to the CMYK palette.

Note: *In the Color panel, you may need to choose Show Options from the Color panel
menu to see all of the CMYK sliders.*

8   With the Gradient box selected, position the eyedropper cursor (✏) in the color bar at the bottom of the Color panel, and drag or click to select a new color. Notice the change to the gradient fill in the selected background shape.

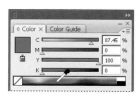

Gradient box color selected.   *The result.*

You can also drag the Color panel sliders or enter values in the percent text fields to select a color. The selected gradient box changes to reflect your choice.

9   With the left gradient stop still selected, enter these CMYK values in the Color panel: C=**0**, M=**0**, Y=**0**, and K=**0**. (To move between text fields, press Tab.) Press Enter (Windows) or Return (Mac OS) to apply the last value typed.

10   In the Gradient panel, select the end gradient stop on the right.

11   In the Color panel, choose CMYK from the panel menu (▾≡) to switch to the from Grayscale to CMYK.

12   Change the end color to green by entering these values in the Color panel: C=**75**, M=**19**, Y=**100**, and K=**40** (Press Tab to move between each text field.) Press Enter or Return to apply the last value typed.

Now you'll save the new gradient in the Swatches panel.

13 Click the Swatches tab to bring the panel to the front of its group. (If the Swatches panel isn't visible on-screen, choose Window > Swatches to display it.)

14 To save the gradient, drag it from the Fill box in the Tools panel or the Gradient panel and drop it on the Swatches panel; or select it in the Fill box in the Tools panel or in the Gradient panel, and click the New Swatch button (🖻) at the bottom of the Swatches panel.

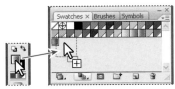

Drag gradient swatch from Fill box to Swatches panel.

15 In the Swatches panel, double-click the new gradient swatch to open the Swatch Options dialog box. Type **Background** in the Swatch Name text field, and click OK.

16 To display only gradient swatches in the Swatches panel, click the Show Swatch Kinds menu button (🖳.) at the bottom of the Swatches panel and choose Show Gradient Swatches from the pop-up menu.

Display only gradient swatches.

17 Try out some of the different gradients in the selected rectangle.

Notice that some of the gradients have several colors. You'll learn how to make a gradient with multiple colors later in this lesson.

18 Deselect the artwork by choosing Select > Deselect, and then choose File > Save.

Adjusting the direction of the gradient blend

Once you have painted an object with a gradient fill, you can adjust the direction that the gradient colors blend in the object. Now you'll adjust the gradient fill in the background shape.

1 Use the Selection tool (▶) to select the rectangle in the background.

2 Select the Gradient tool (▣) in the Tools panel.

Select gradient-filled object.

The Gradient tool.

The Gradient tool works only on selected objects that are filled with a gradient.

3 Click and drag the cursor from the top to the bottom of the selected background rectangle to change the position and direction of the gradient's starting and ending colors. Hold the Shift key down while dragging to constrain the gradient to 45 degree angles.

Drag Gradient tool straight down with Shift key held down.

The result.

You can edit a gradient multiple times with the Gradient tool. For example, drag within the rectangle to create a short gradient with distinct color blends; drag a longer distance outside the rectangle to create a longer gradient with more subtle color blends. You can also drag from the ending color to the starting color and vice versa to transpose the colors and reverse the direction of the blend.

4   With the background rectangle still selected, choose Object > Lock > Selection.

5   Use the Selection tool (➤) to select the rectangle behind the "Evening News" text. Notice that it's painted with a radial-type gradient (as indicated in the Gradient panel).

You can create linear or radial gradients. Both types of gradients have a starting and an ending color. With a radial gradient, the starting color of the gradient defines the center point of the fill, which radiates outward to the ending color.

6   Select the Gradient tool (▣) in the Tools panel.

7   Click and drag the cursor across the selected rectangle behind the "Evening News" text from the center out to change the position and direction of the gradient's starting and ending colors. Try several different variations.

Drag to edit radial gradient   *A subtle difference.*

8   Deselect the artwork by choosing Select > Deselect, and then choose File > Save.

Adding colors to a gradient

Every gradient in Adobe Illustrator has at least two gradient stops. By editing the color mix of each stop and by adding gradient stops in the Gradient panel, you can create custom gradients.

Now you'll paint some type that has been converted to path outlines with a linear gradient fill, and edit the colors in it.

1   Use the Selection tool (🡑) and click to select the capital letter E in the type Evening News. Choose Select > Same > Fill & Stroke.

The Evening News type has already been converted to path outlines so you can fill it with a gradient. (To convert type to path outlines, select it and choose Type > Create Outlines. See Lesson 7, "Working with type," for more information.)

2   Choose Object > Group to group the letters.

Select letter outlines and group type.

By grouping the letters, you'll fill each individual letter with the same gradient at once. Grouping them allows you to edit the gradient fill globally.

3   In the Tools panel, click the Gradient button (◼) below the Fill and Stroke boxes to paint the type outlines with the current gradient fill—in this case, with the radial gradient that was last selected in the background shape.

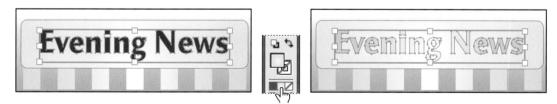

Paint selected type with last-selected gradient fill.

To edit the colors in a gradient, click on the gradient stops below the gradient bar.

4   Choose Window > Gradient if the Gradient panel is not showing. In the Gradient panel, choose Linear to from the Type menu to change the fill to a linear gradient, and then type **90** into the Angle field to change the direction of the gradient.

5   Click the left gradient stop to select it so that you can adjust the starting color of the gradient.

The Color panel displays the color of the currently selected gradient stop in the Fill box.

Now you'll change the display of the Swatches panel so that you can choose any color from it.

6   At the bottom of the Swatches panel, click the Show Swatch Kinds button (▣.) and choose Show All Swatches from the pop-up menu that appears.

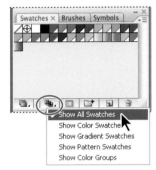

Show all swatches.

7   With the left gradient stop selected in the Gradient panel, hold down Alt (Windows) or Option (Mac OS) and click a color swatch in the Swatches panel to assign the color to the gradient. (We selected the White color swatch.)

Holding down Alt/Option as you click a color swatch applies the color to the selected gradient stop in the gradient rather than to the selected objects in the artwork.

Colors in gradients can be assigned as CMYK process colors, RGB process colors, Web Safe RGB colors, or spot colors.

Now you'll add intermediate colors to the gradient to create a fill with multiple blends between colors.

8   In the Gradient panel, click anywhere below the gradient slider (color bar) to add a stop between the other gradient stops.

You add a color to a gradient by adding a gradient stop. When you add a new gradient stop, a diamond appears above the gradient slider to mark the color's new midpoint.

9 With the new gradient box selected, hold down Alt (Windows) or Option (Mac OS) and click a color swatch in the Swatches panel to assign it to the gradient. (We selected the Yellow color swatch.)

Observe how the new color looks in the Evening News type.

10 With the right gradient stop selected in the Gradient panel, hold down Alt (Windows) or Option (Mac OS) and click a color swatch in the Swatches panel to assign the color to the gradient. (We selected the red evening news color swatch.)

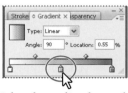 

Select the gradient box and   *The result.*
change the middle color.

11 To adjust the midpoint between two colors, drag the diamond icon between the yellow and white color stops to the right.

Drag a diamond icon to adjust
the color midpoint.

Note: *You can delete a color in a gradient by dragging its gradient stop downward and out of the Gradient panel.*

Another way to apply a color to the gradient is to sample the color from the artwork using the Eyedropper tool or drag a color swatch onto a color stop.

12 Select the center gradient stop in the Gradient panel. Select the Eyedropper tool ( ) in the Tools panel. Hold down Shift and click a color in the artwork. (We sampled the light blue color from the necklace of the newswoman in this example.)

Holding down Shift as you click with the Eyedropper tool applies the color sample to the selected gradient box in the gradient rather than replacing the entire gradient with the color in the selected Evening News type.

Select Gradient stop   *Shift-click to apply sample to selected stop in gradient.*   *The result.*

13 The Evening News text will look better without the middle swatch of the gradient. To delete a swatch from a gradient, click and drag the middle stop off of the Gradient panel. Drag the diamond icon to the left until Location reads 50% (approximately).

Click and drag the stop.   *The result.*

Next you'll save the new gradient.

14 In the Swatches panel, choose New Swatch from the panel menu, type a name for the gradient in the Swatch Name text field (we named it "News type"), and click OK to save the new gradient.

15 Deselect the artwork by choosing Select > Deselect, and then choose File > Save.

Creating smooth-color blends

You can choose several options for blending the shapes and colors of objects to create a new object. When you choose the Smooth Color blend option, Adobe Illustrator CS3 combines the shapes and colors of the objects into many intermediate steps, creating a smooth graduated blend between the original objects.

Now you'll combine two shapes of the anchorwoman's hair into a Smooth color blend.

1   In the Layers panel (Window > Layers if it's not visible), click on the arrow to the left of the broadcaster layer to view the sublayers. Click on the eye to the left of the first two <Group> sublayers and the Hair sublayer to turn them off. This will make it easier to see the objects you will be blending.

2   Using the Selection tool (▸), click one of the right lines to select it, and then Shift-click to select the second right line.

Both objects have a stroke and no fill. Objects that have strokes blend differently than those that have no stroke.

3   Choose Object > Blend > Blend Options.

4   In the Blend Options dialog box, for Spacing choose Smooth Color (if it's not already selected), and click OK.

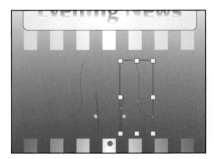

Select right two shapes.

Set blend options.

This action sets up the blend options, which remain set until you change them. Now you'll apply the blend.

5   Choose Object > Blend > Make.

Result.

When you make a smooth-color blend between objects, Adobe Illustrator CS3 automatically calculates the number of intermediate steps necessary to create a smooth transition between the objects. This type of blend can be done with lines and closed shapes.

Note: *To release a blend and revert to the original objects, select the blend and choose Object > Blend > Release.*

6   Repeat steps 2 and 5 for the 2 lines on the left side as well. The blend settings are remembered (that's why you won't have to repeat steps 3 and 4). This will complete the anchorwoman's hair.

7   Choose Object > Show All to reveal all of the hidden content.

Blending intermediate steps

Now you'll create a series of blended shapes among three different-colored shapes that make up the necklace of the anchorwoman by specifying the number of steps in the blend and using the Blend tool.

1   Click away from the artwork to deselect it, and then double-click the Blend tool (⊞) to open the Blend Options dialog box.

2   For Spacing, choose Specified Steps, type **4** for the number of steps, and click OK.

3   Using the Blend tool, click the left light blue rounded rectangle with the tool's upper hollow square, and then click the blue circle to make a blend between them.

A new object is created that blends the shapes and their colors together in four steps.

4   Now click the other light blue circle to complete the blended path.

Click objects with Blend tool to   *Result.*
create a blend.

Note: *To end the current path and continue blending other objects on a separate path, click the Blend tool in the Tools panel first, and then click the other objects.*

Modifying the blend

Now you'll modify the shape of the path or spine of the blend using the Convert Anchor Point tool.

1   Select the Direct Selection tool (🔍) from the Tools panel and click in the center of the darker blue circle of the necklace to select that anchor point. In the Control panel, click the Convert Selected Anchor Points To Smooth button (⬛) to smooth the curve.

Now you'll adjust the spacing between the center shapes on the blend.

2   Using the Convert Anchor Point tool (⌐), from the same group as the Pen tool (✒) in the Tools panel, select the left anchor point of the spine (at the center of the light blue circle on the left)—don't release the mouse button—and drag up to lengthen the direction line and stretch out the spacing between the blend steps.

3   Using the Convert Anchor Point tool (⌐), select the right anchor point of the spine (at the center of the light blue circle on the right)—don't release the mouse button—and drag down to lengthen the direction line and stretch out the spacing between the blend steps.

Select end and middle anchor points and drag direction handles to reshape blend path.

💡 *A quick way to reshape the blend's path is to wrap it around another path or object. Select the blend, select the other object or path, and then choose Object > Blend > Replace Spine.*

You can modify the blend instantly by changing the shape or color of the original objects. If you want to change the appearance of the necklace more, choose the Direct Selection tool (⬧) and click on the center anchor point of the blend, then drag up a little bit. This will reshape the necklace.

Now you'll delete an anchor point on an object and reshape the object to modify the blend.

4   Zoom in closer on the center blue circle of the necklace by using the Zoom tool (🔍) or the Navigator panel.

5   With the Selection tool (▶), click the center blue circle of the necklace to select it.

6   Select the Delete Anchor Point tool (✒) from the same group as the Convert Anchor Point tool in the Tools panel and click the top point on the circle to delete it. Notice how changing the shape of the center blue circle affects the shape of the intermediate steps in the blend.

7 Select the Direct Selection tool (⟨⟩) in the Tools panel and drag an anchor point on the bottom of the center blue circle out to extend the shape.

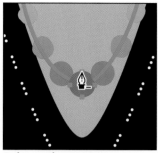 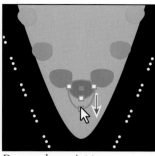 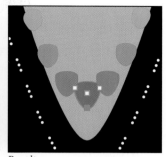

Delete anchor point on original object.

Drag anchor point to reshape object.

Result.

💡 *You can switch the starting and ending objects in the blend without affecting the shape of the spine by selecting the blend and choosing Object > Blend > Reverse Spine.*

8 Choose Select > Deselect, then File > Save.

Combining blends with gradients

You can blend objects that are filled with gradients to create different effects of color blending. The two lines of boxes in the artwork are filled with gradients. (See "Exploring on your own" at the end of this lesson to learn how to create them.)

Now you'll blend the gradient-filled lines to create a multicolored blend in the artwork.

1 Double-click the Hand tool (✋) in the Tools panel to fit the artwork in the window.

2   Select the Blend tool (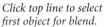) in the Tools panel and click the top line of boxes to select the first object for the blend. Then click the corresponding point on the bottom line of boxes to create the blend. (If you don't click the corresponding point, you'll get a distorted result.)

The current blend settings for four specified steps are applied to the blend. You can change these settings for an existing blend.

Click top line to select first object for blend.   *Click corresponding point on bottom line.*   *Result.*

3   Click the Selection tool (⬆) to select the bounding box of the new blend, and choose Object > Blend > Blend Options.

4   In the Blend Options dialog box, select Preview, type a number in the text field (we specified 2 steps), and press Tab to see the effect in the artwork. Click OK.

Change number of steps in the blend.   *Result.*

5   Click away from the artwork to deselect it.

Now you'll adjust the blend by changing a gradient color in one of the original objects.

6   Select the Direct Selection tool (⇡) in the Tools panel, and select one of the original line of boxes. (We selected the bottom line of boxes.)

Select original object.

7   In the Gradient panel, click a gradient stop to select a color in the gradient fill. (We selected the middle stop to select the middle color of the gradient.)

8   Hold down Alt (Windows) or Option (Mac OS), and click a color in the Swatches panel to apply it to the selected gradient stop. (We selected the yellow color swatch.)

Holding down Alt/Option as you click applies the color swatch to the selected gradient stop rather than to the selected line of boxes.

> 💡 *You can paint the individual steps in the blend with separate gradients or colors by expanding the blend. Select the blend and choose Object > Blend > Expand.*

9   To view your final artwork, press Tab to hide the Tools panel and all open panels.

Pressing Tab toggles between hiding and showing the Tools panel and panels. Pressing Shift+Tab toggles between hiding and showing just the panels (and not the Tools panel).

10   Choose Select > Deselect to deselect the artwork.

11   Choose File > Save. Choose File > Close to close the file.

To learn more about working with blends see "Blending objects" in Illustrator Help.

Exploring on your own

The two lines that create the background in the artwork were created by applying a dashed stroke to two straight lines, and then they were converted to path outlines so that they could be filled with gradients. To create a gradient-filled line like those in the artwork, do the following:

1   Choose File > New to create a new document and draw a straight line using the Pen tool.

2   Select the line, remove the fill, paint the stroke with a color, and increase the stroke weight to **20 pt**.

3   With the line selected, and the Stroke panel showing (Window > Stroke if you don't see it), turn on the Dashed Line option. Type **25** into the first dash field.

4   Choose Object > Path > Outline Stroke.

Notice that the stroke color has switched with the fill of None, so now you can fill the object with a gradient.

Review

▶ **Review questions**

1 What is a gradient fill?

2 Name two ways to fill a selected object with a gradient.

3 What is the difference between a gradient fill and a blend?

4 How do you adjust the blend between colors in a gradient?

5 How do you add colors to a gradient?

6 How do you adjust the direction of a gradient?

7 Describe two ways to blend the shapes and colors of objects.

8 What is the difference between selecting a smooth-color blend and specifying the number of steps in a blend?

9 How do you adjust the shapes or colors in the blend? How do you adjust the path of the blend?

▶ **Review answers**

1 A gradient fill is a graduated blend between two or more colors, or tints of the same color.

2 Select an object and do one of the following:

• Click the Gradient box in the Tools panel to fill an object with the default white-to-black gradient or with the last selected gradient.

• Click a gradient swatch in the Swatches panel.

• Make a new gradient by clicking a gradient swatch in the Swatches panel and mixing your own in the Gradient panel.

• Use the Eyedropper tool to sample a gradient from an object in your artwork, and then apply it to the selected object.

3 The difference between a gradient fill and a blend is the way that colors combine together—colors blend together within a gradient fill and between objects in a blend.

4   You drag the gradient's diamond icons or stops in the Gradient panel.

5   In the Gradient panel, click beneath the gradient bar to add a gradient stop to the gradient. Then use the Color panel to mix a new color, or in the Swatches panel Alt+click (Windows) or Option+click (Mac OS) a color swatch.

6   You click and drag with the Gradient tool to adjust the direction of a gradient. Dragging a long distance changes colors gradually; dragging a short distance makes the color change more abrupt.

7   You can blend the shapes and colors of objects by doing one of the following:

•   Clicking each object with the Blend tool to create a blend of intermediate steps between the objects according to preset blend options.

•   Selecting the objects and choosing Object > Blend > Blend Options to set up the number of intermediate steps, and then choosing Object > Blend > Make to create the blend.

Objects that have painted strokes blend differently than those with no strokes.

8   When you select the Smooth Color blend option, Illustrator automatically calculates the number of intermediate steps necessary to create a seamlessly smooth blend between the selected objects. Specifying the number of steps lets you determine how many intermediate steps are visible in the blend. You can also specify the distance between intermediate steps in the blend.

9   You use the Direct Selection tool to select and adjust the shape of an original object, thus changing the shape of the blend. You can change the colors of the original objects to adjust the intermediate colors in the blend. You use the Convert Anchor Point tool to change the shape of the path, or spine, of the blend by dragging anchor points or direction handles on the spine.

Lakeside Designs

The variety of brush types in Adobe Illustrator CS3 lets you create a myriad of effects simply by painting or drawing on paths. You can choose from the provided Art, Calligraphic, Patterns and Scatter brushes, or create new ones from your Illustrator artwork. Use the Paintbrush tool or the drawing tools to apply brushes to artwork, and use the Scribble effect to add some free form scribbles to the image.

10 | Working with Brushes

In this lesson, you'll learn how to do the following:

- Use the four brush types: Art, Calligraphic, Pattern, and Scatter.
- Change the brush color and adjust brush settings.
- Create new brushes from Adobe Illustrator artwork.
- Apply brushes to paths created with drawing tools.
- Use the Scribble Effect for artwork and text.

Getting started

Adobe Illustrator CS3 brushes let you apply artwork to paths to decorate them with patterns, figures, textures, or angled strokes. You can modify the brushes provided with Adobe Illustrator CS3, and you can create your own brushes. Brushes appear in the Brushes panel.

You apply brushes to paths using the Paintbrush tool or the drawing tools. To apply brushes using the Paintbrush tool, you choose a brush from the Brushes panel and draw in the artwork. The brush is applied directly to the paths as you draw. To apply brushes using a drawing tool, you draw in the artwork, select a path in the artwork, and then choose a brush in the Brushes panel. The brush is applied to the selected path.

You can change the color, size, and other features of a brush. You can also edit paths after brushes are applied.

In this lesson, you'll learn to use the four brush types in the Brushes panel, including how to change brush options and how to create your own brushes. Before you begin, you'll need to restore the default preferences for Adobe Illustrator CS3. Then you'll open the finished art file for this lesson to see what you'll create.

1 To ensure that the tools and panels function exactly as described in this lesson, delete or deactivate (by renaming) the Adobe Illustrator CS3 preferences file. See "Restoring default preferences" on page 3.

2 Start Adobe Illustrator CS3.

Note: If you have not already copied the resource files for this lesson onto your hard disk from the Lesson10 folder from the Adobe Illustrator CS3 Classroom in a Book CD, do so now. See "Copying the Classroom in a Book files" on page 2.

3 Choose File > Open, and open the L10end.ai file in the Lesson10 folder, located inside the Lessons folder in the AICIB folder on your hard drive.

4 If you like, choose View > Zoom Out to make the finished artwork smaller, adjust the window size, and leave it on your screen as you work. (Use the Hand tool (🖑) to move the artwork where you want it in the window.) If you don't want to leave the image open, choose File > Close.

To begin working, you'll open an existing art file set up with guides to draw the artwork.

5 Choose File > Open to open the L10start.ai file in the Lesson10 folder inside the AICIB folder on your hard drive.

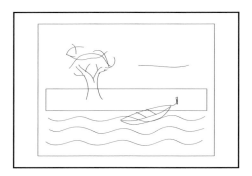

6   Choose File > Save As. In the Save As dialog box, name the file **Brushes.ai,** and choose the Lesson10 folder. Leave the file format set to Illustrator (*.AI), and click Save. In the Illustrator Options dialog box, accept the defaults settings and click OK.

Using Art brushes

Art brushes stretch artwork evenly along a path. Art brushes include strokes resembling various graphic media, such as the Charcoal-Feather brush. Art brushes also include images, such as the Arrow brush, and text, such as the Type brush, which paints the characters *A-R-T* along a path. In this section, you'll use the Charcoal-Feather brush to draw the trunk and limbs of a tree.

The start file has been created with locked paths that you can use to create and align your artwork for the lesson. The paths are locked and cannot be selected, moved, modified, or printed (unless they are unlocked).

Drawing with the Paintbrush tool

Now you'll use the Paintbrush tool to apply a brush to the artwork.

1   In the Tools panel, click the Paintbrush tool (✐) to select it.

You will next select a brush in the Brushes panel to be applied to the artwork.

2   Choose Window > Brushes to open the Brushes panel.

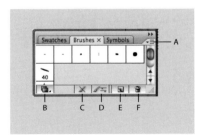

A. Opens the Brushes panel menu.
B. Brush Libraries Menu
C. Remove Brush Stroke.
D. Options of Selected Object.
E. New Brush. F. Delete Brush.

By default, brushes appear as icons. You can also view brushes by name. When viewed by name, a small icon to the right of the brush name indicates the brush type.

3   In the Brushes panel, choose List View from the panel menu (⊞).

From the Brushes panel menu you can also choose which types of brushes are displayed in the Brushes panel to reduce the panel size and make it easier to find the brushes you want to use. Open the panel menu again and choose Show Calligraphic Brushes. Then repeat the step to choose Show Scatter Brushes and Show Pattern Brushes and deselect those options, leaving only the Art brushes visible in the Brushes panel. A check mark next to the brush type in the Brushes panel menu indicates that the brush type is visible in the panel.

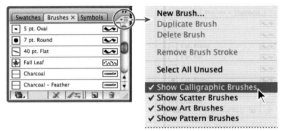

Showing and hiding brush types.

4   Select the Charcoal-Feather art brush in the Brushes panel.

Brushes are applied to paths as a stroke color. If you have a fill color selected when you apply a brush to a path, the path will be stroked with the brush and filled with the fill color. Use a fill of None when applying brushes to prevent the brushed paths from being filled. Later in this lesson you'll use a fill color with a brush. For more information on stroke and fill color, see Lesson 6, "Color and Painting."

5   In the Control panel, click on the Fill box and choose the None (⊘) swatch.

6   Use the Paintbrush tool (✐) to draw a long, upward stroke to create the left side of the tree trunk, tracing over the guides as you draw. Don't worry if your stroke doesn't follow the guide exactly. You'll remove the guides at the end of the lesson, so that they won't show through the finished artwork.

7 Draw a second upward stroke to create the right side of the tree trunk, using the guide to place your drawing.

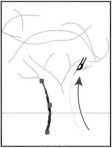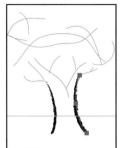

Draw with the Paintbrush tool. *Last path drawn remains selected.*

Each path remains selected after you draw it, until you draw another path.

8 Choose File > Save to save your work.

Editing paths with the Paintbrush tool

When you draw with the Paintbrush tool, the last path you draw remains selected by default. This feature makes it easy to edit paths as you draw. If you draw over the selected path with the Paintbrush tool, the part of the selected path that you drew over is edited. You can disable or set a tolerance for path editing in the Paintbrush tool Preferences dialog box.

Now you'll use the Paintbrush tool to edit the selected path.

1   Place the Paintbrush tool (✐) near the top of the selected path (the right side of the tree trunk) and draw upward.

The selected path is edited from the point where you began drawing over it. The new path is added to the selected path (instead of becoming a separate path).

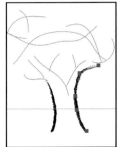

Draw over selected path Selected path is edited.
to edit it.

When drawing with the Paintbrush tool, you may want paths to remain unselected so that you can draw over paths without altering them, and create layered or overlapping strokes. You can change the Paintbrush tool preferences to keep paths unselected as you draw.

2   Choose Select > Deselect.

3   In the Tools panel, double-click the Paintbrush tool (✐) to display the Paintbrush tool Preferences dialog box. You use this dialog box to change the way the Paintbrush tool functions.

4   Click the Keep Selected option to deselect it, and click OK. Now paths will not remain selected after you finish drawing them, and you can draw overlapping paths without altering the earlier paths.

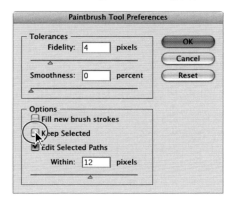

Now you'll draw the limbs of the tree.

5   Draw shorter strokes to create the limbs of the tree.

When the Keep Selected option is turned off, you can edit a path with the Paintbrush tool by selecting the path with the Selection tool (▶) or by selecting a segment or point on the path with the Direct Selection tool (▷) and then redrawing the path with the Paintbrush tool.

6   Press Ctrl (Windows) or Command (Mac OS) to toggle to the Selection tool, and select from the artwork a limb that you want to redraw.

Pressing Ctrl/Command temporarily selects the Selection tool (or the Direct Selection or Group Selection tool, whichever was used last) when another tool is selected.

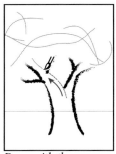

Draw with the   *Path remains*   *Select path to edit it.*
Paintbrush tool.   *unselected.*

7 Use the Paintbrush tool to draw over the selected path.

You can also edit paths using the Smooth tool (✎) and the Path Eraser tool (✐) (located under the Pencil tool (✐) in the Tools panel) to redraw or remove parts of a path drawn with the Paintbrush tool.

After you apply a brush to an object, it's easy to apply another brush to the paths to change the appearance of the object.

8 Choose the Selection tool (▶) and drag a marquee to select the tree trunk and branches.

9 Click on the Brush Libraries Menu button (📖.) at the bottom of the Brushes panel and choose the Artistic > Artistic_Ink library.

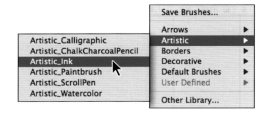

10 In the Artistic_Ink brushes panel, click on the panel menu button (▤) and choose List View from the panel menu. Click the Dry ink 1 brush. The new brush is applied to the selected paths in the artwork. Close the Artistic_Ink panel.

Notice how the Dry Ink 1 brush is added to the Brushes panel. Every brush you click on to apply from a library will be added to the Brushes panel.

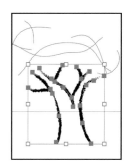

Charcoal-Feather strokes selected.

Selecting the Dry Ink 1 brush.

Dry Ink 1 brush applied.

11 Click outside the artwork to deselect it and view the tree without selection highlights.

12 Drag a selection marquee to select the tree again.

13 Click several other brushes in the Brushes panel to see the effects of those brushes in the artwork. When you have finished, click the Charcoal-Feather brush again to reapply that brush.

14 Click outside the artwork to deselect it.

15 Choose File > Save to save your work.

As you complete the rest of this lesson, use the methods you learned in this section to edit paths as you draw with the Paintbrush tool. You can use the brushes, editing paths with the Keep Selected option if you want strokes to remain selected as you draw, or you can use the Selection tool to select strokes to be edited.

Using Scatter brushes

Scatter brushes randomly spread an object, such as a leaf, a ladybug, or a strawberry, along a path. In this section, you'll use the Fall Leaf Scatter brush to create leaves on the tree. You'll start by adjusting options for the brush to change its appearance in the artwork.

Changing brush options

You change the appearance of a brush by adjusting its settings in the Brush Options dialog box, either before or after brushes have been applied to artwork. The changes you make appear when you apply the brush to artwork, but do not appear in the brush icon in the Brushes panel.

1 In the Brushes panel, choose Show Scatter Brushes from the panel menu (▾≡) to select that option. Then choose Show Art Brushes to deselect that option.

Note: If the Brush type is already checked, selecting it again hides the type in the Brushes panel.

2   Double-click the Fall Leaf brush to open the Scatter Brush Options dialog box. Brush options vary according to the type of brush. For Scatter brushes, you can set either fixed values or a (random) range of values for the brush size, spacing, scatter, and rotation. If you have a pressure-sensitive drawing tablet attached to your computer, you can also set the pressure of the stylus using the Pressure option.

3   Set the following values, either dragging the slider or entering values, and pressing the Tab key to move between the text fields:

•   For Size, set the size of the brush object relative to the default (100%) by choosing Random and entering **40%** and **60%**.

•   For Spacing, set the distance between brush objects on a path relative to 100% (objects touching but not overlapping) by choosing Random and entering **10%** and **30%**.

•   For Scatter, indicate how far objects will deviate from either side of the path, where 0% is aligned on the path, by choosing Random and entering **–40%** and **40%**.

•   For Rotation relative to the page or path, enter **–180°** and **180°**. Rotation relative to Page should be set by default, so leave it there.

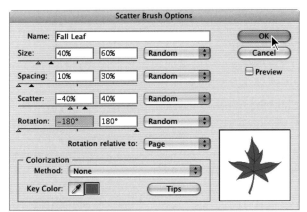

Double-click.
Fall Leaf brush   *Set brush options.*

4   Click OK.

In addition to the features you adjusted in this section, you can change the color of a brush. You'll change the color of the Fall Leaf brush and another brush later in this lesson.

Applying a Scatter brush to paths

Now you'll use the Fall Leaf brush with its adjusted settings to draw leaves on the tree in the artwork. First you'll select and lock the tree. Locking an object prevents it from being altered while you work on other objects in the artwork.

1   Use the Selection tool (▶) to drag a marquee around all parts of the tree to select them.

2   Choose Object > Lock > Selection.

The bounding box around the tree disappears, and the tree is locked.

3   Select the Fall Leaf Scatter brush.

4   Use the Paintbrush tool (✎) to draw strokes with the Fall Leaf brush above the tree branches, using the guides to help place your paths. Remember that if you want to edit paths as you draw, you can use the Keep Selected option for the Paintbrush tool or select paths with the Selection tool.

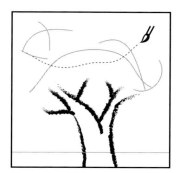  

Drawing with Paintbrush tool.   *Fall Leaf brush applied to artwork.*   *The result.*

5   Choose File > Save.

Changing the color attributes of brushes

Now you'll change the color of the Fall Leaf brush in the artwork.

Before you change the brush color, it's helpful to understand how Adobe Illustrator CS3 applies color to brushes.

To change the color of Art, Pattern, and Scatter brushes, you use one of three colorization methods—models for applying color to the artwork in a brush. To change the color of Calligraphic brushes, you simply select the brush and choose a stroke color. (See Lesson 6, "Color and Painting," for information on choosing a stroke color.) You can change the color attributes of a brush before and after you apply the brush to artwork.

When you apply a brush to artwork, Adobe Illustrator CS3 uses the current stroke color for the brush only if a colorization method is chosen. Selecting brush strokes and choosing a new stroke color applies that new color to the brush. If no colorization method is set, Adobe Illustrator CS3 uses the brush's default color. For example, the Fall Leaf brush was applied with its default color of red (not the current stroke of black) because its colorization method was set to None.

To colorize Art, Pattern, and Scatter brushes, select one of the following options in the Brush Options dialog box—None, Tints, Tints and Shades, and Hue Shift:

* **Tints** displays the brush stroke in tints of the stroke color. Portions of the art that are black become the stroke color, portions that aren't black become tints of the stroke color, and white remains white. If you use a spot color as the stroke, Tints generates tints of the spot color. Choose Tints for brushes that are in black and white, or when you want to paint a brush stroke with a spot color.

* **Tints and Shades** displays the brush stroke in tints and shades of the stroke color. Tints and Shades maintains black and white, and everything between becomes a blend from black to white through the stroke color. Because black is added, you may not be able to print to a single plate when using Tints and Shades with a spot color. Choose Tints and Shades for brushes that are in grayscale.

- **Hue Shift** uses the key color in the brush artwork, as shown in the Key Color box. (By default, the key color is the most prominent color in the art.) Everything in the brush artwork that is the key color becomes the stroke color. Other colors in the brush artwork become colors related to the stroke color. Hue Shift maintains black, white, and gray. Choose Hue Shift for brushes that use multiple colors.

Note: *Brushes colorized with a stroke color of white may appear entirely white. Brushes colorized with a stroke color of black may appear entirely black. Results depend on the original brush colors.*

Changing brush color using Hue Shift colorization

Now you'll change the color of the Fall Leaf brush using the Hue Shift colorization method.

1   Choose the Selection tool (⬉), and drag a selection marquee to select the Fall Leaf strokes in the artwork.

2   Hold down the Shift key and click on the Stroke color to the left of the word Stroke in the Control panel. This links to the Color panel. If you prefer to not use the Control panel, choose Window > Color instead.

3   Click in the color spectrum bar to select a color for the Fall Leaf brush. (We chose an orangish-red color.)

4   In the Brushes panel, double-click the Fall Leaf brush to view the Scatter Brush Options dialog box for the brush. Move the dialog box off to the side so that you can see your artwork as you work.

You'll select a colorization method for the brush. For brushes set to a default colorization method of None, you must choose a colorization method before you can change the brush color. Brushes set to the Tints, Tints and Shades, or Hue Shift colorization method, by default, automatically apply the current stroke color to the brush when you use it in the artwork.

Note: *To find a brush's default colorization setting, double-click the brush in the Brushes panel to view the Scatter Brush Options dialog box, and then select the setting in the Method pop-up menu in the Colorization section.*

5   In the Colorization section in the dialog box, choose Hue Shift from the Method pop-up menu.

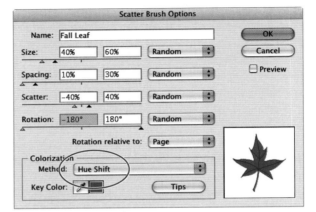

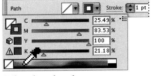

Select brush color.   *Set colorization method.*

The Key Color swatch in the Colorization section indicates the brush color that will shift to the new stroke color. The Key Color box displays the default key color (in this case, the leaf's red color) or the key color you select. For this lesson, you'll use the default key color.

It can be useful to select a new key color if a brush contains several colors and you want to shift different colors in the brush. To select a different key color, you click the Key Color Eyedropper (✐) in the dialog box and position the Eyedropper on the desired color in the preview (such as one of the black veins in the leaf), and click. The new key color shifts to the stroke color when you use the brush in the artwork (and other colors in the brush will shift correspondingly).

6   Click Preview to preview the color to be applied by the colorization method.

The selected Fall Leaf strokes are colorized with the current stroke color (the color you selected in step 3). This color will appear when you apply the Hue Shift colorization method.

7   If desired, choose the Tints, or Tints and Shades, colorization method from the pop-up menu to preview the change. Then return to the Hue Shift method.

8   Click OK. At the alert message, click Apply to Strokes to apply the colorization change to the strokes in the artwork. You can also choose to change only subsequent brush strokes and leave existing strokes unchanged.

Once you select a colorization method for a brush, the new stroke color applies to selected brush strokes and to new paths painted with the brush.

9   Choose Window > Color. Click on the Stroke color to bring it forward and then click the color spectrum bar in several different places to try other stroke colors for the selected brush strokes.

10   When you are satisfied with the color of the Fall Leaf brush strokes, click away from the artwork to deselect it.

11   Choose File > Save.

Changing brush color using Tints colorization

Now you'll apply a new color to the Charcoal - Feather brush in the Art Brushes section of the Brushes panel, and then use the brush to draw bark for the tree in the artwork.

You'll begin by selecting the brush in the Brushes panel.

1   In the Brushes panel menu, choose Show Art Brushes, if it is not already checked. If Show Scatter Brushes is checked, then choose it to hide those brushes.

You'll display the Brush Options dialog box for the Charcoal - Feather brush to see the default colorization settings for the brush and change the brush size.

2   Choose the Charcoal - Feather brush in the Brushes panel.

3   Select the Paintbrush tool and draw two paths to fill the center of the tree.

4   Choose the Selection tool and Shift-click on both paths to select them.

5   Click on the Options of Selected Object button (✒) in the Brushes panel to reveal the Stroke Options (Art Brush) dialog box. The brush's original color is black. Options of Selected Object allows you to edit just the selected paths.

6   In the Stroke Options (Art Brush) dialog box, note that the Charcoal - Feather brush is set by default to the Tints colorization method.

The Tints colorization method replaces black with the stroke color. Neither the Tints and Shades nor the Hue Shift colorization method works with black brushes. Both methods replace the original black color with black, leaving the brush unchanged.

7   In the Size section of the dialog box, enter **350%** for Width to change the size to a more appropriate scale for drawing in the artwork.

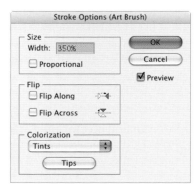

Click the
Options of Selected Object.

Charcoal - Feather brush with width of 350%
and default Tints colorization method.

8   Click OK to accept the settings and close the dialog box.

9   With the two paths still selected, Shift-click on the Stroke color in the Control panel and choose a light brown color for the color of the tree. Click off the page to deselect all items.

Note: If you find strokes disappearing as you create new ones, deselect Keep Selected from the Paintbrush options.

Because the Charcoal - Feather brush is all one color, the Tints colorization method applies the new stroke color as one color (rather than varied tints of the color). When the original brush contains several colors, the Tints colorization method applies a different tint for each color in the brush.

Using a fill color with brushes

When you apply a brush to an object's stroke, you can also apply a fill color to paint the interior of the object with a color. When you use a fill color with a brush, the brush objects appear on top of the fill color in places where the fill and the brush objects overlap.

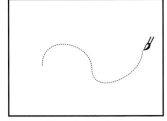
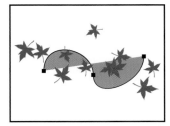

*Choose
fill color.*   *Draw with paintbrush.*   *Brush objects appear on top of fill.*

Now you'll use the Paintbrush tool to draw a canoe at the edge of the grass with an Art brush. You'll begin by selecting the brush in the Brushes panel.

1   In the Brushes panel, click on the Brush Libraries Menu button (.) at the bottom of the Brushes panel and choose the Artistic > Artistic_Ink library. Click on the Tapered Stroke brush to add it to the Brush panel. Close the Artistic_Ink library.

The Tapered Stroke brush uses the Tints colorization method by default. To change the color of the Tapered Stroke brush, you'll simply select a stroke color.

2 In the Control panel, click on the Stroke color and choose the Canoe Stroke color for the edges of the canoe. (It will be one of the brown swatches).

Now you'll use the Paintbrush tool to draw the edges of the canoe. Use the guides to align your drawing.

3 Use the Paintbrush tool ( ) to draw a crescent shape to make the side and bottom of the canoe:

- Draw a long stroke from left to right to make the side edge of the canoe. Do not release the mouse button.
- While still holding down the mouse button, draw a second long stroke beneath the first, from right to left, connecting the two strokes at the right endpoint of the object, to make a crescent shape. When you have drawn the second stroke, release the mouse button.

You may have to draw the crescent shape more than once to create a shape with a single path. Remember that you can edit paths as you draw. Use the Direct Selection tool ( ) to select a segment of the path that you want to redraw.

Don't worry if your drawing doesn't match the guides exactly. What's important is drawing the shape as one path, without releasing the mouse button, so that you can fill the object correctly. (If a shape is made of separate paths, the fill color is applied to each path separately, yielding unpredictable results.)

4 Draw a third long stroke for the top side of the canoe. Then draw two shorter strokes for the crossbars. (Draw the top side and crossbars as separate paths, releasing the mouse button after each one.)

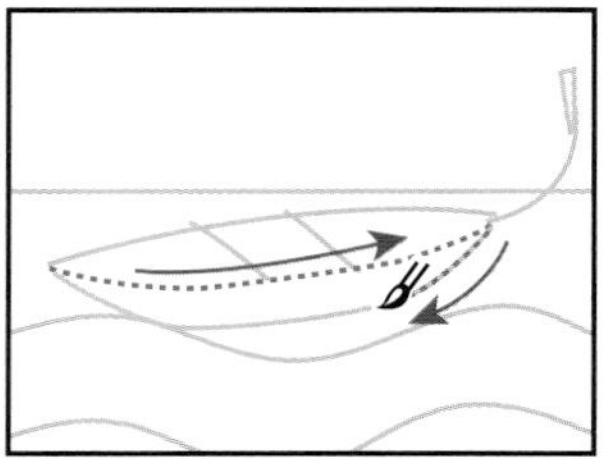

Draw crescent as one path.

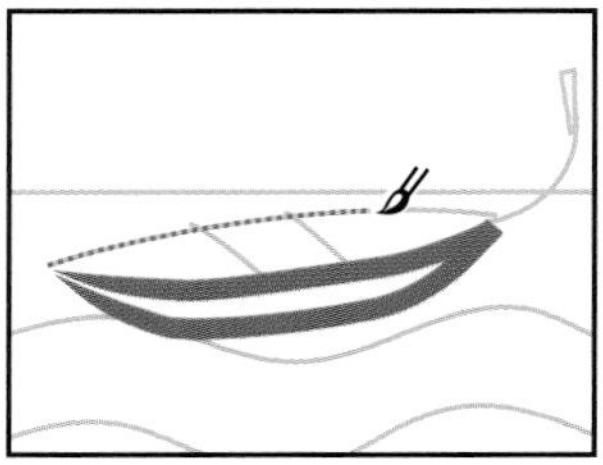

Add top.

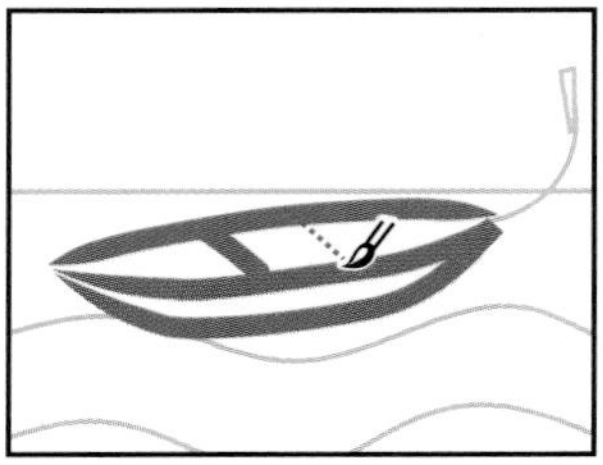

Add crossbars.

Now you'll fill the side of the canoe with a color.

5   Choose the Selection tool (↖), and select the crescent shape you drew for the lower side and bottom of the canoe.

6   Select the Fill color box in the Control panel, when the Swatch panel appears, choose to select the Canoe Fill swatch.

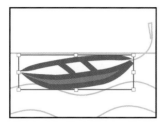

Selected shape is filled.

7   Click outside the artwork to deselect it.

8   Choose File > Save.

Using Calligraphic brushes

Calligraphic brushes resemble strokes drawn with the angled point of a calligraphic pen Calligraphic brushes are defined by an elliptical shape whose center follows the path. Use these brushes to create the appearance of hand-drawn strokes made with a flat, angled pen tip.

You'll use a Calligraphic pen to draw water below the canoe. You'll begin by selecting the brush, and then choose a color for the brush.

1   If not already selected, in the Brushes panel, choose Show Calligraphic Brushes from the panel menu (▼≡). Then choose Show Art Brushes from the menu to deselect that option.

2   In the Brushes panel, select the 40 pt. Flat brush.

3   In the Control panel, click the Stroke color and choose the Waves blue swatch.

Calligraphic brushes use the current stroke color when you apply the brushes to artwork. You do not use colorization methods with Calligraphic brushes.

4   In the Color panel, click the Fill box and choose None (⊘). A fill of None with brushes prevents paths from being filled when you apply the brush.

5   Select the Paintbrush tool (✎), and draw wavy lines for the water surface. The paths you draw use the stroke color you selected in step 3.

Now you'll change the shape of the 40 pt. Flat brush in the Brush Options dialog box to change the appearance of the strokes made with the brush.

6   In the Brushes panel, double-click the 40 pt. Flat brush to display the Calligraphic Brush Options dialog box.

You can change the angle of the brush (relative to a horizontal line), the roundness (from a flat line to a full circle), and the diameter (from 0 to 1296 points) to change the shape that defines the brush's tip, and change the appearance of the stroke that the brush makes. Now you'll change the diameter and angle of the brush.

7   Enter **35 pt** for Diameter. In the Name text field, enter **35 pt Oval**. Notice that the weight of the Calligraphic brush strokes in the artwork decreases. Enter -**20** for the angle. The Preview window in the dialog box shows changes you make to the brush.

8   Click OK. At the alert message, click Apply to Strokes to apply the change to the strokes in the artwork.

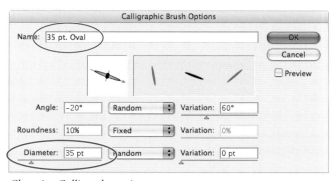

40 pt Flat brush.   *Changing Calligraphy options.*

9   With the Selection tool, Shift-click on the three blue wavy lines.

10   Click the Transparency panel tab or choose Window > Transparency to view the Transparency panel. Type in **45** for the Opacity of the wavy lines.

11   Ctrl/Command+click outside the artwork or choose Select > Deselect to deselect it.

12   Choose File > Save.

Using Pattern brushes

Pattern brushes paint a pattern made up of separate sections, or tiles, for the sides (middle sections), ends, and corners of the path. When you apply a Pattern brush to artwork, the brush applies different tiles from the pattern to different sections of the path, depending on where the section falls on the path (at an end, in the middle, or at a corner). You'll open an existing Pattern Brush library and choose a Dashed Circle pattern to represent a chain. There are hundreds of interesting pattern brushes you can choose from when creating your own projects—from dog tracks to teacups.

1   If not already selected, in the Brushes panel, choose Show Pattern Brushes from the panel menu.

2   In the Brushes panel, click on the Brush Libraries Menu button at the bottom of the Brushes panel and choose the Borders > Borders_Dashed library. A separate panel appears with various dashed borders that are ready to use.

3   Choose List View from the Borders_Dashed panel menu.

Choosing from the   *Dashed_Circles 1.4 added*
Borders_Dashed library.   *to the Brushes library.*

4   Choose Select > Deselect and then click the Dashed Circles 1.4 brush to add it to the Brushes panel. Close the Borders_Dashed panel.

5   Double-click on the Dashed Circles 1.4 pattern brush you just added to the Brushes panel. This displays the Pattern Brush Options dialog box for the brush.

The Pattern Brush Options dialog box displays the tiles in the Dashed Circles 1.4 brush. The first tile on the left is the Side tile, used to paint the middle sections of a path. The second tile is the Outer Corner tile. The third tile is the Inner Corner tile.

Pattern brushes can have up to five tiles—the Side, Start, and End tiles, plus an Outer Corner tile and an Inner Corner tile to paint sharp corners on a path. Some brushes have no corner tiles because the brush is designed for curved paths, not sharp corners. In the next part of this lesson, you'll create your own Pattern brush that uses corner tiles.

Now you'll change the scale of the Pattern brush so that the brush is in scale with the rest of the artwork when you apply it.

6   In the Pattern Brush Options dialog box, enter **20%** in the Scale text field, and click OK.

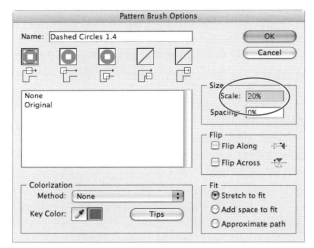

Dashed Circles 1.4 brush.   *Dashed Circles with tiles scaled 20%.*

7   Select the Paintbrush tool (✐), and draw a path that loops around the base of the tree. Then draw a second path that leads from the loop around the tree to the canoe.

Draw the stroke as two separate paths, rather than one path, to avoid creating a path with a sharp angle. (Because the Dashed Circle brush does not include corner tiles, the brush uses Side tiles to paint sharp angles. The Side tiles appear severed at sharp corners, and the rope appears to be cut.)

 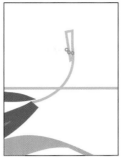  

Draw the first portion.   *Result.*   *Draw the second portion.*   *Draw the third portion.*

Now you'll draw the stake and wrap the chain around it.

8 Choose Select > Deselect to deselect all of the artwork on the page.

9 Choose the Pen tool ( ) from the Tools panel and click four times around the stake guides to create a closed path, clicking back on the first point drawn to close the path. From the Fill box in the Control panel, choose a dark brown color. Make sure that the Stroke is set to None ( ).

Now you will select a portion of the chain you created earlier in the lesson and move it in front of the stake to make the chain appear to go around the stake.

10 Choose Select > Deselect to deselect the stake.

11 Choose the Selection tool ( ), and then select the first and third portions of chain you drew. (Be careful not to select the stake.)

12 Choose Object > Arrange > Bring to Front.

   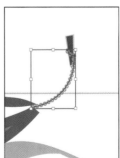

Draw the stake.   *Close the path.*   *Fill the stake with a color.*   *Select two portions of
chain and bring to front.*

13 Choose File > Save.

Creating brushes

You can create new brushes of all four brush types, using artwork in an Adobe Illustrator CS3 file as the basis for the brush. In this section, you'll use artwork provided with the lesson to create a new Pattern brush with three tiles: a yellow bar for the Side tile, and a blue circle for the Outer Corner tile and Inner Corner tile.

Creating swatches for a Pattern brush

You create Pattern brushes by first creating swatches in the Swatches panel with the artwork that will be used for the Pattern brush tiles. In this section, you'll use the yellow line and blue circle drawings included with the artwork file to create swatches.

1   Use the scroll bars, the Hand tool (✋), or the Navigator panel to display the scratch area to the right of the artboard to view the yellow line and blue circle drawings located there.

🄰 For information on moving to different areas of the document window, see Lesson 1, "Getting to Know the Work Area."

Shapes that will make up the pattern brush.

2   Choose Object > Unlock All.

Bounding boxes and selection highlights appear around the shapes, indicating that the objects are unlocked and selected. The tree, which you locked earlier in the lesson, is unlocked and selected. (The tree can be unlocked because you've finished drawing in the area of the tree.)

3   Using the Selection tool (▶), click outside the artwork to deselect the objects.

4   Click the Swatches panel tab to view the Swatches panel. (If the panel isn't visible on-screen, choose Window > Swatches.)

Now you'll create a pattern swatch.

5   With the Selection tool (🢂), drag the circle shape into the Swatches panel. The new swatch appears in the Swatches panel.

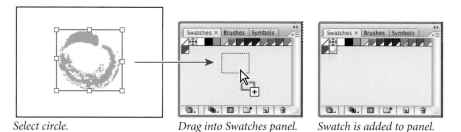

Select circle.   *Drag into Swatches panel.*   *Swatch is added to panel.*

6   Click away from the artwork to deselect.

7   In the Swatches panel, double-click the new pattern swatch you just created. Double-clicking the swatch changes the current fill or stroke box to that swatch and opens the Swatch Options dialog box.

8   Name the swatch **Corner**, and then click OK.

9   Now repeat steps 5 through 8 to create a pattern swatch of the yellow line art:

•   Use the Selection tool to drag the line into the Swatches panel. The new swatch appears in the Swatches panel.

•   Click away from the artwork to deselect.

•   In the Swatches panel, double-click the swatch.

•   Name the swatch **Side**, and then click OK.

📘 For more information on creating pattern swatches, see "About patterns" in Illustrator Help.

Creating a Pattern brush from swatches

To create a new Pattern brush, you apply swatches from the Swatches panel to tiles in the Brush Options dialog box. Now you'll apply the pattern swatches made in the previous steps to tiles for a new Pattern brush.

First you'll open a Brush Options dialog box for a new Pattern brush.

1   Click the Brushes panel icon to view the panel, or choose Window > Brushes.

2   Choose Select > Deselect.

3   In the Brushes panel, click the New Brush button.

4   Select New Pattern Brush and click OK.

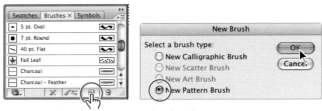

Create new brush.   Select brush type.

You'll apply the Side swatch to the Side tile for the New Pattern Brush.

5   In the Pattern Brush Options dialog box, select the Side tile box (the far left tile box).

6   In the pattern swatches scroll list, select the Side swatch. The Side swatch appears in the Side tile box.

Next you'll apply the Corner swatch to the Outer Corner tile and Inner Corner tile for the new Pattern brush.

7 In the Pattern Brush Options dialog box, select the Outer Corner tile box (the second tile box from the left). In the pattern swatches scroll list, select the Corner swatch. The Corner swatch appears in the Outer Corner tile box.

In the Pattern Brush Options dialog box, select the Inner Corner tile box (the middle tile box). In the pattern swatches scroll list, select the Corner swatch. The Corner swatch appears in the Inner Corner tile box.

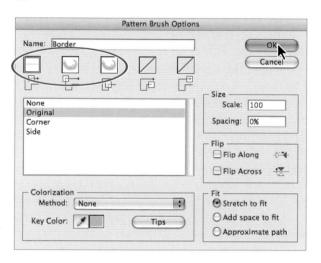

You won't create a Start tile or End tile for the new brush. (You'll apply the new brush to a closed path in the artwork later in the lesson, so you won't need Start or End tiles at this time. When you want to create a Pattern brush that includes Start and End tiles, you add those tiles the same way as you did the Side and Corner tiles.)

8 In the Name text field, name the brush **Border**. Then click OK.

The Border brush appears in the Pattern brush section in the Brushes panel.

Note: When you create a new brush, the brush appears in the Brushes panel of the current artwork only. If you open another file in Adobe Illustrator CS3, the Border brush won't appear in that file's Brushes panel.

To save a brush and reuse it in another file, you can create a brush library with the brushes you want to use. For more information, see "Work with brush libraries" in Illustrator Help.

Painting with the Pattern brush

So far in this lesson, you've used the Paintbrush tool ( ) to apply brushes to paths. You can also apply brushes to paths created with any drawing tool—including the Pen, Pencil, Ellipse, and Rectangle tools—and the other basic shape tools. In this section, you'll use the Rectangle tool to apply the Border brush to a rectangular border around the artwork.

When you use drawing tools to apply brushes to artwork, you first draw the path with the tool and then select the brush in the Brushes panel to apply the brush to the path.

First you'll set the fill and stroke color to None.

1   In the Tools panel, click the Fill box and click the None button (⬜). Then click on the Stroke box and click the None button (⬜).

2   Use the Navigator panel or the Zoom tool ( ) to reduce the view of the artwork. Now you'll draw a border with the Rectangle tool and apply the brush to the path.

3   Select the Rectangle tool (■). Drag to draw a rectangle on the artboard, following the outer guide.

4   In the Brushes panel, choose Thumbnail View from the panel menu ( ).

5   In the Brushes panel, click the Border brush.

The rectangle path is painted with the Border brush, with the Side tile on the sides and the Corner tile on the corners.

Draw rectangle.

Select Pattern brush.

Brush is applied to rectangle path.

6 Ctrl+click (Windows) or Command+click (Mac OS) outside the art to deselect it. Now you'll draw a curved path using the Border brush.

7 In the Brushes panel, double-click the Borders Pattern brush to view the Pattern Brush Options dialog box for the brush.

You'll change the scale and spacing of the brush for a different look.

8 Under Size, enter **130%** for Scale. Click OK.

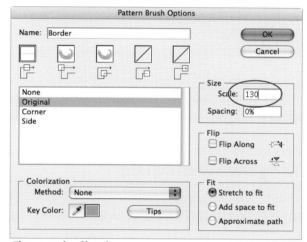

Select Border Pattern brush.   Change scale of brush.

9 At the Brush Change alert message, click Leave Strokes to keep the border brush strokes as they are.

The Leave Strokes option preserves paths in the artwork that are already painted with the brush. The changes you made to the brush will apply to subsequent uses of the brush. Now you'll use the brush to paint a curved path in the artwork.

10 Select the Paintbrush tool (🖌) and draw a smooth curve to the right of the tree. Use the guides for placement.

Apply Pattern brush to path with paintbrush.   *Result.*

The path is painted with the Side swatch from the Border brush (the Side tile in the brush). Because the path does not include sharp corners, the Outer Corner tile and Inner Corner tile (the corner tiles) are not applied to the path.

Applying the Scribble Effect

The Scribble effect is a feature in Illustrator CS3 that lets you apply loose or mechanical-like scribbling to fills and strokes. This includes fills of gradients and patterns.

You will create the grass using the Scribble Effect and its options.

1 Create a rectangle over the tree to create the grass. Fill the rectangle with the Green swatch from the Swatches panel and give it a Stroke of None (⬜).

Create a rectangle using guides for the grass.

2 With the grass still selected, choose Object > Arrange > Send to Back.

3 Choose Effect > Stylize > Scribble.

The Scribble Options dialog box appears, giving you choices that range from changing the width of the scribbled stroke to curviness and spacing.

4   Choose options in the Scribble Options dialog box to make the grass look more like grass. (We used the following settings: Angle **67˚**, Path Overlap **0 pt**, Variation **5 pt**, Stroke Width **3 pt**. The curviness was set to be more angular with a setting of **5%**, but variations were made to make the strokes look less mechanical with a Curviness Variation setting of **1%**. Spacing between the strokes was set to **6 pt** with a variation of **.5 pt**.) Click OK.

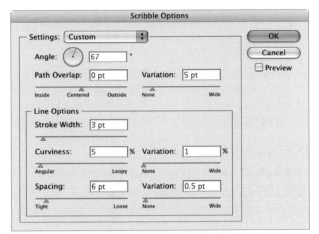

Using the Scribble Options to create grass.   Result.

5   Select the Type tool (**T**) and click above the curved shape to the right of the tree. Before typing, set up character attributes. Click on Character in the Control panel or choose Window > Type > Character. (We chose Myriad Pro Black, which comes with Adobe Illustrator CS3). Change the font size and leading to **24 pt**.

6   Type **Lakeside Designs**.

You've completed the artwork for the lesson. Now you'll hide the drawn guides so you can view the artwork in its finished form.

7   Choose Window > Layers to open the Layers panel. Click the eye icon to the left of the Guides layer to hide the drawn guides.

8   Choose File > Save to save your work. Choose File > Close to close the file.

Exploring on your own

Applying brushes

Practice applying brushes to paths you create with drawing tools (just as you applied the Pattern brush to a path drawn with the Rectangle tool in the final section of the lesson).

1   Choose File > New, to create a document for practice.

2   In the Brushes Libraries Menu button (▣.), from the Decorative category, choose Decorative_Scatter.

3   Use the drawing tools (the Pen or Pencil tool, and any of the basic shapes tools) to draw objects. Use the default fill and stroke colors when you draw.

4   With one of the objects selected, click a brush in the Decorative Scatter panel to apply the brush to the object's path.

As you select a Scatter brush, it is automatically added to the Brushes panel.

5   Repeat step 4 for each object you drew.

6   Double-click on a used Scatter brush listed in the Brushes panel to display the Scatter Brush Options dialog box for one of the brushes you used in step 4, and change the color, size, or other features of the brush. After you close the dialog box, click Apply To Strokes to apply your changes to the brush in the artwork.

🔲 You can also create your own brush libraries. See "Work with brush libraries" in Illustrator Help.

Creating brushes

Use one of the basic shapes tools to create artwork to use as a new Scatter brush.

1   Select a basic Shape tool in the Tools panel, and draw an object, keeping it selected.

2   Click the New Brush button at the bottom of the Brushes panel.

Note: You can use more than one object to create the new brush. All selected objects in the artwork will be included in the brush. If you use a brush to create artwork for a new brush, remember to expand the brush strokes before creating the new brush.

3   In the New Brush dialog box, select New Scatter Brush, and click OK.

The Brush Options dialog box for the new brush appears with the selected objects displayed in the brush example. The new brush is named Scatter Brush 1 by default.

4   Enter a new name for the brush. Then click OK to accept the settings for the brush.

5   Select the Paintbrush tool (✐) and draw a path. The new brush is applied to the path.

6   Double-click the new brush to display the Brush Options dialog box. Change the brush settings to try out different versions of the brush. When finished, click OK.

Review

▶ ## Review questions

1   Describe each of the four brush types: Art, Calligraphic, Pattern, and Scatter.

2   What is the difference between applying a brush to artwork using the Paintbrush tool and applying a brush to artwork using one of the drawing tools?

3   Describe how to edit paths with the Paintbrush tool as you draw. How does the Keep Selected option affect the Paintbrush tool?

4   How do you change the colorization method for an Art, Pattern, or Scatter brush? (Remember, you don't use colorization methods with Calligraphic brushes.)

5   How can you make the Scribble effect more mechanical rather than loose and flowing?

▶ ## Review answers

1   The following are the four brush types:

•   Art brushes stretch artwork evenly along a path. Art brushes include strokes that resemble graphic media (such as the Charcoal-Feather brush used to create the tree). Art brushes also include objects, such as the Arrow brush.

•   Calligraphic brushes are defined by an elliptical shape whose center follows the path. They create strokes that resemble hand-drawn lines made with a flat, angled calligraphic pen tip.

•   Pattern brushes paint a pattern made up of separate sections, or tiles, for the sides (middle sections), ends, and corners of the path. When you apply a Pattern brush to artwork, the brush applies different tiles from the pattern to different sections of the path, depending on where the section falls on the path (at an end, in the middle, or at a corner).

•   Scatter brushes scatter an object, such as a leaf, along a path. You can adjust the Size, Spacing, Scatter, and Rotation options for a Scatter brush to change the brush's appearance.

2   To apply brushes using the Paintbrush tool, you select the tool, choose a brush from the Brushes panel, and draw in the artwork. The brush is applied directly to the paths

as you draw. To apply brushes using a drawing tool, you select the tool and draw in the artwork; then you select the path in the artwork and choose a brush in the Brushes panel. The brush is applied to the selected path.

3   To edit a path with the Paintbrush tool, simply drag over a selected path to redraw it. The Keep Selected option keeps the last path selected as you draw with the Paintbrush tool. Leave the Keep Selected option turned on (the default setting) when you want to easily edit the previous path as you draw. Turn off the Keep Selected option when you want to draw layered paths with the paintbrush without altering previous paths. When the Keep Selected option is turned off, you can use the Selection tool to select a path and then edit the path.

4   To change the colorization method of a brush, double-click the brush in the Brushes panel to view the Brush Options dialog box. Use the Method pop-up menu in the Colorization section to select another method. If you choose Hue Shift, you can use the default color displayed in the dialog box preview; or you can change the key color (the new color that will appear) by clicking the Key Color Eyedropper, and clicking a color in the preview. Click OK to accept the settings and close the Brush Options dialog box. Click Apply to Strokes at the alert message if you want to apply the changes to existing strokes in the artwork.

Existing brush strokes are colorized with the stroke color that was selected when the strokes were applied to the artwork. New brush strokes are colorized with the current stroke color. To change the color of existing strokes after applying a different colorization method, select the strokes and select a new stroke color.

5   Using the Scribble Option, you can keep the choices for Curviness Variation and Spacing Variation to a minimum to make the scribble more mechanical.

Effects are commands that change the look of an object. It's easy to turn two-dimensional artwork into three-dimensional shapes using the 3D effect, apply drop shadows and much more. Effects are live, which means you can apply an effect command to an object and then continue to modify the effect's options or remove the effect at any time using the Appearance panel.

11 | Applying Effects

In this lesson, you'll learn how to do the following:

- Understand the differences between Filters and Effects.
- Use Warp Effects to create a banner logotype.
- Use Pathfinder and Distort and Transform Effects.
- Use Photoshop Effects to add texture to objects.
- Create 3D objects from 2D artwork.
- Map artwork to the faces of the 3D objects.

Getting started

In this lesson, you'll create several objects using the Texture, Warp, 3D Effects features and more in Illustrator CS3. Before you begin, you'll need to restore the default preferences for Adobe Illustrator. Then you'll open a file containing the finished artwork to see what you'll create.

1 To ensure that the tools and panels function exactly as described in this lesson, delete or deactivate (by renaming) the Adobe Illustrator CS3 preferences file. See "Restoring default preferences" on page 3.

2 Start Adobe Illustrator.

Note: If you have not already copied the resource files for this lesson onto your hard disk from the Lesson11 folder from the Adobe Illustrator CS3 Classroom in a Book CD, do so now. See "Copying the Classroom in a Book files" on page 2.

3 Choose File > Open, and open the L11end.ai file in the Lesson11 folder, located inside the Lessons folder within the AICIB folder on your hard drive.

This file displays a completed illustration of a gift certificate.

4   Choose View > Zoom Out to make the finished artwork smaller, adjust the window size, and leave it on your screen as you work. (Use the Hand tool (🖐) to move the artwork where you want it in the window.) If you don't want to leave the image open, choose File > Close.

Using live effects

The Effect menu commands alter the appearance of an object without changing the underlying object. Applying an effect to an object automatically adds the effect to the object's appearance attribute. You can select and edit the effect at any time by double-clicking on the effect in the Appearance panel.

Many Effect commands also appear in the Filter menu, but only the Effect commands are fully editable. Filters change the underlying object, and the changes can't be modified or removed after the filter is applied. But one advantage to reshaping an object with a filter command is that you have immediate access to the new or modified anchor points created by the filter. (An effect must be expanded before you have access to the new points.)

You can apply more than one effect to an object. In this part of the lesson, you'll apply three effects to the lemon—a pathfinder effect to make the inner part of the lemon, a Distort & Transform effect to finish the inner part of the lemon, and a texture using a Photoshop effect called Grain to create the rind.

The finished Gift Certificate.

1   Choose File > Open, and open the L11start.ai file in the Lesson11 folder, located inside the Lessons folder within the AICIB folder on your hard drive.

LOTS O' LEMON

2   Choose File > Save As. In the Save As dialog box, name the file **Gift.ai**, and choose the Lesson11 folder. Leave the file format set to Illustrator (*.AI), and click Save. In the Illustrator Options dialog box, leave the Illustrator options at their default settings, and click OK.

3   Use the Hand tool (✋) to move the artwork to the left so you can see off the right side of the artboard. There are several pieces to a logo, including a lemon.

4   Select the Star tool (✰) in the Tools panel. Click once on the page and in the star dialog box enter **80 pt** for Radius 1, **14.5 pt** for Radius 2 and **12 pt** for Points, click OK. Don't worry about the stroke or the fill of the star. You are using it to punch through the yellow shape beneath it to create the lemon wedges.

5   With the Selection tool, position the star over the unfinished lemon in the lower right corner off the artboard.

Note: Make sure to position the star so that it leaves a straight edge at the top of the lemon.

6   Shift + click on the center lemon shape to choose the star and the top gradient filled shape, then choose Object > Group to group them together.

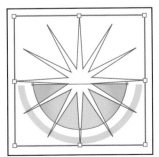

Set the star settings.   *Position the star and group the objects.*

7   Choose Effect > Pathfinder > Subtract to subtract the top shape (the star) from the bottom shape (the lemon part). It will still look like two separate shapes when selected. To commit to the effect, choose Object > Expand Appearance.

Effects are live, which means that they are still editable. To commit to the effect and change the underlying object, you can expand the appearance.

Effect > Pathfinder > Subtract
and Expand Appearance result.

Next you will change the appearance of the wedges you just created using the Roughen effect.

8   With the lemon wedge shapes still selected, choose Effect > Distort & Transform > Roughen. In the roughen dialog box, choose 3% for Size, 13/in for the Detail and the Smooth option. Click OK.

You can experiment with these settings, but you will change them later in this lesson.

9   Choose Select > Deselect to deselect the shapes.

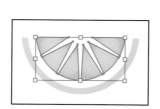
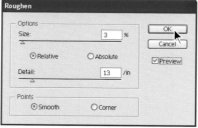

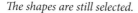

The shapes are still selected.   *Change the Roughen settings.*   *The result.*

10   Choose the Selection tool (➤) in the Tools panel. Then click to select the yellow edge of the lemon.

You will next apply an effect to the lemon rind to make it look more realistic.

11 With the lemon edge selected, choose Effect > Texture > Grain to open the Effect Gallery. In the Grain settings on the right, choose **49** for Intensity, **55** for Contrast and the Clumped Grain Type. Click OK.

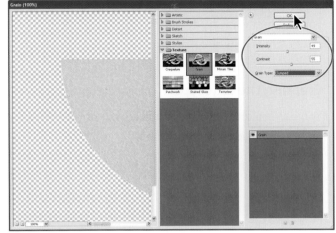

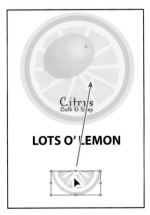

Object selected.

Edit the Grain effect settings in the Effect Gallery.

12 With the Selection tool still selected, drag across the shapes that make up the lemon slice and choose Object > Group to group them together. Drag the lemon slice onto the Citrus logo above it.

13 Choose the Rotate tool (⟳) and from the upper right corner, click and drag around the right corner to rotate the lemon slice. Choose Select > Deselect.

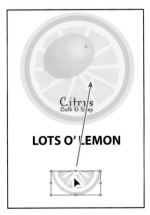
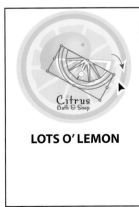
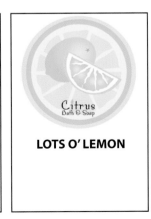

14 Choose File > Save to save your work.

Next you will create a warp effect with the text and then edit the effect.

Creating a banner logo with the Warp effect

You will use a Warp effect to create the banner logo. Warp effects distort objects, including paths, text, meshes, blends, and raster images. Because Warp effects are live, you can apply a warp to your artwork, and then continue to modify or remove the effect at any time using the Appearance panel.

Creating the logotype

You can make a warp from objects in your artwork, or you can use a preset warp shape or a mesh object as an envelope.

1   Choose the Selection tool (⬆) in the Tools panel. Then click to select the "Lots O' Lemon" type.

2   Choose Effect > Warp > Rise.

3   In the Warp Options dialog box, select Preview to preview the effect of changes.

4   Drag the Warp Options dialog box by its title bar so you can see the dialog box and the selected type in the artwork.

5   Set the Bend amount to **93%** to create a ribbon effect. Click OK.

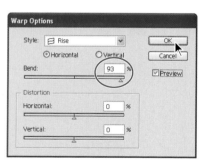
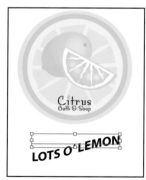

Use the Warp effect to distort the text.

6   With the Selection tool (⬆), click on the ":Lots O' Lemon" type if it is not still selected, and while holding the Shift key down, drag it up into the center of the Citrus logo above it.

7   Choose Object > Arrange Bring to Front if it's not on the top of the other objects.

8   Choose File > Save to save your work.

Stylizing the banner and logotype

To complete the banner and logotype, you'll add some sophistication by offsetting a stroke around the text and adding a colored drop shadow.

1   With the Selection tool (▲), click on the "Lots O' Lemon" type if it is not still selected.

2   If the Appearance panel is not visible, choose Window > Appearance.
Notice that the Appearance panel lists the Warp: Rise effect that has been applied to the text.

3   From the Appearance panel menu (▤), choose Add New Stroke. Leave the color as black, and in the Control panel choose a stroke weight from the pop-up menu of **1pt**.
You can add multiple strokes to one object, and apply different effects to each one, giving you the opportunity to create unique and interesting artwork.

Add a new stroke.

4   With the Stroke selected in the Appearance panel, choose Effect > Path > Offset Path. Change the Offset to **2 pt**, and click OK. This creates an outline around the text.

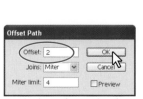

Apply the Offset Path effect.   *The result.*

Now you will add a colored drop shadow to the text.

5   In the Appearance panel, click on the word Type. This assures that the drop shadow applies to the text and not to just the offset stroke.

6   Choose Effect > Stylize > Drop Shadow, and check the Preview checkbox. Change the X Offset to **4 pt**, the Y Offset to **4 pt**, and the Blur to **2 pt**.

7   Click on the color square to the right of the Color radio button. Pick an orange color. (We picked C=10%, M=50%, Y=75%, K=0%.) Click OK.

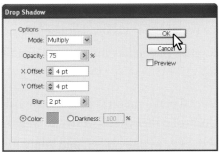

Select Type on the   Change the Drop Shadow options,   The result.
Appearance panel.   including the shadow color.

8   Click OK to close the Drop Shadow dialog box.

9   With the Selection tool, click off the artwork to deselect, or choose Select > Deselect.

10   File > Save.

Editing an effect

Effects are live, so they can be edited once applied to an object. This can be done within the Appearance panel by double-clicking on the name of the effect. This will display that effect's dialog box. Changes you make will update the artwork. In this section, you will edit the drop shadow effect applied to the text.

1   With the Selection tool (➤), click on the "Lots O' Lemon" text and make sure that the Appearance panel is showing. If it isn't, choose Window > Appearance or click on the panel icon.

2   Double-click on the Drop Shadow effect listed. You may need to scroll down in the Appearance panel to see this.

3   In the Drop Shadow dialog box that appears, change the Opacity value to 50% and click OK.

4   To finish off, choose the Selection tool and drag across all of the logo parts. Choose Object > Group to group them together.

5   Click on the Symbols panel icon or choose Window > Symbols to reveal the Symbols panel. Drag the grouped logo onto the Symbols panel to create a symbol. In the Symbol Options dialog box that appears, name the symbol Can top and choose Graphic as the symbol Type. Click OK.

To learn more about symbols, visit Lesson 13, "Working with Symbols."

6   Choose Select > Deselect and save the file by choosing File >Save. Keep this file open for the next lesson.

Creating the 3D cylinder

In this part of the lesson, you'll use two-dimensional shapes as the foundation for creating three-dimensional objects. Using the 3D effect, you can control the appearance of 3D objects with lighting, shading, rotation, and other properties.

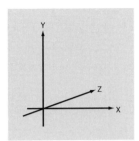

The 3D effect takes advantage of the x, y, and z axes.

There are three ways to create a 3D object:

• Extrude and Bevel—Extends a 2D object along the object's z axis to add depth to the object. For example, if you extrude a 2D ellipse, it becomes a cylinder.

• Revolve—Sweeps a path or profile in a circular direction around the global y axis (revolve axis) to create a 3D object.

• Rotate—Uses the z axis to rotate 2D artwork in 3D space and change the artwork's perspective.

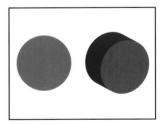 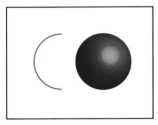 

Extrude and Bevel.   *Revolve.*   *Rotate.*

Using the 3D Extrude effect

In this next section, you will create a can to hold the soap for which you have already created a label.

1   Choose the Ellipse tool (◯) from the Tools panel. Below the "Lots O' Lemon" logo off the artboard on the right, click and release below the logo. In the Ellipse options dialog box, type **285 pt** into the Width text field, and click on the word Height. The values are entered equally, then click OK.

2   Fill the shape with the color Can Yellow from the Swatches panel. Click on the Stroke box in the Control panel and set the Stroke to None (◻).

3   Choose Effect > 3D > Extrude and Bevel, check the Preview checkbox. Click on the title bar of the options window, and drag it to a location that allows you to see your artwork.

The Extrude and Bevel effect has taken the two-dimensional circle and extruded it using the default settings. You will change several options, including the depth and edges.

4   First, click on the gray track cube face on the left side of the dialog box. Experiment with rotating the object in space by clicking and dragging the cube. When you are finished experimenting, choose Off-Axis Bottom from the Position pop-up menu.

5   Make the cylinder taller by using the Extrude Depth slider or typing 75 into the Extrude Depth text field. Check off and on the Preview checkbox to refresh the image.

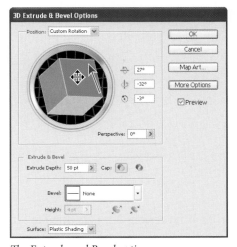

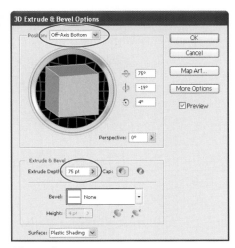

The Extrude and Bevel options.   *The result.*

Cap On or Cap Off?

In the Extrude and Bevel section of the 3D Options window for the Extrude and Bevel effect and the Revolve section of the 3D Options window for the Revolve 3D effect you have a choice to make your object appear solid or hollow.

- Click the Revolve Cap On button to make the object appear solid.
- Click the Revolve Cap Off button to make the object appear hollow.

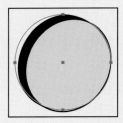 

Cap On.   *Cap Off.*

6   Using the Bevel pop-up menu, experiment with the choice of different bevels to see different variations of edge effects you can easily create.

If you select a bevel from the Bevel pop-up menu, you can add beveling properties to carve away from, or add to the object's surface.

- The Extent Out (🝰) button adds the bevel to the object's shape.
- The Extent In (🝰) button carves the bevel out of the object's original shape.

7   When you are finished experimenting, return to None in the Bevel pop-up menu.

The result.

Note: 3D objects may display anti-aliasing artifacts on screen, but these artifacts disappear when the object is rasterized. Read more about rasterization in the flattening section of Lesson 15, "Printing Artwork and Producing Color Separations."

8   Click OK. Leave the object selected.

9   File > Save. Leave the file open for the next lesson.

Applying the Symbol as mapped artwork

You can apply any 2D artwork stored as a symbol in the Symbols panel to selected surfaces on your 3D object.

Every 3D object is composed of several surfaces. For example, the shape that you just created has three external surfaces. It has a top, a bottom, and a side surface that wraps around the shape. In this next section, you will take the Lots O' Lemon logo that you created and map it to the cylinder.

To map artwork to a 3D object

The following is some helpful information about mapping artwork to 3D objects.

• To move the symbol, position the cursor inside the bounding box and drag; to scale, drag a side or corner handle; to rotate, drag outside and near a bounding box handle.

• To make the mapped artwork fit to the boundaries of the selected surface, click Scale To Fit.

• To remove artwork from a single surface, select the surface using the Surface options, and then either choose None from the Symbol menu or click Clear.

• To remove all maps from all of the 3D object's surfaces, click Clear All.

• To shade and apply the object's lighting to the mapped artwork, select Shade Artwork.

• To show only the artwork map, not the geometry of a 3D object, select Invisible Geometry. This is useful when you want to use the 3D mapping feature as a three-dimensional warping tool. For example, you could use this option to map text to the side of an extruded wavy line, so that the text appears warped as if on a flag.

—From Illustrator Help

1   Since you are editing the existing Extrude and Bevel effect, locate the Appearance panel. Choose Window > Appearance if it is not visible, and double-click on 3D Extrude and Bevel. When the 3D Extrude and Bevel Options appear, drag the window to the side so that you can see your artwork as you make changes.

Note: Any time that you apply an effect, double-click on the named effect in the Appearance panel to edit it. If you were to choose Effect > 3D > Extrude and Bevel again with the can still selected, it would add another instance of the effect unless you cancelled the operation.

2   In the 3D Extrude and Bevel Options dialog box, click Map Art, and check Preview. When the Map Art dialog box appears, notice the options to select a Symbol and a Surface. A window for positioning the mapped artwork appears below.

3   Click on the single arrow to navigate from one surface to another. Notice that as you rotate through the surfaces, a red highlight appears, indicating what surface you have active in the preview window.

4   Choose 1 of 3. You see the top of the cylinder in the preview panel.

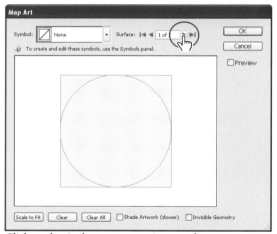

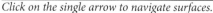

Click on the single arrow to navigate surfaces.

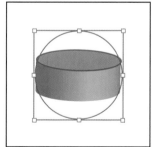

The highlighted surface.

5 From the Symbol pop-up menu, choose the Symbol named Can top.

The Can top Symbol is placed in the preview panel.

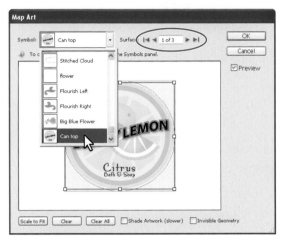

Select the Symbol.   *The result.*

6 In Surface, click on the single arrow and choose 3 of 3.

7 Choose Leaves from the Symbol pop-up window.

8 Use the preview panel to position the Leaves. In this position, the light gray area is visible. Click Shade Artwork to have the side and top art shaded.

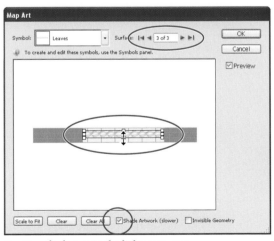

Position the leaves in the light gray area.   *The result.*

9 Click OK, and click OK again.

10 Choose File > Save.

Creating a revolved object

In this next lesson you will create a lemon in the shape of a sphere. To begin with, create an arc that will be revolved to create the sphere.

1 Choose the Rectangle tool (▣) and click once on the artboard away from the artwork. When the Rectangle options dialog box appears, type **85 pt** for the Width and **100 pt** for the Height. Click OK.

2 Press D to return the rectangle back to the default colors of black stroke and white fill.

3 Press Ctrl+5 (Windows) or Command+5 (Mac OS) or choose View > Guides > Make Guides, to turn the rectangle into a custom guide.

4 As a default, guides are locked. To verify that guides are locked, choose View > Guides. If there is a check mark to the left of Lock Guides, they are locked. If there is no check mark, choose Lock Guides to lock them.

5 Using the Pen tool (✒), click on the lower right corner of the rectangle guide, hold the Shift key down and drag to the left until the endpoint of the direction line reaches the lower left corner, and release. This creates a directional line.

6 Click on the upper right corner and holding the Shift key down, drag to the right until the endpoint of the directional line reaches the upper left corner and release. You have created an arc.

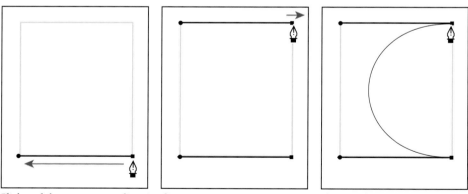

Click and drag to create a direction line.   The complete arc.

7 Choose View > Guides > Clear Guides.

8 Using the Selection tool, make sure the arc is selected.

9   Click on the Fill box in the Control panel. When the Swatches panel appears choose None (☑).

10   Click on the Stroke box in the Control panel. When the Swatches panel appears choose Can Yellow.

11   Choose Effect > 3D > Revolve. Click on Preview to see your changes.

The Revolve option appears. The options appear similar to the Extrude options, but have quite a different effect.

12   Leave the position at the default position of Off-Axis Front.

13   Change the edge from Left Edge to Right Edge. Your arc revolves around the designated edge. The result varies dramatically depending upon the side that you choose. Leave it set to Right Edge. Click OK.

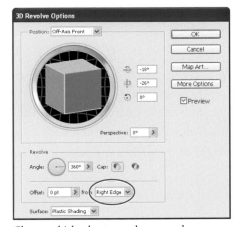

Choose which edge to revolve around.   *Revolve with Left Edge selected.*   *Revolve with Right Edge selected.*

14   File > Save, and keep the file open for the next lesson.

Changing the lighting

In this next lesson, you will use additional options to change the strength and direction of the light source.

1   With the lemon shape selected, double-click on 3D Revolve in the Appearance panel. If the Appearance panel is not visible, choose Window > Appearance. You may also need to scroll in the Appearance panel.

2   Check the Preview checkbox, and click More Options.

Using More Options gives you the opportunity to create custom lighting effects on your 3D object. You will use the preview window in the lower left to reposition the lighting and change the shade color.

3   From the Surface pop-up menu, choose Diffuse Shading.

4   In the preview window, click and drag the white square that represents the light source. This changes the direction of the lighting. For this exercise, drag the light source to the top of the object. Click on the New Light button to add another light source to the lemon shape. Drag the second light source to the right.

*Move the light source by dragging it
and change the Surface.*

5   Click on the Shading Color pop-up menu, and select Custom. Click on the colored Red square to the right of Custom and use the Color Picker to select a dark yellow color, or enter values in the color text fields to the right of the picker window (we used C=0%, M=19%, Y=100%, B=50%), then click OK.

The yellow shape now has a dark yellow shading applied to it.

What are Blend Steps?

Clicking More Options in the 3D options window reveals the Surface option called Blend Steps. Blend Steps controls how smoothly the shading appears across the object's surfaces. Enter a value between 1 and 256. Higher numbers produce smoother shades and more paths than lower numbers.

As a default, this amount is low in order to quickly generate the blend and provide the optimum number of steps for artwork that is viewed on your computer monitor or on the Internet. This low number may cause banding (large, visible shifts of value from one tone to the next) when printing. To learn more about techniques used to avoid banding in gradients, read "To calculate the maximum blend length for gradients" in Illustrator Help.

6   Change the Ambient Light to **40%**, then click OK.

Ambient light controls the brightness on the surface uniformly.

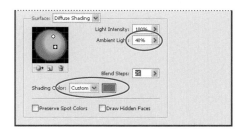

7   Position the lemon closer to the soap tin.

8   Choose File > Save.

Mapping a Photoshop image

You can map artwork from Illustrator and also import artwork from other applications, such as Photoshop. In this next part of the lesson, you will place a Photoshop texture into the document, and apply it to the lemon.

1   Choose File > Place, and locate the image named Lemonskin.psd in the Lesson11 folder. Make sure that Link is unchecked. Files to be used as symbols must be embedded. Click Place.

2   With the Symbols panel visible, use the Selection tool (➤) to drag the image into the Symbols panel. Enter the name newTexture into the Symbol Options dialog box and choose Graphic from the Type option.

3   Delete the placed image.

4   Select the lemon, and double-click on 3D Revolve in the Appearance panel.

5   Click on Map Art, and then select the outer surface of the lemon. You may have one or more surfaces if the arc edges are not perfectly aligned. Use the Next Surface arrow pointing to right to navigate through the surfaces and choose the one that highlights the outer surface.

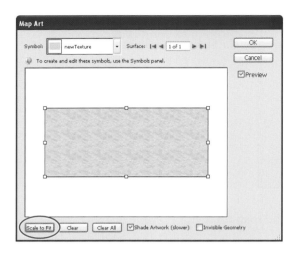

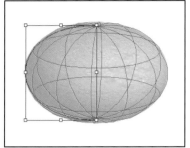

6 Once the surface is located, choose the newTexture symbol from the Symbol pop-up menu.

Note: If you pick the wrong surface to apply the symbol to, choose Clear to clear the symbol and try mapping to another surface.

7 Press Scale to Fit, and check Shade Art. Click OK, and OK again.

Map a Photoshop image.

The texture now wraps around the lemon shape. Next you will clone the 3D objects to add more to the artboard.

8 Using the Selection tool, select the lemon shape you just created. Hold down the Alt (Windows) or Option (Mac OS) key, and drag the shape next to itself (to the left and down), releasing the mouse first. This clones the shape and gives you a total of two spheres. Move them closer to the tin and choose Object > Arrange > Bring to Front so that they are in front of the tin.

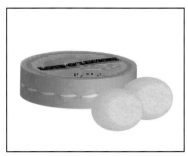

Use Alt/Option to clone the sphere.

Adjusting the lighting

Since 3D objects do not share lighting, you will edit the existing Extrude and Bevel applied to the ellipse you used to create the soap tin.

1   Using the Selection tool (➤), click on the Lemon soap tin.

2   Double-click on 3D Extrude and Bevel to open the 3D options window.

3   In the lighting preview pane, drag the light to the top of the shape. This makes the lighting more consistent with the lemon shapes. We added a second light source to the tin in a similar position to where it was on the sphere. Click OK.

4   With the Selection tool still selected, select the tin and both spheres by Shift+clicking or dragging across them. Move them onto the artboard in the middle of the gift certificate.

Off the artboard on the right, there is a green stem. You can place that on one of the lemons if you like. Choose Object > Arrange > Bring to Front if it disappears.

5   Choose File > Save. Leave the file open for the next lesson.

The completed illustration with a green stem added.

💡 *Once you have applied the 3D effect to an object, it remains a live effect. In other words, you can change the scale of the object or change the color, and the 3D effect remains.*

Note: Do not rotate objects with the 3D effects applied to them; you will get unexpected results. To rotate a 3D object, double-click on the Appearance panel 3D effect, and rotate the item in space using the Position preview window.

6   Once you have rearranged objects as you like, you have completed the lesson. Choose File > Save, then choose File > Close.

Exploring on your own

On your own, try to create an additional item for the artwork in this lesson. Choose File > Open, and locate the file in the Lesson11 folder named L11strt2.ai.

1   Choose the Selection tool, and then Select > All.

2   Drag the artwork into the Symbols panel.

3   Double-click on the Symbol in the Symbols panel and name it **Soap**.

4   With the artwork still selected, choose Edit > Clear, or press the Delete key.

5   Choose the Rectangle tool (▭), and click once on the artboard. Enter the values of **325 pt** for the width and **220 pt** for the height; click OK.

6   Choose Effect > 3D > Extrude and Bevel, and experiment with different positions and settings.

7   Choose Map Art, and map the Symbol that you created (Soap) to the top of the box.

8   Click OK and then click OK again when you are finished.

Take the illustration further by creating your own symbols and applying them to the other faces of the box.

Creating your own revolved artwork

This is when you have the opportunity to create your own 3D shape. In this next lesson you will create a path and adjust the offset to create a vase. An example of the path that we use is in the file named paths.ai in the Lesson11 folder, but it can be much more worthwhile to apply your own path and see the interesting results you can achieve.

1   Choose View > Show Rulers, or Ctrl+R (Windows) or Command+R (Mac OS).

2   Create a vertical guide by clicking on the vertical ruler and dragging it out to a blank area on your artboard.

3   Choose the Pen tool (✒) and create a vertical path with several curves, representing the curves that will be replicated in the 3D shape. If it is easier, use the Pencil tool (✏) to draw a path. The size of the path is not important at this time, it can be scaled later.

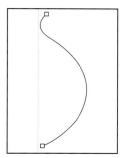

Create a path to revolve.

4   Using the Fill box in the Control panel, select a color for the fill, and choose None in the Stroke fill box.

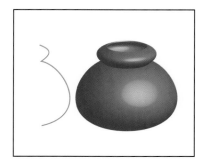

Example of curves and the resulting 3D shape.

5   Choose Effect > 3D > Revolve, and check the Preview checkbox.

6   Depending upon the effect you want to achieve, you can change the axis from the Left Edge to the Right Edge.

7   To make the 3D object wider, choose an offset. The slider moves rather quickly, so type **50** into the Offset text field. If necessary, uncheck and recheck Preview to see the results.

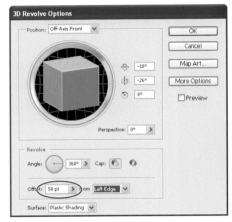

Offset at 50 pt.   *Result.*

If the lighting options are not visible, click on the More Options button to add an additional light source to the vase.

8   In the lighting preview window, click on the New button (⊠) to add another light source. Position the lights so that one is on the lower left and the other is in the upper right of the preview object.

9   Change the Ambient Light to **25%**.

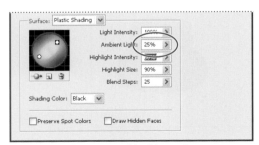

Click the new button to add additional light sources.

10   Click OK.

11   File > Close and don't save the file.

Review

Review questions

1 What are the three types of 3D effects that are available? Give a good example of why you would use each one.

2 How can you control lighting on a 3D object? Does one 3D object's lighting affect other 3D objects.

3 What are the steps to mapping artwork to an object?

4 Once a 3D object is created, what is the best way to rotate it?

Review answers

1 Using the 3D effect, you can choose from Extrude and Bevel, Revolve, and Rotate.

• Extrude and Bevel—Uses the z axis to give a 2D object depth by extruding the object. For example, a circle becomes a cylinder.

• Revolve—Uses the y axis to revolve an object around an axis. For example, an arc becomes a circle.

• Rotate—Uses the z axis to rotate 2D artwork in 3D space and change the artwork's perspective.

2 By clicking the More Options button in the 3D options window, you can change the light, the direction of the light, and the shade color. Options for one 3D object's lighting do not affect other 3D objects.

3   Map an artwork to an object by following these steps:

a Select the artwork and hold down the Alt/Option key and click on the New Symbol icon in the Symbols panel.

b Select the object that is to be 3D and choose Effects > 3D > Extrude and Bevel or Revolve.

c Click on Map Art.

d Select the surface using the arrows.

e From the Symbol pop-up menu, select the symbol.

f Click OK, and then click OK again.

4   Once you have created a 3D object, it is best to double-click on the 3D effect in the Appearance panel and use the Position preview window to position it in space. Using the Rotate tool will lead to unexpected results.

You can alter the look of an object without changing its structure using appearance attributes—fills, strokes, effects, transparency, blending modes, or any combination of these object properties. You can edit or remove appearance attributes. You can also save them as Graphic styles and apply them to other objects. You can also edit an object that has a Graphic style applied to it, plus edit the Graphic style—an enormous time-saver!

12 | Applying Appearance Attributes and Graphic Styles

In this lesson, you'll learn how to do the following:

- Create an appearance attribute.

- Reorder appearance attributes and apply them to layers.

- Copy and remove appearance attributes.

- Save an appearance as a Graphic Style.

- Apply a Graphic Style to a layer.

- Select appropriate resolution settings for printing or exporting files with transparency.

Getting started

In this lesson, you'll enhance the basic design for a Web page by applying appearance attributes and Graphic Styles to the type, background, and three buttons on the page. Before you begin, you'll restore the default preferences for Adobe Illustrator CS3. Then you will open the finished art file for this lesson to see what you'll create.

1 To ensure that the tools and panels function exactly as described in this lesson, delete or deactivate (by renaming) the Adobe Illustrator CS3 preferences file. See "Restoring default preferences" on page 3 in the Introduction.

2 Start Adobe Illustrator CS3.

Note: If you have not already copied the resource files for this lesson onto your hard disk from the Lesson12 folder from the Adobe Illustrator CS3 Classroom in a Book CD, do so now. See "Copying the Classroom in a Book files" on page 2.

3   Choose File > Open, and open the L12end.ai file located in the Lesson12 folder inside the Lessons folder within the AICIB folder on your hard drive.

The artwork in this file is a design mock-up of a Web home page. The design for the completed page includes several Graphic Styles and effects, including overlapping gradients, transparent type, Drop Shadows, and texturized and shaded graphics.

4   If you like, choose View > Zoom Out to make the design mock-up smaller, adjust the window size, and leave it on-screen as you work. (Use the Hand tool ( ) to move the artwork where you want it in the window.) If you don't want to leave the artwork open, choose File > Close.

Note: The final version (L12end.ai) does not have text on the red circle. You will be adding that to the file for practice later in the lesson.

Document Startup Profiles

In Adobe Illustrator CS3, there are New Document Profiles that set up a document for print, web, video, and more. For example, if you are designing a web page mock-up, you could use a Web Document Profile, which automatically displays the page size and units in web settings (pixels), changes the Color Mode to RGB, and the Raster Effects to 72 ppi. Details relating to Raster Effects are found in Lesson 15, "Printing Artwork and Producing Color Separations."

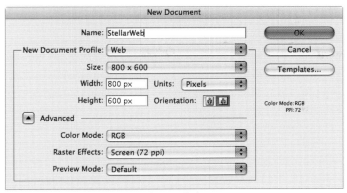

New Document dialog box set for a web document.

Using appearance attributes

You can apply appearance attributes to any object, group, or layer by using effects and the Appearance and Graphic Styles panels. An appearance attribute is an aesthetic property—such as a fill, stroke, transparency, or effect—that affects the look of an object, but does not affect its basic structure. An appearance attribute can be changed or removed at any time without changing the underlying object or any other attributes applied to the object.

The advantage to using the Appearance panel to add effects or other attributes is that these effects or other attributes can be selected and edited at any time.

For example, if you apply a Drop Shadow effect to an object, at any time, you can change the drop shadow distance, blur, or color. You can also copy that effect and apply it to other shapes, groups, or layers. You can even save it as a Graphic Style and use it for other objects or other files. In contrast, if you create a drop shadow by applying the Drop Shadow filter to an object, you cannot edit the filter results, copy the filter effect, or apply it to other objects globally

The Appearance panel contains the following types of editable attributes:

* **Stroke** lists some stroke attributes (stroke type, brush, color transparency, and effects). All other stroke attributes are displayed in the Stroke panel.

* **Fill** lists all fill attributes (fill type, color, transparency, and effects).

- **Transparency** lists opacity and blending mode.

- **Effect** lists commands in the Effect menu.

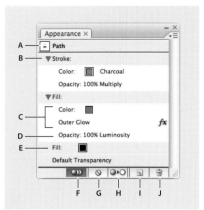

A. Selected Object.
B. Stroke color with paintbrush and opacity applied.
C. Fill color and Effect applied.
D. Fill opacity and blending mode.
E. Second fill color and effects.
F. New Art Has Basic Appearance.
G. Clear Appearance.
H. Reduce to Basic Appearance.
I. Duplicate Selected Item.
J. Delete Selected Item.

Note: Later in this lesson, you will learn about flattening artwork using effects that take advantage of transparency. Flattening is an easy and necessary step for files that will be printed. If your artwork is to be printed, make sure that you create files in the CMYK color mode. Flattening is not necessary if your final output is for the Web.

Adding appearance attributes

You'll start by selecting the star shape and adding to its basic appearance using the Appearance panel.

1   Choose File > Open, and open the L12start.ai file, located in the Lesson12 folder inside the Lessons folder within the AICIB folder on your hard drive.

2   Choose File > Save As. In the Save As dialog box, name the file **StellarWeb.ai**, and choose the Lesson12 folder. Leave the file format set to Illustrator (*.AI), and click Save. In the Illustrator Options dialog box, accept the default settings and click OK.

3   Choose Window > Workspace > [Panel].

4   Using the Selection tool (↖), select the star shape.

5   Click on the Layers tab to open the Layers panel. In the Layers panel, expand the Star Button layer so that you can see its contents. Notice that the star shape is selected, as indicated by the square to the right of the layer name, and its path is targeted, as indicated by the circle icon (◎) to the right of the path name.

6   Notice the stroke and fill attributes of the star shape listed in the Appearance panel. (If the panel isn't visible on-screen, choose Window > Appearance to display it; a check mark indicates that the panel is open on-screen.)

Star selected.

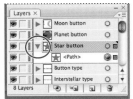
Expanded Star Button layer.

Stroke and fill attributes.

7   In the Appearance panel, click the Stroke attribute to select it.

Selecting the Stroke attribute lets you change just the stroke in the artwork.

8   In the Transparency panel, choose Multiply from the blending mode pop-up menu.

You can expand and collapse the stroke attributes in the Appearance panel by clicking the triangle (▸) to the left of the attribute in the panel list.

9   While continuing to use the Selection tool, press and hold the Ctrl+spacebar (Windows) or Command+spacebar (Mac OS) and click the star shape to zoom in to about 200%. Inspect the stroke around the star to see how it has changed. The effect of the Multiply blending mode is similar to drawing on a page with transparent marker pens.

Strokes are centered on a path outline—half of the stroke color overlaps the filled star shape and half of the stroke color overlaps the background gradient.

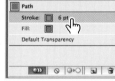
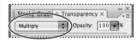

Selected star shape.   *Select Stroke.*   *Choose Multiply blending mode.*

Reordering appearance attributes

Now you'll change the appearance of the Multiply blending mode by rearranging the attributes in the Appearance panel.

1   Resize the Appearance panel so that you can view all of its contents. Click the Fill attribute and drag it above the Stroke attribute. (This technique is similar to dragging layers in the Layers panel to adjust their stacking order.)

 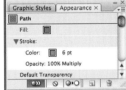 

Drag Fill attribute above Stroke attribute.   *The result.*

Moving the Fill attribute above the Stroke attribute changes the look of the Multiply blending modes on the stroke. Half the stroke has been covered up. Blending modes work only on objects that are beneath them in the stacking order.

You'll now add another stroke to the object using the Appearance panel.

2   With the star shape still selected, choose Add New Stroke from the Appearance panel menu (⊡≡). A stroke is added to the top of the appearance list. It has the same color and stroke weight as the first stroke.

3   In the Color panel, click on the panel menu button (⊡≡) and choose Show Options from the panel menu. RGB should be chosen, but if not, choose it from the panel menu, and then use the sliders or text fields to change the color to a dark orange. (We used a color mix of R=255, G= 73, and B=0.)

RGB color mode is chosen because you are working with a Web document.

4   Type **2 pt** into the Stroke weight text field in the Control panel. Press Enter or Return.

You'll rearrange the order of the appearance attributes to prepare for adding live effects in the next part of the lesson.

5   In the Appearance panel, click on the triangle to the left of the 6-point Stroke attribute to collapse the attribute, then drag it to the very top of the Appearance attributes list. (It should be directly above the 2-point stroke.)

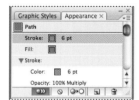
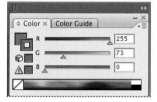

Add new stroke.   *Change stroke color.*   *Rearrange stroke order.*

6   Choose Select > Deselect and then File > Save to save the artwork.

Using Graphic Styles

A Graphic Style is a named set of appearance attributes. By applying different Graphic Styles, you can quickly and globally change the appearance of an object.

For example, you may have a symbol on a map that represents a city, with a Graphic Style applied that paints the symbol green with a drop shadow. You can use that Graphic Style to paint all of the cities' symbols on the map. If you change your mind, you can change the fill color of the style to blue. All the symbols painted with that Graphic Style will then be updated automatically.

The Graphic Styles panel lets you create, name, save, and apply various effects and attributes to objects, layers, or groups. Just like attributes and effects, Graphic Styles are completely reversible. For example, you could apply a style to a circle that contains the Zig Zag effect, turning the circle into a starburst. You can revert the object to its original appearance with the Appearance panel, or you can break the link with that Graphic Style and edit one of its attributes without affecting other objects that are painted with the same Graphic Style.

Graphic Styles can also be applied to text. Adobe Illustrator CS3 allows you to preserve the color of type when applying a graphic style by deselecting Override Character Color from the Graphic Styles panel menu.

Creating and saving a Graphic Style

Now you'll save and name a new Graphic Style using the appearance attributes you just created for the star button.

1   Click the Graphic Styles tab to bring the panel to the front of its group. (If the Graphic Styles panel isn't visible on-screen, choose Window > Graphic Styles; a check mark indicates that the panel is open on-screen.)

2   Drag the Graphic Styles panel from the Dock on the right side of the workspace by the panel tab. Resize the Graphic Styles panel so that all the default styles are visible and there is empty space at the bottom.

3   Make sure that the star shape is still selected so that its appearance attributes are displayed in the Appearance panel.

The appearance attributes are stored in the appearance thumbnail, named Path, in the Appearance panel.

4   In the Appearance panel, drag the Path appearance thumbnail onto the Graphic Styles panel.

5   When a thick black border appears on the inside of the panel, release the mouse button. The border indicates that you are adding a new style to the panel.

The path thumbnail in the Appearance panel will change to "Path: Graphic Style."

Drag object's appearance thumbnail onto Styles panel to save appearance attributes as new style.

6   In the Graphic Styles panel, choose Graphic Style Options from the panel menu. Name the new style **Star Glow**. Click OK.

Notice in the Appearance panel that Path is now followed by Path: Star Glow. This indicates that a graphic style called star glow is applied to the selected object.

7   Choose Select > Deselect to deselect the star shape, and then choose File > Save.

Applying a Graphic Style to a layer

Once a Graphic Style is applied to a layer, everything added to that layer will have that same style applied to it. Now you'll create a new Graphic Style, and apply it to a layer. Then you'll create a few new shapes on that layer to see the effect of the style.

1   Choose Window > Workspace > [Panel].

2   In the Appearance panel, click the Clear Appearance button at the bottom of the panel. Then select the No Selection appearance name or thumbnail.

The Clear Appearance option removes all appearance attributes applied to an object, including any stroke or fill.

3   Choose Effect > Stylize > Drop Shadow.

Use the default settings. If desired, click the radio button to the left of the color swatch in the Drop Shadow dialog box, then click on the color swatch to change the shadow color. (We picked a red color of R=215, G=65, and B=4.) Click OK to exit the Color Picker, and click OK again to apply the effect.

Note: Because the Drop Shadow appearance has no stroke or fill, its thumbnail will be blank. Once attributes are applied to a shape, the drop shadow will appear.

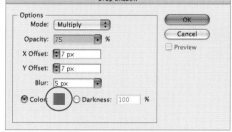

Clear Appearance.   *Choose Effect > Drop Shadow and edit.*   *Result.*

When creating a new style, the Graphic Style panel automatically uses the current appearance attributes displayed in the Appearance panel.

4   In the Graphic Styles panel, Alt+click (Windows) or Option+click (Mac OS) the New Graphic Style button at the bottom of the panel, and type **Drop Shadow** as the name of the new style. Click OK.

Now you'll target the Planet Button layer, to apply a drop shadow to all the shapes on that layer.

5   In the Layers panel, click the triangle to the left of the Planet button layer to expand the layer. Then click the target indicator (◎) to the right of the Planet button layer. (Be careful not to target the mesh-filled path, the <Mesh> sublayer. If you target the path, only the planet shape will have a drop shadow.)

6   In the Graphic Styles panel, click the Drop Shadow style to apply the style to the layer.

7   Choose Select > Deselect to deselect the planet shape.

Now you'll test the layer effect by adding some shapes to the Planet Button layer.

8   Select the Star tool (☆) in the same group as the Rectangle tool (▢) in the Tools panel.

9   Click the Color tab to bring the panel to the front of its group, or choose Window > Color to display it. In the Color panel, choose a fill color (we used R=129, G=23, B=136 for a purple color) and a stroke of None.

10   With the Planet Button layer still selected, draw several small stars around the planet shape.

Because the Drop Shadow style contains only an effect, and no stroke or fill, the objects retain their original stroke and fill attributes.

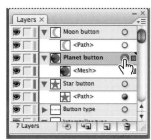

Layer targeted.   *Graphic Style applied to layer.*   *Stylized artwork added to layer.*

11 Notice the following icons on the right side of a layer in the Layers panel, indicating whether any appearance attributes are applied to the layer or whether it is targeted:

(◉) Indicates that the layer, group, or object is targeted but has no appearance attributes applied to it.

(○) Indicates that the layer, group, or object is not targeted and has no appearance attributes applied to it.

(◉) Indicates that the layer, group, or object is not targeted but has appearance attributes applied to it.

(◉) Indicates that the group is targeted and has appearance attributes applied to it. This icon also designates any targeted object that has appearance attributes more complex than a single fill and stroke applied to it.

12 Choose File > Save to save the artwork.

Applying existing Graphic Styles

Adobe Illustrator comes with a panel of pre-made Graphic Styles that you can apply to your artwork. Now you'll finish the button designs by adding an existing style to the Moon button layer.

It is a good idea to use the Layers panel to select the objects or layers to which you want to apply styles. Effects or styles vary, depending on whether you're targeting either a layer or an object, or group within a layer. Now you'll select the Moon button shape, not the layer.

1 In the Layers panel, click the triangle (▶) to expand the Moon button layer.

2 Select the <Path> sublayer to select it. Then click the target indicator (◉) to the right of the <Path> sublayer to target it. Targeting the sublayer selects the path in the artwork.

Note: If you target a layer or sublayer by mistake, Ctrl/Command-click the target indicator to remove it.

3   Select the Moon gradient from the Swatches panel to fill the selected path.

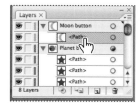  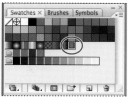

Select path in Layers panel.   Target path in Layers panel. Change fill color to Moon gradient.

Now you'll apply a Graphic Style to the Moon button layer. The style contains a color, which you'll apply to the layer in place of the moon's existing color.

4   In the Layers panel, click the target indicator (◎) for the Moon button layer.

5   Either choose Window > Graphic Styles or click the Graphic Styles tab to bring the panel to the front of its group. In the Graphic Styles panel, click the Green relief style to apply it to the layer.

6   Choose File > Save to save the artwork.

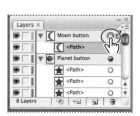  

Layer selected.   Graphic Style applied.   The result.

Next you'll type some text and apply an existing graphic style to it.

7   Choose Select > Deselect.

8   In the Layers panel, choose the Planet button layer and select the Type tool (**T**). Click to create a text frame on the button and type START.

9   Choose Edit > Select All to select the text. In the Control panel, choose Myriad Pro from the Font menu, Black from the Style menu, and 36pt from the font size pop-up menu.

10 Use the Selection tool (➤) to Shift-click on the text and the Planet button. Release the Shift key and click once more on the Planet button. By clicking again on the Planet button, you set it as the key element. That means that other objects align to it. Choose Vertical Align Center (▥) and Horizontal Align Center (▤) from the Align options in the Control panel.

11 Choose Select > Deselect.

12 With the Selection tool, click on the text to select it. From the Graphic Styles panel menu, choose Override Character Color to turn off the option. Then click on Graphic Styles Libraries menu button (▥) and choose the Neon Effects library.

13 From the Neon Effects library, click on the Thin Violet Neon graphic style to apply it to the text. If Override Character Color had been left on, the fill would be transparent.

Choose the neon graphics style.   The result.

When applying graphic styles to type, you have the option of overriding the character color or not. This can be very useful when working with type.

Applying an appearance to a layer

You can also apply simple appearance attributes to layers. For example, to make everything on a layer 50% opaque, simply target that layer and change the opacity in the Transparency panel.

Next you'll target a layer and change its blending mode to soften the effect of the type.

1 In the Layers panel, click the downward triangle next to the Moon button layer to collapse the layer.

2 If necessary, scroll to the Star type layer. Then click the target indicator (○) for the Star type layer. This action selects everything on the layer and targets all of its objects.

3 In the Transparency panel, choose Soft Light from the blending mode menu.

4 Choose File > Save to save the artwork.

Star Type layer targeted.   *Soft Light mode applied.*   *The result.*

Copying, applying, and removing Graphic Styles

Once you've created several Graphic Styles and appearances, you may want to use them on other objects in your artwork. You can use the Graphic Styles panel, the Appearance panel, the Eyedropper tool (🖋), or the Paint Bucket tool (🖴) to apply and copy appearance attributes.

Next you'll apply a style to one of the objects using the Appearance panel.

1 Choose Select > Deselect.

2 Use the Selection tool (▶) to click the star shape to select it.

3 In the Appearance panel, drag the appearance thumbnail (labeled Path: Star Glow) onto the moon shape to apply those attributes to it.

You can apply styles or attributes by dragging them from the Graphic Styles panel or the Appearance panel onto any object. The object doesn't have to be selected.

Star shape attributes.   *Drag thumbnail onto new object to apply the same attributes.*

4 Choose Select > Deselect.

Next, you'll apply a style by dragging it directly from the Graphic Styles panel onto an object.

5   In the Graphic Styles panel, drag the Green relief graphic style thumbnail onto the moon shape in the artwork.

6   Release the mouse button to apply the style to the shape.

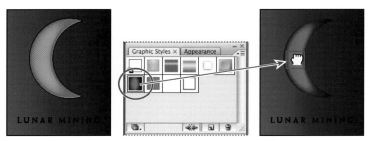

Drag graphic style thumbnail onto object (selected or not) to apply the style.

Now you'll use the Layers panel to copy an attribute from one layer to another.

7   Expand the Layers panel to see all of the layers. In the Layers panel, click on the Planet button layer to select it. Alt+drag (Windows) or Option+drag (Mac OS) the appearance indicator from the Planet button layer onto the appearance indicator of the Button type layer.

Using Alt or Option copies one layer effect onto another, as indicated by the hand cursor with the plus sign. To move an appearance or style just from one layer or object to another, simply drag the appearance indicator.

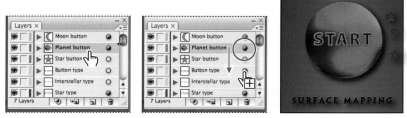

Alt/Option drag the appearance attributes from one layer to another.

Now you'll remove an appearance from a layer using the Layers panel.

8   In the Layers panel, click the target indicator to the right of the Button type layer.

9   Drag the appearance indicator to the Trash button at the bottom of the Layers panel to remove the appearance attribute.

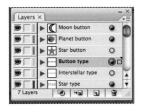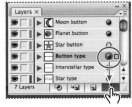

Drag appearance indicator to Trash button to remove attributes.

Another way to remove attributes of a selected object or layer is to use the Appearance panel. Select the object and then click the Reduce to Basic Appearance button at the bottom of the panel to return the object to its original state (including any stroke or fill) before the appearance attribute or style was applied.

10 Choose File > Save, and then File > Close.

Exploring on your own

Now that you've learned the basic steps to creating and using effects and Graphic Styles, experiment with different combinations of appearance attributes to fashion interesting special effects. Try combining different styles to produce new ones.

For example, here's how to merge two existing styles to create a brand new style:

1 Choose File > New to open a new file.

2 If the Graphic Styles panel isn't visible on-screen, choose Window > Graphic Styles to display it.

3 In the Graphic Styles panel, select Thick Aqua Neon style.

4 Add another style to the selection by Ctrl-clicking (Windows) or Command-clicking (Mac OS) the style named Chiseled.

5 Choose Merge Graphic Styles from the Graphic Styles panel menu.

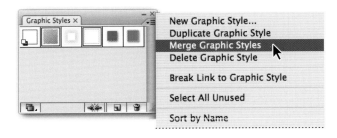

6   Name the new style **merged style** in the Style options dialog box, and click OK.

7   On the artboard, draw a shape or create text. Then apply the new style.

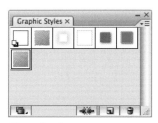

Merged styles.   *The result.*

If you want to edit the style and save it again, do the following:

1   To replace a style, Alt+drag (Windows) or Option+drag (Mac OS) the appearance thumbnail onto the style you are replacing in the Graphic Styles panel.

2   The style being replaced displays a thick black border when you position the cursor over it.

Review

▶ Review questions

1   Name two types of Appearance attributes.

2   How do you add a second stroke to an object?

3   What's the difference between applying a Graphic Style to a layer versus applying it to an object?

4   How do you remove an appearance using the Layers panel?

▶ Review answers

1   The Appearance panel contains the following types of editable attributes:

- Fill attributes (fill type, color, transparency, and effects).
- Stroke attributes (stroke type, brush, color transparency, and effects).
- Transparency attributes (opacity and blending mode).
- Effects from the Effect menu.

2   From the Appearance panel menu, choose Add New Stroke. A stroke is added to the top of the appearance list. It has the same color and stroke weight as the original stroke.

3   Once a Graphic Style is applied to a layer, everything you add to that layer will have that style applied to it. For example, if you create a circle on Layer 1 and then move it to Layer 2, which has a Drop Shadow effect applied, the circle would adopt that effect. When a style is applied to a single object, nothing else on that object's layer is affected by the object's style. For example, if a triangle has a Roughen effect applied to its path, and you move it to another layer, it will still retain the Roughen effect.

4   In the Layers panel, click the target indicator of a layer. Drag the appearance indicator down to the Trash icon in the Layers panel to remove the appearance. You can also remove the appearance of a selected object or layer by using the Appearance panel. Select the object and click the Reduce to Basic Appearance button to return the object to its original state before the appearance attribute or style was applied.

Enjoy Washington!

The Symbols panel lets you apply multiple
objects by painting them onto the page.
Symbols used in combination with the
symbolism tools offer options that make
creating repetitive shapes, such as grass,
or stars in the sky, easy and fun. You can
also use the Symbols panel as a database
to store artwork and map symbols to 3D
objects. Symbols can also provide excellent
support for SWF and SVG export.

13 | Working with Symbols

In this lesson, you'll learn how to do the following:

- Apply symbol instances.
- Create a symbol.
- Use the symbolism tools.
- Modify and redefine a symbol.
- Store and retrieve artwork in the Symbols panel.

Getting started

In this lesson, you'll finish artwork for a poster. Before you begin, restore the default preferences for Adobe Illustrator; then open a file containing the final version of the finished artwork to see what you are going to create.

1   To ensure that the tools and panels function exactly as described in this lesson, delete or deactivate (by renaming) the Adobe Illustrator CS3 preferences file. See "Restoring default preferences" on page 3.

2   Start Adobe Illustrator CS3.

Note: If you have not already copied the resource files for this lesson onto your hard disk from the Lesson13 folder from the Adobe Illustrator CS3 Classroom in a Book CD, do so now. See "Copying the Classroom in a Book files" on page 2.

3   Choose File > Open and open the file named 13end.ai in the Lesson13 folder within the AICIB folder on your hard drive.

If you like, choose View > Zoom Out to reduce the view of the finished artwork, adjust the window size, and leave it on your screen as you work. (Use the Hand tool (✋) to move the artwork where you want it in the window.) If you don't want to leave the image open, choose File > Close.

4   To begin working, you'll open an existing art file set up for the artwork. Choose File > Open to open the 13start.ai file in the Lesson13 folder, located inside the Lessons folder within the AICIB folder on your hard drive.

5   Choose File > Save As. In the Save As dialog box, name the file **poster.ai** and navigate to the Lesson13 folder. Leave the file format set to Illustrator (*.AI), and click Save. In the Illustrator Options dialog box, leave the defaults settings and click OK.

Working with symbols

A symbol is an art object that is stored in the Symbols panel and can be reused. For example, if you create a symbol from an object in the shape of a blade of grass, you can then add instances of that grass multiple times to your artwork without using the complex artwork multiple times. The grass instance is linked to the grass symbol in the Symbols panel and can be altered using symbolism tools or edited and replaced; all instances of the symbol linked to that original symbol are also updated. You can turn that grass from brown to green instantly! Symbols save time and greatly reduce file size. They can also be used in conjunction with Flash to create SWF files or artwork for Flash.

Illustrator comes with a series of symbol libraries that you can use, ranging from Tiki icons to Hair and Fur. These symbol libraries are accessed from the Symbols panel or by choosing Window > Symbol Libraries.

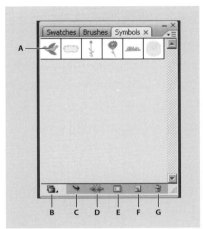

A. Symbols
B. Symbol Libraries Menu.
C. Place Symbol Instance.
D. Break Link to Symbol.
E. Symbol Options.
F. New Symbol.
G. Delete Symbol.

Illustrator symbols and Flash integration

You can move Illustrator artwork into the Flash editing environment or directly into Flash Player. You can copy and paste artwork, save files in SWF format, or export artwork directly to Flash. In addition, Illustrator provides support for Flash dynamic text and movie clip symbols.

A symbol workflow in Illustrator is similar to symbol workflow in Flash:

Symbol creation

- When you create a symbol in Illustrator, the Symbol Options dialog box lets you name the symbol and set options specific to Flash: movie clip symbol type (which is the default for Flash symbols), Flash registration grid location, and 9-slice scaling guides. In addition, you can use many of the same symbol keyboard shortcuts in Illustrator and Flash (such as F8 to create a symbol).

Isolation mode for symbol editing

Symbol properties and links

Static, dynamic, and input text objects

—From Illustrator Help

Using Illustrator Symbol Libraries

You will first start by adding some clouds to this image from an existing symbol library. Then you will create your own symbol to use as the leaves for the tree.

1   If the Symbols panel is not visible, choose Window > Symbols.

2   From the Symbol Libraries Menu button (🖿) choose the Nature library. The Nature panel opens floating out in the Workspace. This library is external to the Illustrator file you are working on, but you can import any of the symbols into the document and use them in the artwork.

3   Click on the Cloud 1 symbol in the Nature symbol library to add it to the Symbols panel library. Close the Nature library panel.

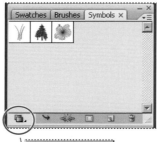
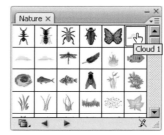
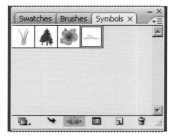

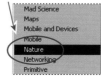

Click the Symbol Libraries Menu.   *Click on the Cloud 1 symbol.*   *The symbol Cloud 1 is added to*
button and choose Nature library.   *the Symbols panel.*

4   If the Layers panel is not visible, choose Window > Layers. Click on the Sky layer to choose it.

5   Using the Selection tool (▸), click and drag the Cloud 1 symbol onto the artboard, over the sky Drag out 3 more clouds and position them around the sky.

Next you will resize the symbol instances on the page.

6   With the Selection tool still selected, click on one of the instances of the Cloud 1 symbol on the page. Holding down the Shift key, drag a corner to make the cloud larger. Scale all of the clouds to varying sizes using the same method.

Resize clouds.

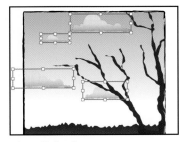
Select all clouds.

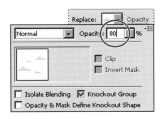
Change transparency.

Note: Symbol instances can have many transformations applied to them, but try changing the fill color and you'll see that property is controlled by the symbol in the Symbols panel.

Next you will edit the cloud symbol so that all of the instances are affected.

Editing Symbols

If there are symbol instances on the page, you can edit the symbol by double-clicking on an instance on the page. When you edit an instance, all occurrences will be updated as well.

1   With the Selection tool ( ) double-click on one of the clouds on the page. A warning dialog box will appear. Click OK to continue. This will take you into Isolation mode.

The cloud may appear to change in size. That's because you are looking at the original symbol before you resized it on the page.

2   Click on the cloud to select it. Notice that you can't click on any other objects on the page.

3   If the Gradient panel is not visible, choose Window > Gradient or click on it's tab in the Dock. Make sure that the Fill box is selected in the Tools panel.

4   Choose More Options from the Gradient panel menu. Drag the diamond icon located above the slider to adjust the midpoints of the gradient's color stops.

5　With the Selection tool, double-click off the cloud or click the Exit Isolation Mode button (◄) at the upper-left corner of the artboard. This will exit Isolation Mode and let you edit the rest of the content.

Double-click on a cloud, then click　*Drag the midpoint*　*All of the clouds change as a result.*
to select it.　*of the gradient to the left.*

6　Choose File > Save and leave the document open.

Creating Symbols

Illustrator also lets you create your own symbols. Symbols can be made from objects including paths, compound paths, text, raster images, mesh objects, and groups of objects. Symbols can even include active objects, such as brush strokes, blends, effects, or other symbol instances.

Note: You cannot use non–embedded placed art as a symbol, nor can you use certain kinds of groups, such as groups of graphs.

Now you will draw an object and create your own symbol.

1　If the Layers panel is not visible, choose Window > Layers. Click on the Leaves layer to select it.

2　Off the right edge of the artboard, select the Pencil tool (✐) from the Tools panel. Click and draw a leaf shape, starting and ending on the same point. When you've drawn all the way around the shape and approach the beginning of the shape, hold down the Alt (Windows) or Option (Mac) to close the path.

Note: Draw the leaves in proportion to the tree. Since this is vector art, you can draw bigger and scale it smaller.

3　From the Control panel, click on Fill and choose the Dark Green swatch from the Swatches panel that appears. With the Selection tool (▸), Alt (Windows) or Option (Mac) drag 2 copies of the leaf you drew.

4   If the Color panel is not visible, choose Window > Color. Select one of the copied leaves and change the color fill in the Color panel to a lighter green by typing in 75%. Now select the other copied leaf and change the color fill in the Color panel to a light green by typing in 50%.

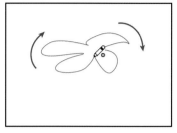

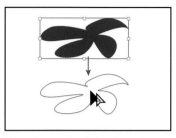

Drawing and closing the leaf shape with the Pencil tool.

Choosing a color fill and copying the leaf twice.

The resulting leaves

5   If the Symbols panel is not visible, choose Window > Symbols. With the Selection tool, select the darkest green leaf and drag it into the Symbols panel.

6   When the Symbol Options dialog box appears, enter leaf1 for the Name and choose Graphic as the Type. Click OK to create the symbol.

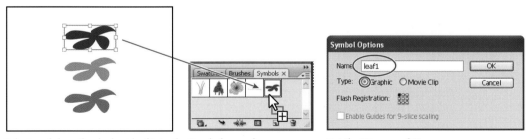

Select and drag the darkest leaf into the Symbols panel.

Set the Name and Type.

7   Repeat the above steps to create symbols for the copied leaves and name the 75% green leaf leaf2 and the 50% leaf, leaf3.

What is 9-slice scaling?

You can use 9-slice scaling (scale-9) in the Symbol Options dialog box to specify component-style scaling for movie clip symbols destined for export to Flash. This type of scaling lets you create movie clip symbols that scale appropriately for use as user interface components, as opposed to the type of scaling typically applied to graphics and design elements.

—From Illustrator Help

Applying a symbol instance

Next you will use the Symbol Sprayer tool to apply the leaves to your illustration.

1   Select the Symbol Sprayer tool ( ) from the Tools panel.

2   Click on the leaf1 symbol that you created in the Symbols panel.

3   Click and drag using the Symbol Sprayer tool, much like an airbrush or can of spray paint, to create the leaves of the tree with your leaf1 symbol. You can also click and release to add fewer leaves.

Use the Symbol Sprayer like an airbrush.

Note: You can release the Symbol sprayer and then keep spraying. All of the symbols you spray on the page are added to a single Symbol Set.

Symbol instances

Keep the following in mind when creating a symbol instance with the Symbol Sprayer:

• All the symbols that appear from each spray become one instance set that you manipulate and edit as a whole.

• You can enlarge or reduce the spraying radius by using the bracket keys ,"[" for a smaller spraying radius, "]" for a larger spraying radius.

• Holding down the Alt (Windows) or Option (Mac OS) key while using the Symbol Sprayer deletes instances.

4   Choose Select > Deselect to deselect the leaf1 symbol set on the page.

5   In the Symbols panel, click on the leaf2 symbol to select it.

6   Click and drag again using the Symbol sprayer, as you did in step 3, to create more leaves of the tree with your leaf2 symbol.

This will give the tree two colors of leaves, giving a more realistic appearance. You can try this with leaf3 as well to give it even more leaves. Just make sure to choose Select > Deselect between.

7 If the Layers panel is not visible, choose Window > Layers. Click on the arrow to the left of the Leaves layer to view the content. Note that for every leaf symbol (leaf1 and leaf2) you have sprayed, there is a new symbol set in the Leaves layer. When spraying with the Symbol Sprayer, symbols are added to a symbol set if it is selected at the time. If not, a new symbol set is created.

Use the Symbol Sprayer.

Result.

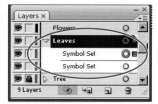

8 Choose Select > Deselect, then File > Save to save the file.

Using the symbolism tools

In this next lesson, you will use the Symbol Sizer and Spinner tools to alter the look of individual symbol instances.

Editing symbols using the symbolism tools

There are seven symbolism tools hidden inside the Symbol Sprayer tool. Symbolism tools are used for changing the density, color, location, size, rotation, transparency, or style of symbol sets.

Symbolism tools

What do the Symbolism tools do?

Symbol Shifter tool—Moves symbol instances around. It can also change the relative paint order of symbol instances in a set.

Symbol Scruncher tool—Pulls symbol instances together or apart.

Symbol Sizer tool—Increases or decreases the size of symbol instances in an existing symbol set.

Symbol Spinner tool—Orients the symbol instances in a set. Symbol instances located near the cursor orient in the direction you move the cursor. As you drag the mouse, an arrow appears above the cursor to show the current orientation of symbol instances.

Symbol Stainer tool—Colorizes symbol instances. Colorizing a symbol instance changes the hue toward the tint color, while preserving the original luminosity, so black or white objects don't change at all.

Symbol Screener tool—Increases or decreases the transparency of the symbol instances in a set.

Symbol Styler tool—Applies the selected style to the symbol instance.

You can switch to the Symbol Styler tool when using any other symbolism tool, by clicking a style in the Styles panel.

Now you will select the leaf1 symbol set and edit the leaves using the Symbol Sizer and Symbol Spinner tools.

1　In the Layers panel, click in the top symbol set's selection column (between the target button and the scroll bar) to select the symbol set.

2　In the Tools panel, click and hold down the mouse button on the Symbol Sprayer tool and select the Sizer tool ( ). Click and drag over your symbol instances to scale up some of the leaves. Hold down Alt (Windows) or Option (Mac OS) while you are using the Symbol Sizer tool to reduce the size of the selected instances.

Select the first symbol set.

Symbol set selected.

Resize with the Sizer tool.

Note: *The Symbol Sizer works better when you click and release over symbol instances, rather than holding down. If the symbols resize too quickly for you, choose Edit > Undo and try again.*

Now you will rotate some of the symbols.

3 Select the Symbol Spinner tool (🖮) and click and drag over the leaves to rotate. The more you move the cursor, the more rotation occurs and the more leaves that are effected.

Rotating the leaves using the symbolism tools.

4 Choose File > Save.

Editing symbols

In the next steps, you will add an additional symbol, then edit and update it.

1 Choose Select > Deselect.

2 If the Layers panel is not visible, choose Window > Layers. Click on the Leaves layer to select it.

3 Using the Selection tool (🖮), click on the Fill color in the Control panel and select None (◻) from the Swatches panel. Click on the Stroke color in the Control panel and select grass green from the Swatches panel for the stroke.

4 Click on the stroke weight in the Control panel, and select **1 pt** from the pop-up menu.

5 Double-click on the Pencil tool (✎) in the Tools panel. From the Pencil Tool Preferences dialog box, deselect the Keep Selected option and click OK.

6   Using the Pencil tool (✐), create several blades of grass. Use at least 10 line segments to make a tuft of grass.

*Create blades of grass to be used
as a symbol.*

7   Switch to the Selection tool and drag a marquee selection to surround the blades of grass. (You could also select one blade and Shift-click to add the others.)

8   With the blades of grass selected, choose Window > Symbols to open the Symbols panel. Click the New Symbol button on the Symbols panel. Name the new symbol **grass** in the Symbol Options dialog box and choose Graphic as the Type. Click OK.

Create a new symbol from the grass.

9   Use the Selection tool to delete the original blades of grass used to create the symbol.

10   In the Tools panel, click and hold down the mouse button on the Symbol Spinner tool and select the Symbol Sprayer tool (⬚). Double-click the Symbol Sprayer tool in the Tools panel to open the Symbolism Tool options dialog box. Change the Intensity to 9 and the Symbol Set Density to 8 and click OK.11   In the Symbols panel, click on the grass symbol you just added. Return to the artboard by clicking and dragging to apply the grass symbol over the base of the tree.

11   In the Control panel, choose a black fill.

12 Select the Symbol Stainer tool (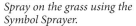). Press the right bracket key] several times to increase the size of the brush. Click and release over the grass instances, giving them a darker stain. Use Alt (Windows) or Option (Mac OS) to decrease the colorization amount and reveal more of the original symbol color for some of the instances of grass. Try different color fills (like the Light green swatch) to achieve a more realistic looking grass.

Spray on the grass using the Symbol Sprayer.

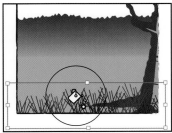

Stain the grass using the Symbol Stainer.

13 Choose File > Save.

Updating a symbol

In this next section, you will edit the grass once, and all instances will be updated.

1 In the Symbols panel, double-click on the grass symbol to edit. A temporary instance of the symbol appears in the center of the artboard..

💡 *You can also click on the Edit Symbol button in the Control panel.*

2 Choose Select > All or drag across the blades of grass with the Selection tool.

3 Click Stroke Weight in the Control panel and choose **2pt** from the menu.

4 Double-click outside of the grass on the artboard or clicking the Exit Isolation Mode button (◀) at the upper-left corner of the artboard to see all of the artwork. The symbol instances are now using the thicker blades of grass.

5 Choose File > Save to save this artwork.

Breaking a link to a symbol

There will come a time when you place symbols in your artwork and one or more of the instances needs to be different. The Symbolism tools will allow you to change instances up to a point. Illustrator also allows you to break the link between a symbol and an instance. This effectively groups the object on the artboard, allowing you to ungroup and edit the points.

Now you will place several instances of a symbol and break the link to one of the instances.

1   If the Layers panel is not visible, choose Window > Layers. In the Layers panel, click on the Flowers layer to select it.

2   In the Symbols panel, drag out 4 copies of the Hibiscus symbol onto the leaves of the tree. Arrange them so that they are spread out with the Selection tool (▶).

> 💡 *Once you drag one instance from the Symbols panel, you can Alt (Windows) or Option (Mac) drag out copies to make more instances.*

3   Select one of the symbol instances of the flower on the page. In the Control panel, click the Break Link button ().

You should now be able to see the points that make up the flower shapes. Also, the object is a group. You will see the word Group on the left end of the Control panel.

Symbol instance selected.   *Link is broken to symbol.*

4   Select the Zoom tool (🔍) and click twice on the selected flower to zoom in. Try not to select the pieces of the flower.

5   Double-click on the flower with the Selection tool to enter Isolation mode. Click on the pink flower shape to select it (not the smaller pieces).

6 Click on the Fill box in the Tools panel and open the Gradient panel by choosing Window > Gradient or clicking on the Gradient panel tab. Alt (Windows) or Option (Mac) click on the light pink color in the gradient ramp.

7 If the Color panel is not visible, choose Window > Color. Drag the Magenta slider to the right until 75% or so is reached.

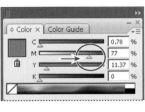

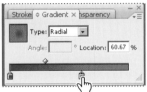

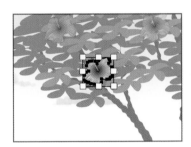

Select the flower shape.   *Alt or Option click the color in   The Result.*
the Gradient ramp and adjust the
Magenta in the Color panel.

8 Double-click somewhere outside of the flower with the Selection tool to exit the Isolation mode. Choose Select > Deselect.

9 Choose File > Save and keep the artwork open.

Storing and retrieving artwork in the Symbols panel

Save frequently used logos or other artwork as a symbol to readily access them when needed.

In this next lesson, you will take symbols you've created so far and save them as a new symbol library that you can share with other documents or other users.

1 In the Symbols panel, click on the Symbol Libraries Menu button (🖿.) and choose Save Symbols from the list that appears.

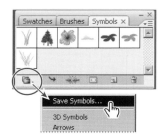

2 In the Save Symbols as Library dialog box, choose a location such as your Desktop to place the library file and name the library file **outdoors.ai**. Click Save.

Note: When you first open the Save Symbols as Library dialog box, you are taken into a Symbols folder. This is where the libraries you create can be stored. Illustrator will recognize any libraries stored here and let you choose them from the Symbol Libraries menu.

💡 *If you save the library into the default folder, you can make subfolders and create a folder structure that suits you. This way you can easily organize the libraries and access them through the Symbol Libraries Menu button or Window > Symbol Libraries.*

3 Save the file and keep it open.

4 Create a new document using File > New. Leave the settings at the defaults and click OK.

5 From the Symbols panel, click on the Symbol Libraries Menu button (🖿.) and choose Other Library... at the bottom of the list that appears. Navigate to the Desktop folder where you saved the outdoors.ai library, choose it and click Open to open it.

The outdoors library will appear as the outdoors panel in the workspace. You can dock it or leave it where it is. It will stay open as long as Illustrator is open. When you close, then open Illustrator, it will not reopen.

6 Drag out any of the Symbols from the outdoors library panel onto your page.

Share libraries this way! You can save them and open the library using Other Library option or open the library directly to open a document that contains the symbols.

7 Choose File > Close and do not save the file.

Mapping a symbol to 3D artwork

You can apply any 2D artwork stored as a Symbol in the Symbols panel to selected surfaces on a 3D object.

You can learn all about mapping symbols to 3D artwork by visiting Lesson 11, "Applying Effects.".

Symbols and Flash integration

Symbols also provide excellent support for SWF and SVG export. When you export to Flash, you can set the symbol type to MovieClip. Once in Flash, you can choose another type if necessary. You can also specify 9-slice scaling in Illustrator so that the movie clips scale appropriately when used for user interface components.

You can move Illustrator artwork into the Flash editing environment or directly into Flash Player. You can copy and paste artwork, save files in SWF format, or export artwork directly to Flash. In addition, Illustrator provides support for Flash dynamic text and movie clip symbols.

You can also use Device Central to see how Illustrator artwork will appear in Flash Player on different handheld devices.

Pasting Illustrator artwork into Flash

You can create graphically rich artwork in Illustrator and copy and paste it into Flash simply, quickly, and seamlessly.

When you paste Illustrator artwork into Flash, the following attributes are preserved:

Paths and shapes	Scalability
Stroke weights	Gradient definitions
Text (including OpenType fonts)	Linked images
Symbols	Blending modes

—From Illustrator Help

Exploring on your own

Try to integrate symbols into illustrations with repeated artwork, such as maps that contain repeated icons and road signs, to creative and customized bullets for text. Symbols make it easy to update logos in business cards or name tags, or any artwork created with multiple placements of the same art.

To place multiple symbol instances, do the following:

1   Select the artwork that is to become a symbol.

2   Drag the art using the Selection tool (↖) into the Symbols panel. Delete the original art once it is in the Symbols panel.

3   To use the first instance, drag the symbol from the Symbols panel to a location on your artboard.

4   Drag as many instances of the symbol as you like, or Alt/Option drag the original instance to clone it to other locations.

5   The symbols are now linked to the original symbol in the Symbols panel. If it is updated, all placed instances will be updated.

Note: You can break the link between the placed symbol by right-clicking (Windows) or Control+clicking (Mac OS) and selecting Break Link to Symbol from the context-sensitive menu or clicking on the Break Link button in the Control panel.

Review

▶ **Review questions**

1   What are three benefits of using a symbol?

2   Name the symbolism tool that is used for changing tints and shades of a symbol.

3   If you are using a symbolism tool on an area that has two different symbols applied, which one becomes affected?

4   How do you update an existing symbol?

5   What is something that cannot be used as a symbol?

6   How do you access symbols from other documents?

▶ **Review answers**

1   Three benefits of using symbols are:

* Easy application of multiple shapes.

* You can edit one symbol, and all instances will be updated.

* You can map artwork to 3D objects.

2   The Symbol Stainer tool changes the tints and shades of a symbol.

3   If you are using a symbolism tool over an area that has two different symbol instances, the symbol active in the Symbols panel will be the only instance affected.

4   To update an existing symbol, double-click on the symbol icon in the Symbols panel or double-click on an instance of the symbol on the artboard. From there, edits can be made in isolation mode.

5   Non-embedded images and groups of graphs cannot be used as symbols.

6   You can access symbols from saved documents by choosing Window > Symbol Libraries > Other Libraries or from the Symbol Libraries menu.

Tech Expo

May 15th - 20th   Seattle Expo Center

You can easily add an image created in an image-editing program to an Adobe Illustrator file. This is an effective method for seeing how a photograph looks incorporated with a line drawing, or for trying out Illustrator special effects on bitmap images.

14 | Combining Illustrator CS3 Graphics with the Creative Suite

In this lesson, you'll learn how to do the following:

- Differentiate between vector and bitmap graphics.
- Create a crop area using the Crop Area tool.
- Place embedded Adobe Photoshop graphics in an Adobe Illustrator file.
- Create a clipping mask from compound paths.
- Make an opacity mask to display part of the image.
- Sample color in a placed image.
- Replace a placed image with another, and update the document.
- Export a layered file to Adobe Photoshop.

Combining artwork

You can combine Illustrator artwork with images from other graphics applications in a variety of ways for a wide range of creative results. Sharing artwork between applications lets you combine continuous-tone paintings and photographs with line art. Even though Illustrator lets you create certain types of raster images, Photoshop excels at many image-editing tasks; once done, the images can then be placed in Illustrator.

To illustrate how you can combine bitmap images with vector art, and work between applications, this lesson steps you through the process of creating a composite image. In this lesson, you will add photographic images created in Adobe Photoshop to a postcard created in Adobe Illustrator. Then you'll adjust the color in the photo, mask the photo, and sample color from the photo to use in the Illustrator artwork. You'll update a placed image and then export your postcard to Photoshop.

Vector versus bitmap graphics

Adobe Illustrator creates vector graphics, also called draw graphics, which are made up of shapes based on mathematical expressions. These graphics consist of clear, smooth lines that retain their crispness when scaled. They are appropriate for illustrations, type, and graphics, such as logos, that may be scaled to different sizes.

Bitmap images, also called raster images, are based on a grid of pixels and are created by image-editing applications such as Adobe Photoshop. In working with bitmap images, you edit groups of pixels rather than objects or shapes. Because bitmap graphics can represent subtle gradations of shade and color, they are appropriate for continuous-tone images such as photographs or artwork created in painting programs. A disadvantage of bitmap graphics is that they lose definition and appear jagged when scaled up.

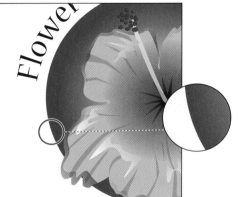

Logo drawn as vector art.

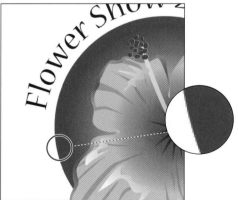

Logo rasterized as bitmap art.

In deciding whether to use Illustrator or a bitmap image program such as Photoshop for creating and combining graphics, consider both the elements of the image and how the image will be used.

In general, use Illustrator if you need to create art or type with clean lines that will look good at any magnification. In most cases, you will also want to use Illustrator for laying out a single page design, because Illustrator offers more flexibility in working with type and with reselecting, moving, and altering images than Photoshop. You can create raster images in Illustrator but its pixel-editing tools are limited. Use Photoshop for images that need pixel-editing, color correcting, painting, and other special effects. Use InDesign for laying out anything from a postcard to a multiple chapter book such as this *Classroom in a Book*.

Getting started

Before you begin, you'll need to restore the default preferences for Adobe Illustrator. Then you'll open the finished art file for this lesson to see what you'll create.

1   To ensure that the tools and panels function exactly as described in this lesson, delete or deactivate (by renaming) the Adobe Illustrator CS3 preferences file. See "Restoring default preferences" on page 3.

2   Start Adobe Illustrator CS3.

3   Choose File > Open, and open the L14end.ai file in the Lesson14 folder, located inside the Lessons folder within the AICIB folder on your hard drive.

4   Choose View > Zoom Out to make the finished artwork smaller, adjust the window size, and leave it on-screen as you work. (Use the Hand tool (✋) to move the artwork where you want it in the window.) If you don't want to leave the image open, choose File > Close.

Now you'll open the start file to begin the lesson.

L14end.ai

5   Choose File > Browse to open the Adobe Bridge.

6   In the Favorites panel on the left, click on My Computer (Windows) or Computer (Mac OS) and navigate to the L14strt.ai file (in the Lesson14 folder, inside the Lessons folder in the AICIB folder, on your hard drive) in the Content panel, and double-click to open the file. Close the Bridge.

For information on working with Adobe Bridge, see "Browse for files using Adobe Bridge" in Illustrator Help.

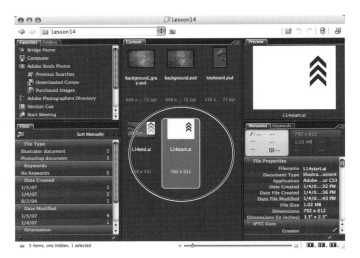

The file has been prepared with two layers: the Text layer and Images layer. You will place images on both. The Images layer also contains objects that you'll make into a mask.

7   Choose File > Save As. In the Save As dialog box, name the file **Postcard.ai**, and navigate to the Lesson14 folder. Leave the file format set to Illustrator (*.AI), and click Save. In the Illustrator Options dialog box leave at the default settings and click OK.

Creating a crop area

Creating a crop area can be accomplished with the Crop Area tool. This defines the area to crop to. For instance, if you create a postcard that is 9"x6" on an 8.5"x11" artboard, it helps to define the area to crop to.

You can create multiple crop areas for your document, but only one crop area can be active at a time. When you have multiple crop areas defined, you can view them all by selecting the Crop tool and pressing Alt. Each crop area is numbered for easy reference. You can edit or delete a crop area at any time, and you can specify different crop areas each time you print or export.

The Crop Area tool works by either double-clicking the tool in the Tools panel, or drawing a crop area on the artboard. In this next lesson, you will create a crop area for a postcard.

1   Double-click the Crop Area tool (⊞) in the Tools panel. In the Crop Area Options dialog box change the Width to 9 in and the Height to 6 in. This will set a crop area that is positioned in the center of the artboard to a 9"x6" postcard size. Click the Show Screen Edge option to create guides around the perimeter of the crop area. Click OK.

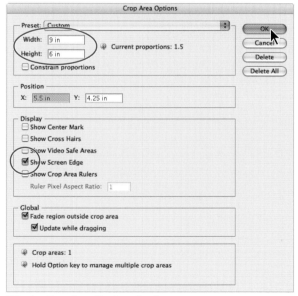

Edit the Crop Area Options for the crop area.   The result after switching to the Selection tool.

2   You should see a gray area on the artboard. That gray area is the area outside of the crop area. The crop area can be resized or moved using the Crop Area tool. To commit the crop area and exit the crop-editing mode, select the Selection tool (➤) from the Tools panel.

When the Crop Area tool is selected, the Control panel shows many of the options found in the Crop Area Options dialog box. Note that you can also create multiple crop areas within a single document by holding the Alt (Windows) or Option (Mac) key.

Placing an Adobe Photoshop file

You can bring artwork from Photoshop (PSD) files into Illustrator using the Open command, the Place command, the Paste command, and the drag-and-drop feature.

Illustrator supports most Photoshop data, including layer comps, layers, editable text, and paths. This means that you can transfer files between Photoshop and Illustrator without losing the ability to edit the artwork. For easy transfer of files between the two applications, adjustment layers that have visibility turned off are imported (though inaccessible) into Illustrator and restored when exported back to Photoshop.

You'll begin by placing a Photoshop file that contains several layer comps in the Illustrator document as an embedded file. Placed files can be embedded or linked. Embedded files are added to the Illustrator file, and the Illustrator file size increases to reflect the addition of the placed file. Linked files remain separate, external files, with a link to the placed file within the Illustrator file. (The linked file must always accompany the Illustrator file, or the link will break and the placed file will not appear in the Illustrator artwork.)

Support for Device N

Illustrator CS3 includes support for Device N rasters. If you create a Duotone, for instance, in Photoshop and place that Duotone into Illustrator, it will now separate properly and print the spot colors.

About layer comps

Designers often create multiple compositions, or comps, of a page layout to show clients. Using layer comps, you can create, manage, and view multiple versions of a layout in a single Photoshop or ImageReady file. Layer comps are fully interchangeable between Photoshop and ImageReady if the image color mode is RGB.

A layer comp is a snapshot of a state of the Layers palette. Layer comps record three types of layer options:

- Layer visibility—whether a layer is showing or hidden.
- Layer position in the document.
- Layer appearance—whether a layer style is applied to the layer and the layer's blending mode.

You create a comp by making changes to the layers in your document and updating the comp in the Layer Comps palette. You view comps by applying them in the document. You can export layer comps to separate files, to a single PDF, or to a web photo gallery.

1   Choose Window > Layers. Drag the top of the Layers panel up so you can see all the layers if necessary.

2   In the Layers panel, select the Images layer if it is not already selected.

When you place an image, it is added to the selected layer. You'll use the Images layer for the placed image. The layer includes artwork for a mask for the image that you'll create later in the lesson.

3   Choose File > Place.

4   Navigate to the keyboard.psd file (in the Lesson14 folder inside the Lessons folder, in the AICIB folder, on your hard drive), and select it. Do not double-click the file or click Place yet.

5   If Link is checked in the Place dialog box, uncheck the Link option.

Note: By deselecting the Link option, the .psd file will be embedded in the Illustrator file. You also have the option to Convert Photoshop layers to objects by deselecting this option.

6   Click Place.

7   In the Photoshop Import Options dialog box, select Black Hands from the Layer Comp pop-up menu, then check the Show Preview option to view the comps.

8   Select the Convert Photoshop layers to objects option and choose Import Hidden Layers to bring in all of the layers. Click OK.

Note: If a color warning dialog box such as Paste Profile Mismatch appears, click OK.

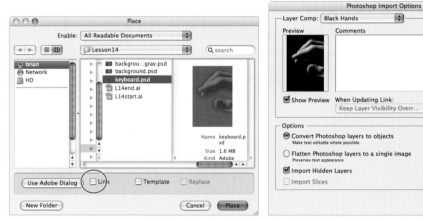

Place the Photoshop file without Link checked.   Select the Layer Comp and other Options.

Rather than flatten the file, you want to convert the Photoshop layers to objects. This is because the keyboard.psd file contains four layers and one layer mask. You will use them later in the lesson.

Now you'll move the placed image.

9   Click the Selection tool (▶) in the Tools panel. Click the center of the image (don't select a bounding box handle as it will resize the image) to select it.

10   In the Control panel, click the word Transform to reveal the Transform panel. Enter **2.5 in** in the X value and **5 in** in the Y value. Choose Flip Horizontal from the Transform panel menu, to flip the image on its center.

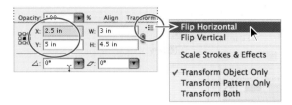

11 Click the toggle arrow (▶) to the left of the Images layer to expand it. Click the toggle arrow (▶) to the left of the keyboard.psd layer to expand it. Notice all of the sublayers of keyboard.psd. These are the result of not flattening the image when it was placed. Click the eye icon (👁) to the left of the keyboard.psd sublayer to toggle the visibility off. The arrows should be the only thing visible on the artboard. Click the Expand triangle (▶) to the left of the keyboard.psd layer to hide it's contents.

12 Choose File > Save

Now you will place an image then duplicate it.

Duplicating a placed image

You can duplicate placed images just as you do other objects in an Illustrator file. The copy of the image can then be modified independently of the original.

Now you'll place the background.psd image and duplicate it in the Layers panel.

1 Choose File > Place and navigate to the background.psd file (in the Lesson14 folder inside the Lessons folder, in the AICIB folder, on your hard drive), and select it. Do not double-click the file or click Place yet.

Note: If a color warning dialog box such as Paste Profile Mismatch appears, click OK.

2 Deselect the Link option if it isn't already and click Place. The image will appear on the artboard. Select the Selection tool and click the image if it is not selected. Click Align to Artboard (▥) and click Horizontal Align Center (▤) and Vertical Align Center (▥) to align the image.

3 Drag the top edge of the Layers panel up to enlarge the Layers panel so that you can see all the contents of the Images layer.

4   Begin dragging the background.psd layer down the list. While dragging hold down the Alt (Windows) or Option (Mac) to duplicate it. Drag until it is at the bottom of the Images layer. Release the mouse button when the indicator bar appears between the last <Path> layer and Text layer. There should now be two background layers.

Note: If you hold down the Alt (Windows) or Option (Mac) before you begin dragging, it may select objects rather than drag and copy the background.psd.

5   Double-click the bottom Background layer and rename it **Masked Background**. Click OK. You will mask this image later in the lesson.

Copy layer by dragging.   *Layer copied.*   *Rename the layer.*

6   Choose File > Save.

Applying Color Edits to a placed image

Color edits can be used to modify colors in placed images in a variety of ways. You can use color edits to convert to a different color mode (such as RGB, CMYK, or grayscale) or to adjust individual color values. You can also use color edits to saturate or desaturate (darken or lighten) colors, or invert colors (create a color negative).

🖳 For information on color modes and modifying colors with color edits, see "About Colors in Digital Graphics" and "Apply an effect or filter" in Illustrator Help.

In this section, you'll adjust colors in the background layer. Later in the lesson, you'll apply a mask to this image and then adjust colors in the Masked Background layer so that the two layers appear in contrasting colors.

1   In the Layers panel, click the background sublayer.

2   Click the eye icon (👁) to the far left of the Masked Background layer to hide it. When you hide a layer, all objects on that layer are deselected, hidden, and locked.

3   In the Layers panel, click the selection column to the far right of the background layer to make sure its contents are selected.

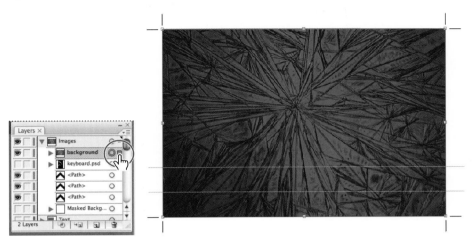

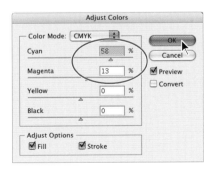

Masked Background layer hidden and contents of background layer selected.

4   Choose Edit > Edit Colors> Adjust Color Balance.

5   In the Adjust Colors dialog box drag the sliders or enter values for the CMYK percentages to change the colors in the image. You can press Tab to move between the text fields. (We used the following values to create more of a blue/purple cast: C=58, M=13, Y=–0, and K=0.). Feel free to experiment a little. Select Preview so that you can see the color changes.

Note: *You may need to turn the Preview on and off to see the results.*

6   When you are satisfied with the color in the image, click OK.

7   Choose File > Save.

▣ You can also use filters to apply special effects to images, distort images, produce a hand-drawn appearance, and create other interesting effects. See "Applying filters and effects to bitmap images" in Illustrator Help.

Masking an image

Masks crop part of an image so that only a portion of the image appears through the shape of the mask. You can make a mask from a single path or a compound path. You can also import masks made in Photoshop files.

Applying a Clipping Mask to an image

In this section, you'll create a clipping mask for the background.psd image and adjust it so that only a small portion of the image is showing.

1   In the Layers panel, click the eye icon area to the left of the Text Layer and the keyboard.psd layer to show the contents for both layers. You may need to scroll in the Layers panel to do this.

2   With the Selection tool still selected, and the background.psd image still selected, click the Mask button (Mask) in the Control panel. This will allow you to easily apply a clipping mask to the image in the shape of the image. Next you will edit this mask.

Note: You can also apply a clipping mask by choosing Object > Clipping Mask > Make.

3   Look in the Layers panel and toggle the arrow to the left of the <Group> that now appears in the top of the Images layer. A <Clipping Path> now shows in the Layers panel. This is the mask. With the Selection tool (▸), click and drag the top bounding point to the guide below the Tech Expo text. Click and drag the bottom, middle bounding point to the bottom guide creating a background image that is masked.

Note: *The key is selecting the mask not the image.*

Notice the Clipping Mask.   *Edit the Clipping Mask after selected.*

4   In the Control panel, click the Edit Contents (◉) button to edit the background.psd again. With the Direct Selection tool (▹) click on the part of the background image that is visible and begin dragging the image upward about an inch, holding down the Shift key as you drag.

Edit Contents button.   *Drag the image using the Direct Selection tool.*

5   Choose Object > Hide Selection to hide the background image.

Creating compound paths and opacity masks

In this section, you'll create a compound path from the arrow pattern on the Images layer and create an opacity mask from the compound path, so that the Masked Background layer appears through the mask. You'll also use an opacity mask that was created in Photoshop and saved as a layer mask.

1   Select the Magic Wand tool (✶) in the Tools panel.

2   Using the Magic Wand tool, click the upper right arrow in the arrow pattern to select all the arrows. Change the Fill color in the Control panel to White.

You can use the Magic Wand tool to select all objects in a document with the same or similar fill color, stroke weight, stroke color, opacity, or blending mode. See "Select objects with the Magic Wand tool" in Illustrator Help.

3   Choose Object > Compound Path > Make.
Notice how all the arrows have been placed onto one layer, called <Compound Path> in the Layers panel.

The Compound Path command creates a single compound object from two or more objects. Compound paths act as grouped objects. The Compound Path command lets you create complex objects more easily than if you used the drawing tools or the Pathfinder commands.

4   With the compound path selected, in the Layers panel click the eye icon area to the left of the Masked Background sublayer to show its contents. You may need to scroll down in the layers panel to see the Masked Background sublayer.

5   With the Selection tool, Shift-click the selection column to the far right of the Masked Background layer. This selects it and adds it to the <Compound Path> selection. (The Selection indicator (■) appears and the Masked Background layer is added to the selection.)

Note: Both the masking object and the object to be masked must be selected in order to create a mask. The masking object also needs to be above the masked object in the Layers panel.

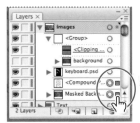

Masked Background and <Compound Path> selected.

6   Click the Transparency panel tab to bring it to the front of its group. (If the Transparency panel isn't visible on-screen, choose Window > Transparency.)

7   From the Transparency panel menu, choose Show Options.

Now you'll mask the Masked Background layer with an opacity mask. This allows you to use the change in luminosity in the overlying flower pattern to affect the background. Similar to a clipping mask, an opacity mask lets you make color and other fine adjustments that you can't make with a clipping mask.

8   From the Transparency panel menu, choose Make Opacity Mask. Make sure that the Clip option is selected.

Preview includes opacity mask.   *Dotted line indicates mask.*

The Masked Background layer is now masked with the arrow pattern, as indicated by the dotted underline beneath the layer name. Next you'll adjust the opacity mask you just created.

9 In the Transparency panel, click on the mask (as indicated by the white arrows on the black background). In the Layers panel, notice that Layers (Opacity Mask) appears. Click the toggle arrow (▶) to the left of the <Opacity Mask> layer to expand it.

 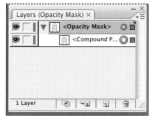

Click to select the opacity mask.   *The Layers panel after.*

10 With the mask selected, in the Control panel, click the Fill color to select a black to white gradient (linear not circular).

11 Select the Gradient tool (▢) in the Tools panel. Holding the Shift key down, start at the top edge of the arrows and drag down.

In Illustrator, much like Photoshop, masks follow this general rule: white shows, black hides. A gradient mask allows you to gradually show an image or other object. Try changing the direction and length of the gradient. Also, try adjusting the Opacity in the Transparency panel to achieve different effects.

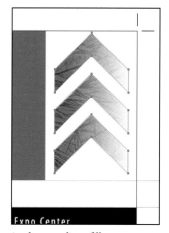 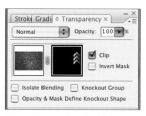 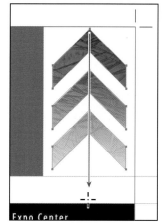

Apply a gradient fill.   *How the mask will look in the Transparency panel.*   *Drag with Gradient tool to change gradient direction.*

12   In the Transparency panel, click the Masked Background image to edit content rather than the mask.

Note: If you forget to stop the opacity mask editing, you can't do much to the other artwork!

13   Choose File > Save.

Editing an imported mask

You've made an opacity mask from artwork created in Illustrator. Now you'll use a mask that was created in Photoshop and imported when you placed the keyboard.psd file. You'll experiment with changing the color of the image and then adjusting the transparency of the opacity mask to tone down the effect.

1   In the Layers panel, click the eye icon area to the left of the background sublayer to turn on the visibility again. Click the toggle arrow (▶) to the left of the keyboard.psd sublayer to expand it, then click the selection column (between the target button and the scroll bar) to the right of the Hands sublayer to select its contents. (The dotted line under its layer name indicates that the Hands layer has an opacity mask applied to it.)

2   In the Transparency panel, change the Blend Mode to Multiply.

3   In the Layers panel, click on the eye icon to the left of the black overlay sublayer to turn its visibility off.

4   Choose Effect > Sketch > Halftone Pattern to open the Filter Gallery. In the Halftone Pattern options, set the Size to 3 and the Contrast to 4. Click OK.

Apply Halftone Pattern to the opacity mask for an interesting effect.

5   Choose File > Save.

Sampling colors in placed images

You can sample, or copy, the colors in placed images, to apply the colors to other objects in the artwork. Sampling colors enables you to easily make colors consistent in a file combining Photoshop images and Illustrator artwork.

In this section, you'll use the Eyedropper tool to sample colors from the placed image, and apply the colors to selected type on the Text layer.

1   In the Layers panel, click the toggle arrow (▶) to the left of the Text layer to expand it, then click the lock icon to the left of the first <Group> below the guides. Click the selection indicator (■) to the right of the <Group> to select the text that has been converted to paths.

2   Select the Eyedropper tool (✒), and Shift-click in the image anywhere to sample a color to be applied to the selected text. (We chose a light blue color from the background.psd right above the text.)

The color you sample is applied to the selected text.

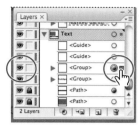

Unlock and select the Group.   *Text with color applied.*

3   Choose File > Save.

To copy appearance attributes using the Eyedropper tool

You can use the Eyedropper tool to copy appearance attributes from one object to another, including character, paragraph, fill, and stroke attributes between type objects. By default, the Eyedropper tool affects all attributes of a selection. To customize the attributes affected by this tool, use the Eyedropper dialog box.

1. Select the object, type object, or characters whose attributes you want to change.

2. Select the Eyedropper tool (✐).

3. Move the Eyedropper tool onto the object whose attributes you want to sample. (When you're correctly positioned over type, the pointer displays a small T.)

4. Do one of the following:

• Click the Eyedropper tool to sample all appearance attributes and apply them to the selected object.

• Shift-click to sample only the color from a portion of a gradient, pattern, mesh object, or placed image and apply the color to the selected fill or stroke.

• Hold down the Shift key and then the Alt (Windows) or Option (Mac OS) key while clicking to add the appearance attributes of an object to the selected object's appearance attributes. Alternatively, click first, and then hold down Shift and then Alt or Option.

Note: You can also click an unselected object to sample its attributes, and Alt-click (Windows) or Option-click (Mac OS) an unselected object to which you want to apply the attributes.

—From Illustrator Help

Replacing a placed image

You can easily replace a placed image with another image to update a document. The replacement image is positioned exactly where the original image was, so you don't have to align the replacement image. (If you scaled the original images, you may have to resize the replacement image to match the original image.)

Now you'll replace the background.psd image with the background_gray.psd image to create a new version of the postcard.

1   Choose File > Save As. In the Save As dialog box, name the file **Postcard2.ai**, and navigate to the Lesson14 folder. Leave the file format set to Illustrator (*.AI), and click Save. In the Illustrator options dialog box, leave at the default settings and click OK.

2   Choose Window > Links.

3   Click the first link in the Links panel to select it. (These links don't have names because we embedded them instead of linking them.) It will be the top blue background image. If it is not, scroll until you see the top blue background image.

4   Click the Relink button (⊕–◘) at the bottom of the Links panel.

5   In the Place dialog box, navigate to the background_gray.psd image in the Lesson14 folder and select it. Make sure that the Link option is selected this time. Click Place to replace the background image with the new one.

The replacement image appears in the Images layer as a background_gray.psd sublayer with no color adjustments applied. When you replace an image, color adjustments you made to the original image are not applied to the replacement. However, masks applied to the original image are preserved. Any layer modes and transparency adjustments you've made to other layers also may affect the image's appearance.

Select image in Links panel   *Result after relinking.*
and replace.

6   Choose File > Save.

You have completed the lesson. If you want to learn how to open and manipulate a layered Illustrator file in Photoshop, continue. If not, skip to "Exploring on your own".

Exporting a layered file to Photoshop

Not only can you open layered Photoshop files in Illustrator, but you can also save layered Illustrator files and then open them in Photoshop. Working with layered files between Illustrator and Photoshop is very helpful when creating and editing web graphics. You can preserve the hierarchical relationship of the layers by selecting the Write Layers option when saving your file. You can also open and edit type objects.

1   Choose File > Export.

2   Navigate to the folder where you'll save the file, and name the file **Postcard2.psd**. Changing the file name preserves your original Illustrator file.

3   Choose Photoshop (PSD) from the Save as Type (Windows) or Format (Mac OS) pop-up menu, and click Save (Windows) or Export (Mac OS).

4   In the Photoshop Export Options dialog box, make sure that CMYK is the Color Model, select Screen (72 ppi) for Resolution, and make sure that Write Layers is selected. Leave the rest of the settings at default (Preserve Text Editability is grayed out because all of the text was already converted to outlines). Click OK.

The Anti-alias option removes jagged edges in the artwork. The Write Layers option lets you export each Illustrator top-level layer as a separate Photoshop layer.

5   Start Adobe Photoshop CS3.

6   Open the Postcard2.psd file that you exported in step 4.

7   Click the Layers tab to view the Layers palette. Notice all of the layers.

8   Choose File > Close to close the file.

Importing Adobe Illustrator graphics in InDesign CS3

How you save and import Illustrator graphics depends on how you want to edit the art once you place it in InDesign.

If you plan to edit a graphic only in Illustrator...

Save the graphic in native Illustrator format (.AI). Some graphics require the extensive drawing tools available in Illustrator or are in their final form and shouldn't be edited. In InDesign, you can place a native Illustrator graphic and transform it as a single object (you can resize or rotate it, for example). Use the Edit > Edit Original command to open the graphic in Illustrator and edit it there.

If you want to adjust layer visibility in InDesign...

Save the Illustrator CS3 file in layered PDF format or native Illustrator format (.AI). For some documents, you want to control the visibility of the layers of a graphic depending on the context. For example, for a multiple language publication, you can create a single illustration that includes one text layer for each language. Using the layered PDF format or native Illustrator format (.AI), you can transform the illustration as a single object in InDesign but you cannot edit the paths, objects, or text within the illustration.

If you want to edit objects and paths in InDesign...

Copy the art from Illustrator and paste it into an InDesign document. For some graphics, you might want to edit them after they're placed in the InDesign document. For example, in a magazine, you might use the same design element in each issue, but want to change its color every month. If you paste a graphic into InDesign and edit it there, you cannot set layer transparency or edit the text.

Exploring on your own

Now that you know how to place and mask an image in an Illustrator file, you can place other images and apply a variety of modifications to the images. You can also create masks for images from objects you create in Illustrator. For more practice, try the following:

• In addition to adjusting color in images, apply transformation effects (such as shearing or rotating) or filters or effects (such as one of the Artistic or Distort filters/effects), to create contrast between the two images in the flower pattern.

• Use the basic shapes tools or the drawing tools to draw objects to create a compound path to use as a mask. Then place the background.psd image into the file with the compound path, and apply the compound path as a mask.

• Create large type and use the type as a mask to mask a placed object.

Review

Review questions

1   Describe the difference between linking and embedding in Illustrator.

2   How do you create an opacity mask for a placed image?

3   What kinds of objects can be used as masks?

4   What color modifications can you apply to a selected object using filters?

5   Describe how to replace a placed image with another image in a document.

Review answers

1   A linked file is a separate, external file connected to the Illustrator file by an electronic link. A linked file does not add significantly to the size of the Illustrator file. The linked file must accompany the Illustrator file to preserve the link and ensure that the placed file appears in the Illustrator file. An embedded file is included in the Illustrator file. The Illustrator file size reflects the addition of the embedded file. Because the embedded file is part of the Illustrator file, no link can be broken. Both linked and embedded files can be updated using the Replace Link button in the Links panel.

2   You create an opacity mask by placing the object to be used as a mask on top of the object to be masked. Then you select the mask and the objects to be masked, and choose Make Opacity Mask from the Transparency panel menu.

3   A mask can be a simple or compound path. You can use type as a mask. You can import opacity masks with placed Photoshop files. You can also create layer clipping masks with any shape that is the topmost object of a group or layer.

4   You can use filters to change the color mode (RGB, CMYK, or grayscale) or adjust individual colors in a selected object. You can also saturate or desaturate colors or invert colors in a selected object. You can apply color modifications to placed images, as well as to artwork created in Illustrator.

5   To replace a placed image, select the placed image in the Links panel. Then click the Replace Link button, and locate and select the image to be used as the replacement. Then click Place.

MONDLICHT

The quality and color of your final printed output are determined by the process you follow to prepare an image for print. Whether you're printing a draft of your work on a desktop printer or outputting color separations to be printed on a commercial press, learning fundamental printing concepts helps ensure that your printed results meet your expectations.

15 | Printing Artwork and Producing Color Separations

In this lesson, you'll learn about the following:

- Different types of printing requirements and printing devices.
- Printing concepts and printing terminology.
- Basic color principles.
- How to separate your color artwork for output to print.
- How to use spot colors for two-color printing.
- Special considerations when outputting to print.
- Saving and printing files with transparency effects.

Printing: An overview

When you print a document from a computer, data is sent from the document to the printing device, either to be printed on paper or to be converted to a positive or negative image on film. For black-and-white, grayscale, or low quantities of color artwork, many people use desktop printers. However, if you require large quantities of printed output, such as a brochure or magazine ad, you'll need to prepare your artwork for output on a commercial printing press. Printing on a commercial press is an art that requires time and experience to perfect. In addition to close communication with a printing professional, learning basic printing concepts and terminology will help you produce printed results that meet your expectations.

Note: This lesson assumes that you have a desktop printer for use with the exercises. If you don't have a desktop printer available, you can read the sections and skip the step-by-step instructions.

Different printing requirements require different printing processes. To determine your printing requirements, consider the following: What effect do you want the printed piece to have on your audience? Will your artwork be printed in black and white? Color? Does it require special paper? How many printed copies do you need? If you're printing in color, is precise color matching necessary, or will approximate color matching suffice?

Take a moment to consider several types of printing jobs:

• A black-and-white interoffice newsletter, requiring a low quantity of printed copies. For this type of printing job, you can generally use a 300-600 dpi (dots per inch) desktop laser printer to output the original, and then use a copy machine to reproduce the larger quantity.

• A business card using black and one other color. The term two-color printing typically refers to printing with black and one other color, although it may also refer to printing with two colors that are not black. Two-color printing is less expensive than four-color printing and lets you select exact color matches, called spot colors, which can be important for logos. For precise color matching, two-color printing is done on a printing press; if only an approximate color match is required, you might use a desktop color printer.

• A party invitation using two colors and tints of those colors. In addition to printing two solid colors, you can print tints of the colors to add depth to your printed artwork. Two-color printing is often done on colored paper that complements the ink colors and might be done on a desktop color printer or on a printing press, depending on the desired quantity and the degree of color matching required.

• A newspaper. Newspapers are typically printed on a printing press because they are time-sensitive publications printed in large quantities. In addition, newspapers are generally printed on large rolls of newsprint, which are then trimmed and folded to the correct size.

• A fashion magazine or catalog requiring accurate color reproduction. Four-color printing refers to mixing the four process ink colors (cyan, magenta, yellow, and black, or CMYK) for printed output. When accurate color reproduction is required, printing is done on a printing press using CMYK inks. CMYK inks can reproduce a good amount of the visible color spectrum, with the exception of neon or metallic colors. You'll learn more about color models in the next section.

About printing devices

Now that you've looked at several types of publications and different ways to reproduce them, you'll begin learning basic printing concepts and printing terminology.

Halftone screens

To reproduce any type of artwork, a printing device typically breaks down the artwork into a series of dots of various sizes called a halftone screen. Black dots are used to print black-and-white or grayscale artwork. For color artwork, a halftone screen is created for each ink color (cyan, magenta, yellow, and black); these then overlay one another at different angles to produce the full range of printed color. To see a good example of how individual halftone screens overlay each other at different angles on a printed page, look at a color comics page through a magnifying glass.

The size of the dots in a halftone screen determines how light or dark colors appear in print. The smaller the dot, the lighter the color appears; the larger the dot, the darker the color appears.

Enlarged detail showing dots in halftone screen.

Screen frequency

Screen frequency (also called line screen, screen ruling, or halftone frequency) refers to the number of rows or lines of dots used to render an image on film or paper. In addition, the rows of dots are broken down into individual squares, called halftone cells. Screen frequency is measured in lines per inch (lpi) and is a fixed value you can set for your printing device.

As a general rule, higher screen frequencies produce finer detail in printed output. This is because the higher the screen frequency, the smaller the halftone cells, and subsequently, the smaller the halftone dot in the cell.

However, a high screen frequency alone does not guarantee high-quality output. The screen frequency must be appropriate to the paper, the inks, and the printer or printing press used to output the artwork. Your printing professional will help you select the appropriate line screen value for your artwork and output device.

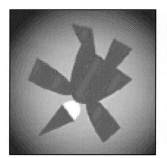 

Low-screen ruling (65 lpi) is often used to print newsletters.

High-screen ruling (150–200 lpi) is used for high-quality books.

Output device resolution

The resolution of a printing device describes the number of dots the printing device has available to render, or create, a halftone dot. The higher the output device resolution, the higher the quality of the printed output. For example, the printed quality of an image output at 2400 dots per inch (dpi) is higher than the printed quality of an image output at 300 dpi. Adobe Illustrator is resolution-independent and will always print at the printing device's highest resolution capability.

The quality of printed output depends on the relationship between the resolution of the output device (dpi) and the screen frequency (lpi). As a general rule, high-resolution output devices use higher screen frequency values to produce the highest quality images. For example, an imagesetter with a resolution of 2400 dpi and a screen frequency of 177 lpi produces a higher quality image than a desktop printer with a resolution of 300 to 600 dpi and a screen frequency of 85 lpi.

About color

Color is produced by a computer monitor and printing device using two different color models (methods for displaying and measuring color). The human eye perceives color according to the wavelength of the light it receives. Light containing the full color spectrum is perceived as white; in the absence of light, the eye perceives black.

The gamut of a color model is the range of colors that can be displayed or printed. The largest color gamut is that viewed in nature; all other color gamuts produce a subset of nature's color gamut. The two most common color models are red, green, and blue (RGB), the method by which monitors display color; and cyan, magenta, yellow, and black (CMYK), the method by which images are printed using four process ink colors.

The RGB color model

A large percentage of the visible spectrum of color can be represented by mixing three basic components of colored light in various proportions. These components are known as the additive colors: red, green, and blue (RGB). The RGB color model is called the additive color model because various percentages of each colored light are added to create color. All monitors display color using the RGB color model.

The CMYK color model

If 100% of red, green, or blue is subtracted from white light, the resulting color is cyan, magenta, or yellow. For example, if an object absorbs (subtracts) 100% red light and reflects green and blue, cyan is the perceived color. Cyan, magenta, and yellow are called the subtractive primaries, and they form the basis for printed colors. In addition to cyan, magenta, and yellow, black ink is used to generate true black and to deepen the shadows in images. These four inks (CMYK) are often called process colors because they are the four standard inks used in the printing process.

Spot colors

Whereas process colors are reproduced using cyan, magenta, yellow, and black inks, spot colors are premixed inks used in place of, or in addition to, CMYK colors. Spot colors can be selected from color-matching systems, such as the PANTONE® or TOYO™ color libraries.

Many spot colors can be converted to their process color equivalents when printed; however, some spot colors, such as metallic or iridescent colors, require their own plate on press.

Use spot color in the following situations:

• To save money on one-color and two-color print jobs. (When your printing budget won't allow for four-color printing, you can still print relatively inexpensively using one or two colors.)

• To print logos or other graphic elements that require precise color matching. You want the printer in Boston to use the same color of red as the printer in New York.

• To print special inks, such as metallic, fluorescent, or pearlescent colors.

Getting started

Before you begin, you must restore the default preferences for Adobe Illustrator CS3. Then you'll open the art file for this lesson.

1   To ensure that the tools and panels function exactly as described in this lesson, delete or deactivate (by renaming) the Adobe Illustrator CS3 preferences file. See "Restoring default preferences" on page 3.

2   Start Adobe Illustrator CS3.

3   Choose File > Open, and open the L15strt1.ai file in the Lesson15 folder, located inside the Lessons folder within the AICIB folder on your hard drive.

4   Choose File > Save As. In the Save As dialog box, name the file **Circus.ai**, and navigate to the Lesson15 folder. Leave the file format set to Illustrator (*.AI), and click Save. In the Illustrator Options dialog box, leave at the defaults and click OK.

What is color management?

Color-matching problems result from various devices and software using different color spaces. One solution is to have a system that interprets and translates color accurately between devices. A color management system (CMS) compares the color space in which a color was created to the color space in which the same color will be output, and makes the necessary adjustments to represent the color as consistently as possible among different devices.

A color management system translates colors with the help of color profiles. A profile is a mathematical description of a device's color space. This is also referred to as a device's color gamut, the range of color that it can interpret. Obviously, there will be some devices capable of seeing more color (or having a larger color gamut) than others. This is why Adobe applications use ICC profiles, a format defined by the International Color Consortium (ICC) as a cross-platform standard to keeping color within a device's gamut.

In this lesson you will see how to use Color Settings to prepare an Illustrator CS3 file for print output.

Setting up color management in Adobe applications

The default color settings are sufficient for most users. However, you can change the color settings by doing one of the following:

If you installed Creative Suite 3 and use multiple Adobe applications, use Bridge to choose a standard color management configuration and synchronize color settings across applications before working with documents.

If you use only one Adobe application, or if you want to customize advanced color management options, you can change color settings for a specific application.

For this example, you will choose North America Prepress 2. If you have the entire suite loaded, try using the Synchronized method. If you did not install the entire Creative Suite 3, use the application method.

Synchronizing color using Adobe Bridge

When you set up color management using Adobe Bridge, color settings are automatically synchronized across applications.

1   Open Bridge.

To open Bridge from another Creative Suite application, choose File > Browse from the application. To open Bridge directly, either choose Adobe Bridge from the Start menu (Windows) or double-click the Adobe Bridge icon (Mac OS).

2   Choose Edit > Creative Suite Color Settings.

3 Select a North America Prepress 2 from the list, and click Apply.

Note: If none of the default settings were to meet your requirements, you could select Show Expanded List Of Color Setting Files to view additional settings. To install a custom settings file, such as a file you received from a print service provider, click Show Saved Color Settings Files.

Color Settings in Adobe Bridge, prior to being Synchronized.

Color Settings after selecting a setting and choosing Apply.

Application color settings

Set up the Color Settings for only Adobe Illustrator CS3.

1   Choose Edit > Color Settings.

2   Select North America Prepress 2 from the Settings menu, and click OK. Your settings may become Unsynchronized, this is OK.

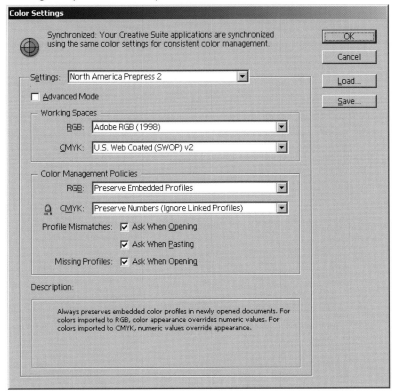

Color Settings in Illustrator CS3.

Note: *By selecting the appropriate profile you are not magically guaranteeing perfect color, but you can expect a more realistic on-screen view of how the printed artwork will appear. Essentially, color management enables the RGB monitor to represent consistent color as it appears when printed in CMYK. Talk to your service provider or printer for more specifications that will help you create more accurate color.*

About missing and mismatched color profiles

For a newly created document, the color workflow usually operates seamlessly: unless specified otherwise, the document uses the working space profile associated with its color mode for creating and editing colors.

However, some existing documents may not use the working space profile that you have specified, and some existing documents may not be color-managed. It is common to encounter the following exceptions to your color-managed workflow:

- You might open a document or import color data (for example, by copying and pasting or dragging and dropping) from a document that is not tagged with a profile. This is often the case when you open a document created in an application that either does not support color management or has color management turned off.

- You might open a document or import color data from a document that is tagged with a profile different from the current working space. This may be the case when you open a document that has been created using different color management settings, or a document that has been scanned and tagged with a scanner profile.

In either case, the application uses a color management policy to decide how to handle the color data in the document.

If the profile is missing or does not match the working space, the application may display a warning message, depending on options you set in the Color Settings dialog box. Profile warnings are turned off by default, but you can turn them on to ensure the appropriate color management of documents on a case-by-case basis. The warning messages vary between applications, but in general you have the following options:

- (Recommended) Leave the document or imported color data as it is. For example, you can choose to use the embedded profile (if one exists), leave the document without a color profile (if one doesn't exist), or preserve the numbers in pasted color data.

- Adjust the document or imported color data. For example, when opening a document with a missing color profile, you can choose to assign the current working space profile or a different profile. When opening a document with a mismatched color profile, you can choose to discard the profile or convert the colors to the current working space. When importing color data, you can choose to convert the colors to the current working space in order to preserve their appearance.

—From Illustrator Help

Printing black-and-white proofs

As a general rule, you should print black-and-white proofs of all your documents at different stages of your work to check the layout and to verify the accuracy of text and graphics before preparing the document for final output.

Now you'll print a draft of the Circus.ai file.

1   In the Circus.ai file, notice the crop marks, the pairs of lines at each corner of the artwork. Crop marks define where the artwork is trimmed after it is printed. The crop marks indicate a bleed, the area of artwork that falls outside the crop marks, and which will be removed when the printed artwork is trimmed. The bleed is used to ensure that the artwork prints to the edge of the trimmed page. For more information on bleed, read "Specifying the bleed area" later in this lesson.

[?] You can set crop marks where you want them directly in the artwork. See "Cropping Artwork" in Illustrator Help.

2   If you're not connected to a black-and-white printer, go on to the next section.

3   Choose File > Print, leave all choices set at the defaults, and click OK (Windows) or Print (Mac OS).

The circus logo is printed in black, white, and shades of gray. Next, you'll soft-proof the color on your monitor screen.

Soft-proofing colors

In a color-managed work flow, you can use the precision of color profiles to soft-proof your document directly on the monitor. Soft-proofing lets you preview on-screen how your document's colors will look when reproduced on a particular output device.

The reliability of soft-proofing completely depends, however, on the quality of your monitor, your monitor profile, and the ambient lighting conditions of your workstation area. In other words, if you are working in an inconsistent environment with varying light throughout the day, you might not get reliable results. For information on creating a monitor profile, see "To calibrate and profile your monitor" in Illustrator Help.

1   Choose View > Proof Setup > Customize. The profile is set to U.S. Web Coated (SWOP) v2. Leave it set to this profile, and click OK.

The View > Proof Colors option is selected by default (indicated by a check mark) so that you can view the artwork as it will look when printed to the selected standard, U.S. Web Coated (SWOP) v2.

Next, you'll change the profile to see what the image will look like if printed on a different output device.

2   Choose View > Proof Setup > Customize.

3   Use the Proof Setup menu to select Euroscale Uncoated v2, and click OK. Because the view is still set to Proof Colors, the image preview automatically shifts colors to display what it would look like were it printed according to the Euroscale Uncoated profile.

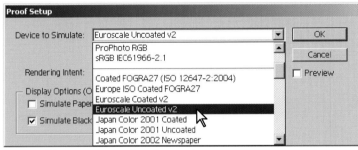

Use Proof Setup to change the color preview.

You'll now return the settings to the SWOP settings.

4   Choose View > Proof Setup > Customize. Set the profile to U.S. Web Coated (SWOP) v2, and click OK.

5   Choose View > Proof Colors to turn off the soft-proofing preview.

Next, you'll work with printing color artwork.

Using the Document Info command

Before you take your color artwork to a prepress professional or begin the process of creating color separations on your own, use the Document Info command to generate and save a list of information about all the elements of your artwork file. The Document Info command displays a panel of information on the objects, linked or placed files, colors, gradients, patterns, and fonts in your document.

If you're working with prepress professionals, be sure to provide them with the Document Info list before delivering your files; they can help you determine what you'll need to include with your artwork. For example, if your artwork uses a font that the prepress house does not have, you'll need to bring or supply a copy of the font with your artwork.

1   Choose Window > Document Info. The Document Info panel appears.

2   In the Document Info panel, select different subjects about the document from the panel menu in the upper right corner. The list box displays information about each subject you select.

3   If you have an object selected in the artwork, choose Selection Only from the Document Info panel menu to display information only on that selected object. It should be selected by default, with a check mark indicating that the Selection Only option is turned on.

The Document Info panel.

You can also view or print the entire contents of the Document Info panel by saving it, and then opening it in a text editor.

4   To save the Document Info text, choose Save from the panel menu, enter a name for the Document Info file, and click Save. You can open the file in any text editor to review and print the contents of the file.

5 When you have looked through the information on the file, you can leave the Document Info panel open onscreen or close it.

Creating color separations

To print color artwork on a printing press, you must first separate the composite art into its component colors: cyan, magenta, yellow, and black, and any spot colors, if applicable. The process of breaking composite artwork into its component colors is called color separation.

You set separation options in the Print dialog box. It's important to note that before setting separation options, you need to discuss the specific requirements of your print job with your printing professional. (You cannot separate to a non-PostScript® printer.)

1 Make sure that the Circus.ai artwork is still open.

2 Select the Selection tool (▶) in the Tools panel. Then click various objects in the artwork to select them.

3 If the Color panel is not visible, choose Window > Color panel. Choose Show Options from the Color panel menu.

As you select different objects, notice that the Color panel reflects the current color's attributes. For example, if you click the flag atop the tent, a PANTONE color swatch appears in the Color panel; if you click the red or green stripe in the clown, the color is mixed using CMYK values.

Selecting a printer description file

The set-up for separations and other options occurs in the Print dialog box.

Important: To be able to continue with this section, your computer must be connected to a PostScript printer. If you are connected to an ink-jet printer or not connected to a printer, the separation options will be dimmed in the Print dialog window.

1   Choose File > Print. The first pop-up window labeled Print Preset is left alone at this point. You will learn how to take your options and turn them into presets later in this lesson.

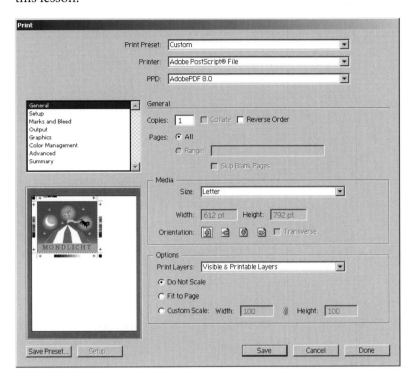

2   First, make sure that you have a printer selected in the Printer pop-up box. If not, select a Postscript printer at this point.

3   Select a PPD.

PostScript Printer Description (PPD) files contain information about the output device, including available page sizes, resolution, available line screen (frequency) values, and the angles of the halftone screens.

Note: A PostScript Printer Description file with limited selections has been placed in the Lesson15 folder for this exercise. When you install Adobe Illustrator, two PPDs are automatically installed in the Utilities folder within the Adobe Illustrator folder, and additional PPDs are provided on the Adobe Illustrator CD.

4   In the PPD pop-up window, choose Other.

5   Navigate to the General.ppd file, located in the Lesson15 folder, inside the Lessons folder within the AICIB folder on your hard drive. Click Open.

The Print dialog box is updated with general printer parameters, and a preview of your artwork is displayed on the lower left side of the dialog box. (The preview of your artwork depends on the page size selected in the Page Size menu. Each output device has a variety of page sizes available; select the desired page size from the Page Size menu in the Print dialog box.)

6   Choose US Letter for the paper size in the Media section.

7   Click on Marks and Bleed in the options window on the left.

In this window you can choose which printer's marks are visible. Printer's marks help the printer align the color separations on the press, and check the color and density of the inks being used.

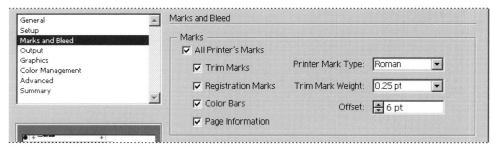

Add all printer's marks, or select just the ones that you want.

8 Click the checkbox to show All Printer's Marks.

The preview shows the crop and other marks in the preview.

 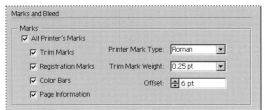

Select printer's marks if not already selected.

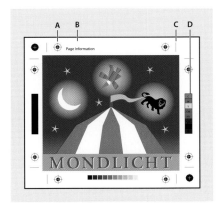

A. Registration mark. B. Page Information.
C. Crop mark. D. Color bar.

Specifying the bleed area

Bleed is the amount of artwork that falls outside the printing bounding box or outside the crop marks and trim marks. You can include bleed in your artwork as a margin of error—to ensure that the ink is still printed to the edge of the page after the page is trimmed or to ensure that an image can be stripped into a keyline in a document. Once you create the artwork that extends into the bleed, you can use Illustrator to specify the extent of the bleed.

Changing the bleed moves the crop marks farther from, or closer to, the image; however, the crop marks still define the same size printing bounding box.

Small bleed.   *Large bleed.*

1   Specify a bleed of **18 pt** by typing it in the Top bleed text field. If the Link button does not have a square surrounding it, click it now to activate equal bleed settings on all sides.

Add a bleed equal on all sides using the Link button.

This means that the artwork extends 18 points beyond the crop marks on your film. The maximum bleed you can set is 72 points; the minimum bleed is 0 points.

The size of the bleed depends on its purpose. A press bleed (that is, an image that bleeds off the edge of the printed sheet) should be at least 18 points. If the bleed is to ensure that an image fits a keyline, it needs to be no more than 2 or 3 points. Your print shop can advise you on the size of the bleed necessary for your particular job.

For more help, use Illustrator Help "Printer's marks and bleed."

Separating colors

1 Click on Output in the Options window on the left side of the Print dialog window. Choose Separations (Host Based).

The circus artwork is composed of process colors and spot colors, which are displayed in the Document Ink Options window.

To the left of the process color names, a printer icon (🖨) is displayed, indicating that a separation will be generated for each color. To the left of the spot color names, a spot color icon (●) is displayed, indicating that the spot colors will be printed as separate colors.

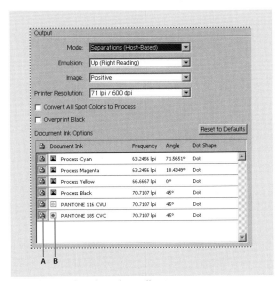

A. Indicates that the color will print.
B. Indicates a spot color.

Illustrator CS3 output mode options

Illustrator CS3 provides three choices for output mode:

• Composite—This mode sends all of the color information in your file to your output device. This is the typical setting for everyday printing to a desktop color printer or a color copier.

• Separations (Host Based)—This mode produces the separations on your computer and sends the separated data to your output device.

• In-RIP Separations—This mode performs color separations at the RIP (Raster Image Processor), leaving the host computer free to perform other tasks. When using this mode the output device receiving the data must support In-RIP separations.

If you were to print color separations at this point, all the colors, including the spot colors in the artwork, would be printed into six separations.

Check the box to the left of Convert all Spot colors to Process. Now the spot colors will be broken down into the CMYK builds, and would be printed into four separations.

Composite image.

Cyan separation.

Magenta separation.

Yellow separation.

Black separation.

2   Uncheck the Convert Spot Color To Process, and the spot colors are no longer grayed out, and the process icon to the left returns to a spot icon, indicating that they are going to print.

As you learned earlier, you can print separations using process colors or spot colors, or you can use a combination of both. You'll convert only the first spot color (PANTONE 116) to a process color because a precise color match isn't necessary. The second spot color, PANTONE 185 CVC, will stay a spot color because a precise color match is desired.

3 To convert Pantone 116 to a process color, click the spot color icon to the left of its name in the list of colors.

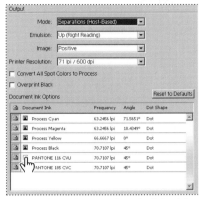

*Click on the color swatch to the left of the color name
to change it to process or spot.*

If you were to print at this point, five separations would be generated: one each for the cyan, magenta, yellow, and black plates (including the spot color converted to a process color); and a single plate for the PANTONE 185 CVC spot color. (This job would require a more specialized press, capable of printing five colors, or the paper would have to be sent back through the press to print the fifth color.)

Composite image.

Cyan separation.

Magenta separation.

Yellow separation.

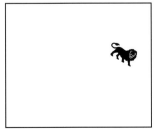

Black separation.

Spot separation.

Specifying the screen frequency

At the beginning of this lesson, you learned that the relationship between the output device resolution and the screen frequency determines the quality of the printed output. Depending on the output device you select, more than one screen frequency value may be available. Your printing professional will direct you to select the screen frequency appropriate to your artwork.

1   In the Printer Resolution pop-up menu, choose 60 lpi/300 dpi from the Halftone menu. The first value, 60, represents the screen frequency (lpi), and the second value, 300, represents the output device resolution (dpi).

Additional separation options, such as Emulsion Up/Down, and Positive or Negative film, should be discussed with your printing professional, who can help you determine how these options should be set for your particular job.

Before printing your separations to a high-resolution output device, it's a good idea to print a set of separations, called proofs, on your black-and-white desktop printer. You'll save time and money by making any needed corrections to your files after reviewing the black-and-white proofs.

2   Click on Save Preset button in the lower left of the Print dialog box to name and save this setting for future use. This customer always uses the same settings, so we will name it with their name **Circus**. In the future you can choose this Preset from the Preset pop-up window at the top. Click OK.

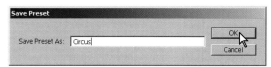

Save frequently used print settings as presets.

3   Choose Print to print separations. Five pieces of paper should be printed—one each for cyan, magenta, yellow, and black, and one for the spot color.

Note: Depending on your chosen printer, you may get a warning message that your PPD doesn't match the current printer. Click Continue to print the proofs.

4   File > Save and close the Circus.ai file.

Working with two-color illustrations

As you learned earlier, two-color printing generally refers to black and one spot color, but may also refer to two spot colors. In addition to printing the two solid colors, you can print tints, or screens, of the colors. Two-color printing is much less expensive than four-color printing and lets you create a rich range of depth and color when used effectively.

Editing a spot color

In this section, you'll open a two-color version of the circus illustration containing black, a spot color, and tints of the spot color. Before you separate the illustration, you'll replace the current spot color with another from the PANTONE color library. Illustrator lets you make global adjustments to spot colors and tints of spot colors using a keyboard shortcut.

1   Choose File > Open, and open the L15strt2.ai file in the Lesson15 folder, located inside the Lessons folder within the AICIB folder on your hard drive.

Because you have set up Illustrator to work with a color management profile, you may be prompted each time you open a new file if you want to change how that file is color managed.

2   At the prompt, select Assign current working space, and click OK.

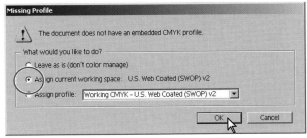

Since Color Management is turned on, you will be prompted
with this window when opening files.

3   Choose File > Save As, name the file **Twocolor.ai**, and select the Lesson15 folder in the Save As dialog box. Leave the file format set to Illustrator (*.AI), and click Save. In the Illustrator Options dialog box, leave at the defaults and click OK.

4   Make sure that the Color panel and the Swatches panel are open and visible; if they aren't, use the Window menu to display them.

5   From the Color panel's menu (arrow in the upper right of the panel) choose to Show Options.

6   Using the Selection tool (➤) click any colored part of the circus tent. Notice the PANTONE 116 C swatch in the Color panel.

Next, you'll replace every instance of the spot color (including any tints of the color) with another spot color.

7   The Swatches panel, like most others, has three different views which you can use. In order to see the swatch color name and the swatch, click on the panel menu in the upper right of the Swatch panel, and choose List View. This provides you with information such as a visual of the swatch, its name and whether it is a process, RGB or spot color.

Change the Swatch panel to List View in order to read the swatch names.

8   Choose Select > Deselect or Ctrl+click (Windows) or Command+click (Mac OS), away from the artwork to deselect it.

9 Choose Window > Swatch Libraries > Color Books > PANTONE solid coated. The PANTONE swatch library appears. From the panel menu, change this panel to be in small list view.

You can choose new spot colors from the swatch library by typing the number of the color you want to use.

10 Choose Show Find Field from the Pantone solid coated panel menu and then click in the Find text field. Type **193**. PANTONE 193 C is selected in the panel.

Next, you'll replace the current PANTONE color with the new PANTONE color.

11 Drag the title bar of the PANTONE Solid Coated swatch library closer to the Swatches panel.

12 If necessary, scroll down on the Swatches panel until Pantone 116 is visible, then hold down Alt (Windows) or Option (Mac OS), and drag the PANTONE 193 C swatch from the PANTONE Solid Coated swatch library onto the PANTONE 116 swatch in the Swatches panel.

As you Alt/Option+drag the swatch, the cursor changes to a crosshair.

The PANTONE 193 C replaces the PANTONE 116 C swatch in the Swatches panel, and the artwork is updated with the new PANTONE Solid color.

Open PANTONE solid coated swatch library.

Select PANTONE 193 C swatch.

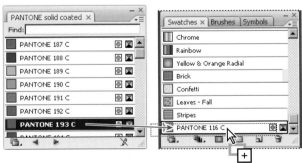

Alt/Option+drag onto swatch to replace in Swatches panel.

Notice that the updated red swatch still is named PANTONE 116 C. You need to rename the updated swatch to avoid confusion about the spot color when your artwork is printed by a commercial press.

13 In the Swatches panel, double-click the updated swatch (still named PANTONE 116 C), and rename the swatch to match its color, PANTONE 193 C. Click OK.

Note: Certain three-digit Pantone values may require you to add a space before entering the value.

Separating spot colors

As you learned in "Separating colors" earlier in this lesson, you can convert spot colors to their process color equivalents, or you can output them to their own separation. When you're working with a two-color illustration, separating spot colors into their process color equivalents is less cost-effective than outputting the spot color to its own separation (converting to four CMYK plates versus one plate for each individual spot color). You'll deselect the Convert to Process option in the Separation Setup dialog box to output each spot color to its own separation.

Composite image.

Separation 1: Black.

Separation 2: Spot color.

1 Choose File > Print.

2 Click on Output in the Options window on the left.

3 Select Separations (Host-Based) for the Mode.

4   You may notice printer icons () to the left of multiple colors. Since this is a two-color job, make sure that you leave on only process black and PANTONE 193 C. Click on the printer icon of any unnecessary colors to turn off printing.

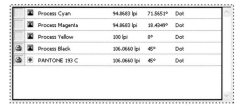

	Process Cyan	94.8683 lpi	71.5651°	Dot
	Process Magenta	94.8683 lpi	18.4349°	Dot
	Process Yellow	100 lpi	0°	Dot
	Process Black	106.0660 lpi	45°	Dot
	PANTONE 193 C	106.0660 lpi	45°	Dot

The printer icon indicates that the color will print.

5   Click Save Preset, and name the Preset **Circus 2-color** to save these separation settings.

6   Click Done to save the settings, but do not print at this time.

7   Save and Close the Twocolor.ai file.

Creating a trap

Trapping is used to compensate for any gaps or color shifts that may occur between adjoining or overlapping objects when printing. These gaps or color shifts occur from misregistration, the result of the paper or the printing plates becoming misaligned during printing. Trapping is a technique developed by commercial print shops to slightly overprint the colors along common edges.

Gap created by misregistration.   *Gap removed by trapping.*

Although trapping sounds simple enough, it requires a thorough knowledge of color and design and an eye for determining where trapping is necessary. You can create a trap in Adobe Illustrator CS3 using two methods: by applying the Trap filter or Trap effect, for simple artwork whose parts can be selected and trapped individually; and by setting a Stroke value for individual objects you want to trap. Like printing, creating a trap is an art that requires time and experience.

About trapping

Where colors printed from separate plates overlap or adjoin one another, press misregistration can cause gaps between colors on the final output. To compensate for potential gaps between colors in artwork, print shops use a technique called trapping to create a small area of overlap (called a trap) between two adjoining colors. You can use a separate, dedicated trapping program to create traps automatically, or you can use Illustrator to create traps manually.

There are two types of trap: a spread, in which a lighter object overlaps a darker background and seems to expand into the background; and a choke, in which a lighter background overlaps a darker object that falls within the background and seems to squeeze or reduce the object.

 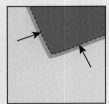

Spread: Object overlaps background.   *Choke: Background overlaps object.*

When overlapping painted objects share a common color, trapping may be unnecessary if the color that is common to both objects creates an automatic trap. For example, if two overlapping objects contain cyan as part of their CMYK values, any gap between them is covered by the cyan content of the object underneath.

Trapping type can present special problems. Avoid applying mixed process colors or tints of process colors to type at small point sizes, because any misregistration can make the text difficult to read. Likewise, trapping type at small point sizes can result in hard-to-read type. As with tint reduction, check with your print shop before trapping such type. For example, if you are printing black type on a colored background, simply overprinting the type onto the background may be enough.

—From Illustrator Help

Overprinting objects

When preparing an image for color separation, you can define how you want overlapping objects of different colors to print. By default, the top object in the Illustrator artwork knocks out, or removes the color of, underlying artwork on the other separations and prints with the color of the top object only. Misregistration may occur when you knock out colors.

Composite image.

First plate.

Second plate.

You can also specify objects to overprint, or print on top of, any of the artwork under them. Overprinting is the simplest method you can use to prevent misregistration (gaps between colors) on press. The overprinted color automatically traps into the background color.

Composite image.

First plate.

Second plate.

You'll select an object in the circus illustration and apply the overprint option. Then you will preview the overprint on-screen.

1   Choose File > Open. Locate and open the Circus.ai file, which you saved in the Lesson15 folder, inside the Lessons folder within the AICIB folder on your hard drive.

2   In the Missing Profile dialog box, select Assign Current Working Space: US Web Coated (SWOP) v2, and click OK.

The color version of the circus illustration appears.

3   Choose View > Zoom In to zoom in on the lion. You'll be able to see the overprint lines better if you magnify the view of the image. (We zoomed in to 400%.)

4   Choose the Selection tool (↖) in the Tools panel. Then click the lion to select it.

5   Click the Attributes tab to bring the panel to the front of its group. (If the Attributes panel isn't open, choose Window > Attributes.)

6   In the Attributes panel, select Overprint Fill.

Now you'll see an approximation of how overprinting and blending will appear in the color-separated output.

7   Choose View > Overprint Preview to see the effect of the overprinted objects. The effect is subtle; look closely at the tip of the flag to see the overprinting.

If an object has a stroke, you can also select the Overprint Stroke option to make sure that the stroke overprints on the object below it as well. Next you'll add a stroke to an object to create a trap.

8   With the Selection tool, select the yellow flag to the left of the lion.

9   Click the Color tab to bring the panel to the front.

10   In the Color panel, drag the yellow fill swatch onto the Stroke box to stroke the flag with the same color as its fill.

11   Click the Attributes tab to bring the panel to the front of its group. Select the Overprint Stroke option.

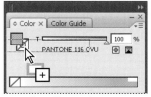

Drag the Fill swatch   *Result.*   *Select Overprint Stroke option.*
onto the Stroke box.

Depending on what you have discussed with your printing professional, you may want to change the amount of trap specified. You'll try out changing the specified trap now.

12   Select the flag shape with the overprint stroke.

13   Click the Stroke tab to bring the panel to the front of its group. Increase the Stroke weight. In Overprint Preview you can see the results.

No Overprint preview.   *Overprint preview.*

Strokes are centered over the object's path. This means that if an object is stroked with the same color as its fill, only half the stroke weight actually overprints. For example, if your printing professional wants a 0.5-point trap added to the yellow flag, you would use a 1-point stroke weight to achieve the trap. Half the stroke will appear inside the fill area, and half will appear outside the fill area.

14   Choose File > Save. Choose File > Close to close the file.

You've finished the lesson. In an ordinary workflow situation, you would now be ready to send your artwork to a commercial press to be printed. Include proofs of color separation setups when you send your electronic file to a printer. Also tell your printer about any traps you created in the artwork. Keep in mind that you must remain in close communication with your printing professional for each print job. Each print job has unique requirements that you must consider before you begin the process of color separation.

Saving and printing files with transparency effects

Now that you have learned to take advantage of Effects and the Appearance panel, you need to learn how to get them to print correctly. Many of the Effects used in this lesson maximize Illustrator's ability to create transparency. Transparency is applied to any object that has been modified to affect an underlying object. Illustrator, InDesign and Photoshop work seamlessly together and will maintain transparency from one application to the other if the proper workflow is followed. This simple workflow includes a final step called flattening, which is necessary for printing.

Flattening is a term used to define the process of converting all transparent objects into a collection of opaque objects that retain the appearance of the original transparent objects when printed.

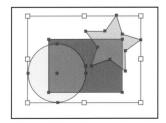
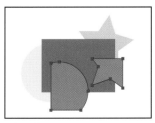

Objects before Flattening.   *After Flattening.*

Illustrator flattens artwork containing transparency before printing or saving the artwork. During flattening, Illustrator looks for areas where transparent objects overlap other objects and isolates these areas by dividing the artwork into components. Illustrator then analyzes each component to determine if the artwork can be represented using vector data or if the artwork must be rasterized.

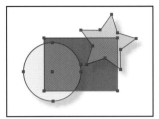

The drop shadow before flattening.

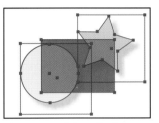

The rasterized drop shadow as a separate object after flattening.

In most cases, the flattening process produces excellent results. However, if your artwork contains complex overlapping areas and you require high-resolution output, you may want to control the degree to which artwork is rasterized. To preserve as much of the vector art in your document as possible, use the Raster/Vector Balance slider in the Document Setup dialog box. Illustrator uses these settings to determine the quality, printing speed, or both, of your artwork.

What is rasterization?

Rasterization is the process of changing vector graphics, vector fonts, gradients, and gradient meshes into bitmap images for display and printing, essentially turning vector artwork into pixels. The higher the ppi (pixels per inch), the better the quality. The amount of ppi or dpi (dots per inch) is referred to as the resolution of the artwork.

Vector Object.

Rasterized at 72 ppi.

Rasterized at 300 ppi.

💡 *In Illustrator CS3, you have the ability to preserve spot color raster in other live effects, including: Rasterize, Feather, Inner/Outer Glow, Gaussian blur, and Radial blur in CMYK and RGB document color spaces.*

Specifying resolution of filters and live effects

For this next exercise, you will create several overlapping shapes with various levels of transparency.

1 Choose File > New, and choose the Basic CMYK profile from the New Document dialog box.

If you plan to print your transparent artwork, the document should be in CMYK mode.

2 Using the shape tools, create any three shapes and overlap them.

3 Assign a different color fill to each, and assign None to the stroke.

4 Using the Transparency panel, apply varying levels of transparency to all three shapes. Exact amounts are not important as long as you can see the underlying shapes.

5 With the three shapes selected, choose Effect > Stylize > Drop Shadow. Accept the default settings, clicking OK.

6 With the three shapes still selected, choose Effects > Pixelate > Pointilize. Leave at the default settings, and click OK.

Create overlapping   *Apply Transparency.*   *Apply Effect.*
shapes with colored fills.

7 Choose File > Save, name the file **shapes.ai**, and select the Lesson15 folder in the Save In menu. Leave the type of file format set to Adobe Illustrator® Document (.AI), and click Save. In the Illustrator Options dialog box, leave at the default settings and click OK.

Using Document Raster Effects Settings

1   Select the Zoom tool (🔍) in the Tools panel. Position the Zoom tool over any shape's drop shadow and click. Continue clicking on the center of the shapes until you have zoomed in to 300%. You should be able to see the pixelated texture of the drop shadow, and the pointilization effect.

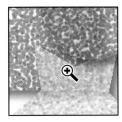

Zoom in to see the details.

Notice the edges of the star shape, with stair-stepping on the angled edges. This is due to the resolution setting for the raster effects. The default setting is 72 ppi.

You will change that setting to improve the quality of the shape's shadow.

2   Choose Effect > Document Raster Effects Settings.

3   Change the Resolution setting to Medium (150 ppi).

4   Leave the other settings as they are, and click OK.

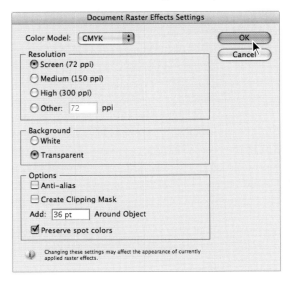

5 Notice that the shadow has become smoother and the pixels have become more precise.

If you were to increase the resolution to 300 ppi, the artwork would be even more well-defined. For this lesson you will leave the setting at 150 ppi.

Now that you have determined the quality of rasterization you want to occur, you will choose your flattening settings using the Flattener Preview panel.

Using the Flattener Preview panel

If you are not sure which objects require flattening, choose Window > Flattener Preview. Use the preview options in the Flattener Preview panel to highlight the areas affected by flattening artwork. Use this information to adjust the flattening options, and save custom flattener presets.

1 On the same shapes.ai file, add another shape. Do not apply transparency or effects to this object.

2 Fill it with a red color from the Swatches panel.

3 Use the Selection tool (➤) to drag the new opaque object on top of any other shape.

4 Choose Window > Attributes and click on the checkbox to Overprint Fill.

5 Choose View > Overprint Preview to show how your overprint will appear when printed.

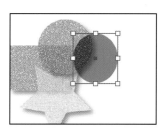
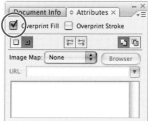

Check the Overprint fill box.

6 Choose Window > Flattener Preview. The Flattener Preview panel can remain open while you work.

7 Click Refresh, and choose Transparent Objects from the Highlight pop-up menu. If necessary, click Refresh again.

All transparent objects are highlighted. Any other objects are gray.

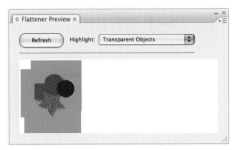

The Flattener Preview panel can show Transparent objects.

8 From the Highlight pop-up menu, choose All Affected Objects. If there were transparent objects on top of non-transparent objects, more objects would appear highlighted.

9 Choose Show Options from the Flattener Preview panel menu.

In Options, you can select different settings and preview the result. Note that the Flattening Preview panel only previews the transparency flattening.

Note: As you change flattening options, click Refresh to update the display in the preview.

10 From the Overprints pop-up menu, choose Simulate for the type of overprinting to use for the preview. Click Refresh.

• **Preserve** to retain overprinting for devices that support it. In most cases, only separations devices support overprinting.

• **Simulate** to maintain the appearance of overprinting in composite output.

• **Discard** to ignore any overprint settings that are present in your document.

11 From the Preset pop-up window, choose High Resolution from the available presets.

• **Low Resolution** is for quick proofs that will be printed on black-and-white desktop printers, as well as for documents that will be published on the Web, or exported to SVG.

Note: The SVG (Scalable Vector Graphics) format is entirely XML-based and offers many advantages to developers and users alike. With SVG, you can use XML and JavaScript to create web graphics that respond to user actions with sophisticated effects such as highlighting, tool tips, audio, and animation.

- ***Medium Resolution*** is for desktop proofs and print-on-demand documents that will be printed on PostScript color printers.

- ***High Resolution*** is for final press output and for high-quality proofs, such as separations-based color proofs. You will now alter the High Resolution setting to create your own custom settings.

12 Specify rasterization settings. Drag the Raster/Vector Balance slider to determine the percentage of rasterization. The settings vary from 0 on the left for the greatest rasterization to 100 on the right for the least rasterization on artwork. Select the highest setting to represent as much artwork as possible using vector data, or select the lowest setting to rasterize all of the artwork. For this exercise, drag the slider to 90%.

Note: You will not see the rasterization in the Flattener Preview panel.

Understand that rasterizing everything in a file degrades some of vector graphics' crisp edges, but maintaining too much of the vector artwork may make a file difficult to print due to printer memory limitations.

13 Specify an output resolution for art and text. In this case, leave the Line Art and Text Resolution at 1200.

If your final output will be separated and printed on a four-color press, you will want to specify a resolution of 1200. If your final output is to be a laser printer or color copier, you can select something lower, such as 600 or 800 dpi. In normal viewing conditions, no difference is visible, but the lower dpi takes less processing time and memory.

14 Set a separate resolution for the Gradients Mesh objects. Generally, these objects require less resolution than solid fill objects. Leave the setting at 300.

15 Leave the Convert All Text to Outlines unchecked. This ensures that the width of text, respectively, remains consistent during flattening.

16 Leave Convert All Strokes to Outlines unchecked. We do not have strokes in this artwork, but if we did, this option would convert all strokes to simple filled paths. This option ensures that the width of strokes stays consistent during flattening, but it will cause thin strokes to appear slightly thicker.

17 Leave the Clip Complex Regions option selected. When selected, this option ensures that the boundaries between vector artwork and rasterized artwork fall along object paths, but it may result in paths that are too complex for the printer to handle.

18 Once you have determined which settings work best for your workflow, choose Save Transparency Flattener Preset... from the panel menu in the upper right of the Flattener Preview.

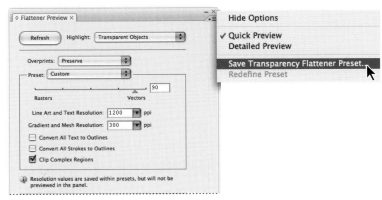

Save your settings as a preset.

19 Name the preset **shapes1** and click OK. You can close the Flattener Preview panel as well.

Note: If you are unsure of which settings to use, contact your printer. A good print provider should be able to discuss the options with you and may even provide a preset that works in their workflow. Learn how to import presets later in this lesson.

Assigning the Flattening preset

Using File > Document Setup, you can either create new flattening settings or assign presets to a document.

1 Choose File > Document Setup.

2 Choose Transparency from the pop-up menu in the Document Setup dialog box.

3 Choose the preset that you created (shapes1) in the Flattener Preview panel.

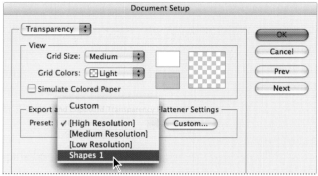

The transparency options in Document Setup.

4   Click OK.

5   Choose File > Save.

Note: You can also create custom flattening settings in the Document Setup window by choosing Custom on the Preset pop-up window and selecting options.

Saving a file with transparency

If you are saving a file that is to be used in other Adobe applications, such as InDesign or Photoshop, keep the transparency live by saving the artwork in the native Adobe Illustrator format. The transparency is supported in these other applications.

In the next exercise, you will save your shape file in two different formats to place into an InDesign or Photoshop document.

1   Choose File > Save As, name the file **shapes1.ai**, and select the Lesson15 folder in the Save As dialog box. Leave the file format set to Illustrator (*.AI), and click Save. In the Illustrator Options dialog box, leave at the default settings and click OK.

2   Open Photoshop or InDesign and choose File > New. Create a letter-sized document.

3   Choose File > Place. Locate the file you saved in the Lesson15 folder named shapes1.ai and click Place.

Using Place to import your file allows the artwork to maintain its transparency.

Note: Though you have the ability to drag and drop artwork from one Adobe application to another, transparency will not be supported.

Saving in the EPS format

Save a file as an Encapsulated Postscript file to use in non-Adobe applications, or if you do not need the transparency to remain live.

1 Return to Adobe Illustrator.

2 Choose File > Save As, name the file **shapes2.eps**, and select the Lesson15 folder in the Save In menu. Set the type of file format to Illustrator EPS, and click Save.

3 In the EPS options window, select the preset you created earlier named shapes1. Click OK.

4 Return to the InDesign or Photoshop document.

5 Choose File > Place and select the file you just saved named shapes2.eps and click Place.

Notice that transparency is not supported. The transparent areas of the artwork do not interact with the rest of the document.

Adobe Illustrator format.   EPS format.

6 Return to Illustrator and choose File > Close, or leave the file open to experiment with other flattening options.

Printing transparent artwork

If your computer is connected to a printer, you can experiment with different flattening settings in the Print dialog box.

1 Choose File > Print.

2 Click on Advanced in the options window.

3 From the Preset pop-up menu, choose a transparency preset or click on Custom to create your own.

Exporting and importing flattening settings

Settings that you create can be accessed by using the Document Setup dialog box, but you can import settings that were created in other documents by choosing Edit > Transparency Flattener Presets.

Export from the document in which you created the preset. Use the Import button to make the settings available to any other document. This can be especially useful if you are working with a printer that can supply presets.

You are now finished with the discussion on flattening. More information can be found using Illustrator help or at Adobe.com. Close any files that you have open.

Saving as Adobe PDF

Adobe Portable Document Format (PDF) is a universal file format that preserves the fonts, images, and layout of source documents created on a wide range of applications and platforms. PDF is the standard for the secure, reliable distribution and exchange of electronic documents and forms around the world. Adobe PDF files are compact and complete, and can be shared, viewed, and printed by anyone with free Adobe Reader® software. In addition, Adobe PDF can preserve all Illustrator data, which means that you can reopen the file in Illustrator without any loss of data.

Adobe PDF is highly effective in print publishing workflows. By saving a composite of your artwork in Adobe PDF, you create a compact, reliable file that you or your service provider can view, edit, organize, and proof. Then, at the appropriate time in the workflow, your service provider can either output the Adobe PDF file directly, or process it using tools from various sources for such post-processing tasks as preflight checks, trapping, imposition, and color separation.

Illustrator files are saved as PDF files by choosing Fils > Save As... and choosing the Adobe PDF (pdf) file format. In the Save Adobe PDF dialog box, you can choose from default Adobe PDF Presets or change them to suit your PDF needs.

🖵 For more help, use Illustrator Help "Creating Adobe PDF files."

PDF Presets

When creating PDFs from Illustrator there are many presets to choose from.

High Quality Print Creates a PDF file for quality printing on desktop printers and proofers. It downsamples color and grayscale images with resolutions above 450 ppi to 300 ppi and prints to a higher image resolution. PDF files created with this settings file can be opened in Acrobat 5.0 and Acrobat Reader 5.0 and later.

Illustrator Default Creates a PDF file in which all Illustrator data is preserved. PDF files created with this preset can be reopened in Illustrator without any loss of data.

PDF/X-1a:2001, PDF/X-3:2002, PDF/X-4:2007: Use these settings to create Adobe PDF documents that are to be checked or must conform to either the PDF/X-1a:2001, PDF/X-3:2002 or PDF/X-4:2007 ISO standards for graphic content exchange. If the file fails compliance checks, a warning message appears that lets you cancel saving the file or continue by saving a file that is not marked as PDF/X-compliant. PDF files created with PDF/X-1a:2001 or PDF/X-3:2002 settings files can be opened in Acrobat 4.0 and Acrobat Reader 4.0 and later. Created PDF documents created with PDF-X-4:2007 can be opened with Acrobat and Adobe Reader 5.0 and later.

Press Quality Creates PDF files for high-quality print production (for example, for digital printing or for separations to an imagesetter or platesetter), but does not create files that are PDF/X-compliant. In this case, the quality of the content is the highest consideration. The objective is to maintain all the information in a PDF file that a commercial printer or prepress service provider needs in order to print the document correctly. This set of options downsamples color and grayscale images with resolutions above 450 ppi to 300 ppi and monochrome images with resolutions above 1800 ppi to 1200 ppi, embeds subsets of fonts used in the document (if allowed), and creates a higher image resolution than the Standard settings. These PDF files can be opened in Acrobat 5.0 and Acrobat Reader 5.0 and later.

Smallest File Size Creates PDF files for displaying on the web, on an intranet, for distribution through an email system for on-screen viewing, or for display on smaller more portable devices (such as handhelds). This set of options uses compression, downsampling, and a relatively low image resolution. It converts all colors to sRGB, and does not embed fonts unless absolutely necessary. These PDF files can be opened in Acrobat 5.0 and Acrobat Reader 5.0 and later.

—From Illustrator Help

Review

▶ **Review questions**

1   How do the RGB and CMYK color gamuts affect the relationship between on-screen colors and printed colors?

2   How can you create a closer match between your on-screen colors and printed colors?

3   What is the benefit of printing interim drafts of your artwork to a black-and-white desktop printer?

4   What does the term color separation mean?

5   What are two ways to output spot colors?

6   What are the advantages of one- or two-color printing?

7   What is trapping?

8   What is a simple method you can use to create trap?

9   Describe what rasterization is.

▶ **Review answers**

1   Each color model has a gamut of color that overlaps but does not precisely match the others. Because monitors display color using the RGB color gamut, and printed artwork uses the smaller CMYK color gamut, there may be times when a printed color cannot precisely match an on-screen color.

2   You can select one of Illustrator's built-in color management profiles to better simulate the relationship between on-screen colors and printed colors. You can choose View > Proof Setup and select an output device profile. Then choose View > Proof Colors to get an on-screen version of how the artwork will look when printed to the selected device.

3   It's a good idea to print black-and-white drafts of your artwork on a desktop printer to check the layout and the accuracy of text and graphics in your publication before incurring the expense of printing to a color printer or imagesetter (for separations).

4   Color separation refers to breaking down composite artwork into its component colors—for example, using the four process colors (cyan, magenta, yellow, and black) to reproduce a large portion of the visible color spectrum.

5   You can convert a spot color to its process color equivalents if a precise color match is not required, or you can output a spot color to its own separation.

6   One- or two-color printing is less expensive than four-color printing, and you can use spot colors for precise color matching.

7   Trapping is a technique developed by commercial print shops to slightly overprint the colors along common edges, and it is used to compensate for any gaps or color shifts that may occur between adjoining or overlapping objects when printed.

8   You can specify objects to overprint, or print on top of, any of the artwork under them. Overprinting is the simplest method you can use to create a trap, which compensates for misregistration on press.

9   Rasterization is the process of changing vector graphics, vector fonts, gradients, and gradient meshes into bitmap images for display and printing, essentially turning vector artwork into pixels. The higher the ppi (pixels per inch), the better the quality. The amount of ppi or dpi (dots per inch) is referred to as the resolution of the artwork.

Index

Production Notes

The *Adobe Illustrator Classroom in a Book* was created electronically using Adobe InDesign CS3. Art was produced using Adobe InDesign, Adobe Illustrator, and Adobe Photoshop. The Myriad Pro and Minion Pro OpenType families of typefaces were used throughout this book.

References to company names in the lessons are for demonstration purposes only and are not intended to refer to any actual organization or person.

Images

Photographic images and illustrations are intended for use with the tutorials.

Images provided by istockphoto.com: Lesson 6.

Images provided by Comstock: Lesson 14.

Image provided by Clipart.com: Lesson 2 (French fries).

Typefaces used

Adobe Myriad Pro and Adobe Garamond Pro, are used throughout the lessons. More information about OpenType and Adobe fonts visit www.adobe.com/type/opentype/.

Team credits

The following individuals contributed to the development of new and updated lessons for this edition of the *Adobe Illustrator CS3 Classroom in a Book*:

Project coordinator, technical writer: Brian Wood

Production: eVolve Computer Graphics, Inc. Training, Brian Wood, T. Elizabeth Atteberry

Proofreading: Wyndham Wood, T. Elizabeth Atteberry

Technical Editors: Jeffrey Hannibal, Wyndham Wood, Michelle Bombeck, T. Elizabeth Atteberry

Tune In To
PeachpitTV

Point your browser to www.peachpittv.com where your favorite authors are bringing their best tips and tricks directly to your desktop.

Missed Photoshop World or Macworld Conference & Expo? Insist on learning from the best? PeachpitTV's newest show, *Author Tips*, features your favorite authors demonstrating their top tips, tricks, and tutorials. You won't want to miss new and upcoming episodes starring Matt Kloskowski, Kevin Ames, Dan Margulis, Ben Willmore, Rich Harrington, and Terry White talking about:

- *Truly Automatic Automations with Adobe Photoshop*
- *Customizing Web Galleries in Adobe Photoshop*
- *Understanding Alpha Channels*
- *Understanding LAB Color*
- *LAB Color: Fixing a Color Cast*
- *Integrating Adobe Bridge*
- *Retouching Interiors*
- *Retouching Portraits: Eye Enhancements*

Photoshop, graphics, design, the Web—you name it— PeachpitTV's *Author Tips* covers everything you need to know to be more creative and get the most from your favorite software.

Also available on iTunes

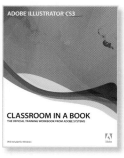
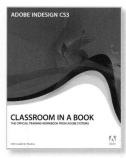
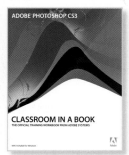

REAL WORLD

Take your skills to the next level!

Industry pros delve under the hood of the Adobe software you use every day to bring you comprehensive references filled with industrial strength production techniques and time-saving tips.

If you're a professional working in the field of digital graphics, publishing, or Web design, you're sure to find these Real World guides to be invaluable resources that you turn to again and again and again.

Real World Adobe InDesign CS3
(ISBN 0-321-49170-X)

Real World Adobe Illustrator CS3
(ISBN 0-321-49621-3)

Real World Adobe Photoshop CS3
(ISBN 0-321-51868-3)

Real World Camera Raw with Adobe Photoshop CS3
(ISBN 0-321-51867-5)